Tricky Design

Tricky Design

The Ethics of Things

Edited by
Tom Fisher and Lorraine Gamman

BLOOMSBURY VISUAL ARTS
LONDON · NEW YORK · OXFORD · NEW DELHI · SYDNEY

BLOOMSBURY VISUAL ARTS
Bloomsbury Publishing Plc
50 Bedford Square, London, WC1B 3DP, UK
1385 Broadway, New York, NY 10018, USA

BLOOMSBURY, BLOOMSBURY VISUAL ARTS and the Diana logo are trademarks of
Bloomsbury Publishing Plc

First published in Great Britain 2019

Cover design: Louise Dugdale
Cover image © Mina De La O / Getty Images

A catalogue record for this book is available from the British Library.

A catalog record for this book is available from the Library of Congress.

ISBN: HB: 978-1-4742-7718-1
          ePDF: 978-1-4742-7720-4
          eBook: 978-1-4742-7719-8

Typeset by Integra Software Services Pvt. Ltd.
Printed and bound in Great Britain

To find out more about our authors and books visit www.bloomsbury.com and
sign up for our newsletters.

Contents

List of Illustrations

Contributors

Shana Agid is an artist/designer, teacher and activist whose work focuses on relationships of power and difference, particularly regarding sexuality, race and gender in visual and political cultures. Agid is Assistant Professor of Arts, Media and Communication at Parsons the New School for Design and holds an MFA in Printmaking and Book Arts and MA in Visual and Critical Studies from California College of the Arts (CCA), and a PhD in Design from RMIT.

Yoko Akama is Associate Professor in communication design at RMIT University, Australia. Her design practice is informed by Japanese philosophy to consider how and what futures can be designed together. Her current work contributes towards the efforts of Indigenous Nations enact self-determination and governance.

Tim Dant recently retired as Professor of Sociology at Lancaster University. He has written about material culture, critical theory and phenomenology. His most recent book *Television and the Moral Imaginary* was published by Palgrave in 2012.

Tom Fisher is Professor of Art and Design at Nottingham Trent University's School of Art and Design. He was once a furniture maker, and is now a musician and musical instrument maker as well as an academic who 'grew up' with the new art history under the influence of Marxists and Feminists in Leeds in the 1970s. His research interests emerge from this mixture. He wrote a PhD about materials and consumption, has done government-funded research on the environmental sustainability of clothing and is concerned with the development of multidisciplinary research in Design. To help pursue this last, he is treasurer of the Design Research Society.

Lorraine Gamman is Professor of Design at Central Saint Martins and the Director of the award-winning *Design Against Crime Research Centre* (DACRC) she founded in 1999. She is the author of *Gone Shopping – the Story of Shirley Pitts, Queen of Thieves*, Bloomsbury (2012) and co-author of numerous recent design research articles on empathy, participatory and socially responsive design. She was Principal Investigator on the AHRC-funded *Extending Empathy* Network (2014–16) and is currently Principal Investigator on AHRC-funded *Design Thinking for Prison Industries* (2014–18), which has developed Makeright an anti-theft design education course and bag label with HMP Thameside and is attempting to scale the project to other UK prisons.

Pras Gunasekera is a designer, researcher and strategist. After graduating from MA Industrial Design, he cofounded Bidean, a more than profit enterprise in design and mental health and subsequently spent eighteen months co-setting up a design studio at HMP Thameside and working part time there to co-deliver Makeright – a design thinking for prison industries course. He is currently employed on the BA Product Design and BA Ceramic Design programmes at Central Saint Martins, where he is also Research Associate with the Design Against Crime Research Centre. In 2017, he was awarded a fellowship from the Winston Churchill Memorial Trust to understand how prison resettlement opportunities in key European countries might benefit from design research methods.

Mahmoud Keshavarz is a Post-Doctoral Fellow within the Engaging Vulnerability Research Program at the Department of Cultural Anthropology, Uppsala University. He has been a Visiting Scholar at Parsons the New School and University of Gothenburg. His research and publications sit at the intersection of design studies, cultural anthropology and politics of movement and migration. His book *The Design Politics of the Passport* is forthcoming in 2018 with Bloomsbury Academics. He is a member of the Decolonizing Design group.

Jeremy Kidwell is Lecturer in Theological Ethics at the University of Birmingham. In his research Jeremy explores the ethical issues that lie at the intersection of 'nature' and 'culture' ranging from ecological ethics, activist studies, religious conceptions of labour to the philosophy of technology. His most recent book *The Theology of Craft and the Craft of Work* (Routledge, 2016) explores an ecological theology of craft, developed in conversation with ancient accounts of craft work and contemporary writing on work and design. Prior to his academic work, Jeremy worked as an engineer and trainer in telecommunications and information technology and he continues to provide consulting services on network security, infrastructure, and the use of information technology in teaching and learning.

Lucy Kimbell is Director of the Innovation Insights Hub and Professor of contemporary design practices at University of the Arts London. She researches design thinking and service design. Lucy's *Service Innovation Handbook* (2014) translates design for managers, who she teaches at Said Business School, University of Oxford.

Ann Light is Professor of Design and Creative Technology at the University of Sussex, where she leads the Creative Technology Research Group. She is a design researcher specializing in social well-being and sustainable futures, the politics of participation and the long-term social and cultural impact of digital networks in post-industrial and developing regions.

Luiza Prado de O. Martins and **Pedro J. S. Vieira de Oliveira** are Brazilian researchers, artists and activists. They have both concluded their PhDs at the University of the Arts Berlin, fully funded by the Brazilian Council of Research and Development (CNPq) and the German Academic Exchange Service (DAAD). Their joint work and research inquires and intervenes, from a decolonizing perspective, on material practices that secure and perpetuate colonial structures of power, focusing on manifestations of gendered and sonic violences. Together they are also two-eighths of the Decolonising Design group.

Nidhi Srinivas is Associate Professor of Management at the New School, and co-founder of the Parsons DESIS Lab. His research dialogues with critical theory in a variety of applied settings, including urban activism, ecological politics, international development and civic design.

Eduardo Staszowski is Associate Professor of Design Strategies at Parsons School of Design, and Director/Co-founder of the Parsons DESIS Lab. He studies design as a method and language, and its role as an intermediary, creating and orienting processes of social innovation and sustainability. He seeks ways to enhance participation in policy development and civic design.

Adam Thorpe is Professor of Socially Responsive Design at Central Saint Martins College, University of the Arts London (UAL). He is Co-director of the Design Against Crime Research Centre and Coordinator of the UAL DESIS Lab (Design for Social Innovation and Sustainability). His research activities are practice based and explore the role of design in addressing societal goals and challenges. He is currently leading the Public Collaboration Lab, researching and prototyping a collaborative learning and doing platform that identifies and leverages synergies between design education and local government.

Cameron Tonkinwise has a background in continental philosophy and continues to research what design practice can learn from material cultural studies and sociologies of technology. His primary area of research and teaching is Sustainable Design. Cameron is widely published on the ways in which Service Design can advance Social Sustainability by decoupling use and ownership – what these days is referred to as the 'Sharing Economy'. He has also been a strong advocate for the importance of critical practice-based design research. Cameron's current focus is Transition Design – design-enabled multi-level, multi-stage structural change towards more sustainable futures.

Acknowledgements

This book originates in a paper that Tom gave at the Design Research Society (DRS) conference in Bangkok, in 2012 – Design as Trickster. That paper derived from thoughts about the conflicted answers that readily emerge when questioning whether design is an inherently positive phenomenon. Clearly it may not be. Lorraine was in the audience and conversation soon established that we had both been thinking along these lines, independently. Lorraine's energy for pursuing these thoughts led us to run a couple of events, titled **Good Things and Bad Things: Tricky Objects, Tricky People, Tricky Processes**, under the auspices of the DRS special interest group 'OPEN: Objects, Practices, Experiences, Networks'. The first was a seminar, in 2013 in Nottingham, and the second a workshop at the 2014 DRS conference at Umea. By this time, the idea for the book was crystallizing, with a 'good things and bad things' Facebook group attracting attention and demonstrating that others shared our interest.

But what made this book possible has been the enthusiasm, dedication and commitment of the contributors. As editors we are indebted to them for this: for responding to our sometimes-misguided editorial comments with positivity and grace; for sharing the passion, engagement and critical precision they all bring to their work with this project. Our thanks go to them, to Silvan Luley of Dignitas for advice on Chapter 11, Hena Ali who helped with administrative work at the outset and to colleagues at Bloomsbury, Rebecca Barden and Claire Constable, who saw the value in tricky things and helped us steer the project to completion.

Foreword

Clive Dilnot

I

For a very long time, from 1945 until very nearly the Millennium, there were only certain ways of thinking and writing correctly about design. One had to take it seriously, but not too seriously – design could not be tasked beyond its own self-imposed limits. Attention to disciplines and boundaries was essential, even while it was permitted to casually use 'design' as a catch-all, sometimes to include the entirety of the world (Papanek: 'All that we do, almost all the time, is design').[1] One had to pay homage to 'problem-solving', albeit with the necessary leavening of creativity (which is what, in this view, differentiated product design from engineering; fashion from dress; the graphic designer from the jobbing printer). Above all, perhaps, one had to be affirmative concerning design, it was 'good' and the more the better, yet precisely in what ways design was 'good' was a difficult question – and one surprisingly little answered. About design's relation to the world (i.e. the world beyond design) little could be said. To ask seriously about its ethics, or its politics, or even substantially about its economics, was very difficult.

On ethics there was, at least between 1945 and 1975, something of an implicit 'social-democratic', slightly egalitarian ethos around design, at least in its more virtuous moments. (Let us say, to characterize it, Pevsner's model of the ethos and ethics of design expressed best in some of his essays of the early 1940s.) Yet not only did all this dissipate very quickly after 1975, when consumption replaced social-democracy (as it has in the United States from the early 1950s) the wider difficulty of how one understood design's relation to the world (other than through consumption) became even more difficult to speak about. Summed up in the classic formulation: 'design *and* society' (or design *and* ethics, design *and* politics, design *and* economics and so on) in each case the 'and' does not connect but marks a conceptual gap (larger in mind than in practice) to be bridged only with acute difficulty. The contradiction is of course blatant. Given that design as a practice (in whatever form or disciplines one likes to consider it) is essentially nothing other than the creation of 'meeting points' as Simon has it, between 'inner' and 'outer' worlds (and we can read these in several ways). But it cannot, as design, be thought if we cannot think these relations (i.e. if cannot think the wealth of relations, situations, institutions, value structures, worlds with which design action necessarily, in each moment, engages).

But this, of course is precisely the point. It has taken us a long time to register, and to begin to respond to these limits to thought. There are exceptions of course. What is in retrospect surprising (especially if we look at design publishing) is how late it was (is) that anything like a more adequate set of critical perspectives and understandings concerning design makes its way into print. As late as 1999 I recall Tony Fry having immense difficulty in finding a publisher for the text he eventually published as *A New Design Philosophy: An Introduction to De-Futuring*.[2] Yet it is not even this that is the true issue. This is rather that the cause of this situation, the limits and boundaries on how design was supposed (how it 'should' and could only) to be thought, had far more consequence, and at deeper levels, than I think, we have yet appreciated.

Of course, limits *were* sensed. This was surely why, across the period that leads up to our own times, successive initiatives have been proposed to try to push at, or get round, or to extend some of these limits: 'design methods' from the 1960s; 'design history' in the 1970s; 'design studies' in the 1980s; 'design research' in the 1990s; 'design thinking' in the 2000s. In each case there are attempts to cohere an approach to thinking specific aspects of design that can begin a push a little beyond the assigned limits to thinking. Yet despite significant and creative work by individuals and organizations (and some institutional gains – conferences, societies, journals, a gradual expansion of design publishing) the results, measured by the standards of hope that characterized the beginning of each initiative, were disappointing. The two most original and creative thinkers in design methods (Christopher Alexander and John Chris Jones) both abdicated from the field precisely in order to be able to more freely think design. Design history, from its promise in the 1970s and 1980s, declined at times into something close to antiquarianism. If it now has global strengths, it also continues to be deeply ambiguous about its intellectual mission. 'Design studies', never constituted an intellectual base adequate to the complexity and depth of the practices that it sought to understand and comprehend. 'Design research' descended rapidly into a 'PhD-ism' (usually borrowing, badly, social-scientific methods to give credibility – but a credibility sustained only by criteria that could not look at the lack of substance generated). 'Design thinking', though its adepts may contest this vigorously, has proved equally unequal to the tasks it set itself.

Nothing individual is meant by these successive (and relative) failures. They do not reflect the often sincere and continuing efforts by many to establish adequate understanding of design. Nor do these comments reflect real achievements. The problem is objective, not subjective. *In every case the base of thought concerning design on which these attempts were made (methodological, historical and so on) was too thin to sustain the effort.* What is remarkable in retrospect is that given these limits on thinking and writing on design that anything could be said at all. What was said had to be so, in effect, against the grain. What was lacking – and what each of these moments in part differently attempted to substitute for – was a form of thought concerning design strong enough, rich enough, sufficiently intertwined enough (a fashionable word from a few years ago might say, sufficiently *rhizomatic*) to be able to bear the weight of thinking the various moments of design (methodological, historical and so on) and for these in turn to be able to feed back into this model. Perhaps, in all this, the most dangerous limit to thought in these years concerned the continual underestimation we were asked to make (indeed, denial of) the *real* complexities, the hybridity, the contradictions and the tensions involved in design. I sadly cannot lay my hands on it, but I recall a line by, I think, the literary critic George Steiner, to the effect that one of, or perhaps *the* most complex mental act that humans can undertake is the translation of a poem from one language to another. Why should we think that the translation from a perception about a human condition or a complex human situation into a material form (I am using 'material' in a very loose sense here) was any less complex?

What all this points to is the sheer difficulty of thinking on design under these conditions. But nowhere, I think, did the astonishing limitations on how, in effect, without explicit rule yet with subtle force, we have been instructed to speak and write on design make themselves so apparent as in the inability to think *well* about the ethics of design.

II

Are we now beginning to escape, even in part, from these limits? Are there signs that thinking about design is finally opening up, in ways almost inconceivable twenty or thirty years ago? I do not want to place *Tricky Design: The Ethics of Things* on any kind of pedestal. The book is not itself *the* or even *an* answer. Yet in its cross-section of authors; in the determination of these authors to attempt to think some very difficult conditions, both substantive, in the world and in design; in its writers' attempts to explore 'ethics' in design from within (i.e. immanently) and do so under the ambit that this 'ethics' is not a matter of unproblematic 'application' but on the contrary is itself 'tricky', the book opens thinking with respect to ethics in at least four dimensions, in terms of

- **things and situations that are 'designed', if often ambiguously** (in the book, through entities and situations as diverse as weaponry in general and handguns in particular; policy formation in the Cabinet Office (UK), the relation of our bodies to other forms of non-human liveliness);
- **the procedures deployed in design, especially in social design** (with community groups and city agencies; in engineering social change; in 'designing' against police abuse and the Prison-Industrial Complex (PIC), in intervening into 'self-choice' in end-of-life);
- **the presuppositions that both the designer and the 'design researcher' bring to the acts of designing** (be they as large as the baggage of colonialism and its histories; the social and political attitudes that inform how we think and often fail to think, of the passport and its implication for lives; or as particular, or so it can seem, of the ethics of research processes – but then these are revealed 'hiding' inside themselves much wider presuppositions concerning persons and conduct);
- **the complex and tricky ethics the designer performs when he or she is acting as a designer** (and the word is exact here, what are the 'trickster' and 'magical' illusions that design deploys in its work?).

In these chapters, thought as totality, something has changed. Or more precisely, something has changed that now becomes evident. At best in the book there is a real profusion of (potentially) new notions and surprise concepts. But what perhaps will most strike the reader used to works touching on ethics is that, usually most serious question: 'How?'; meaning how is ethics, in any substantive moment, to be achieved?

Works on ethics almost by definition tend to be less concerned with *why* this or that? This is all the more evident, usually, in design, where the imperative to action is so predominant. But what makes a difference in this text is the *lack* of rush to 'solutions'. It is precisely the difficulty and even impossibility of 'simply' acting that to an extent unites these very diverse authors. Though many would disavow it, there is something, in a strong sense, of Adorno's famous edicts against 'premature' action.[3] To be sure, there is flowing through the book an ultimately praxiological standpoint, but what is repeatedly of interest is the care which is taken to elucidate the context in which action is to be thought. Here, 'tricky' applies to both the acts to be done and the thing that might be constructed, and above all to the context to which or in which design (as *itself* a 'tricky' thing) is to be deployed.

Something should be said too on the value and force of the choice of the term. No one forgets that Italo Calvino's first of his *Six Memos for the Next Millennium* is lightness: lightness, Calvino insists, that must be understood as thoughtfulness; as that which induces not frivolity but modes of reflection that are able to slip over (or under) the tendency of the world towards petrification, not least of its language and norms.[4] As he rather beautifully and deservedly famously puts it, what is required, what must be valued, is the force of 'the sudden, agile leap of the poet philosopher who raises himself above the world', not to escape it but to show that what lies beneath the moment of the leap, in the weight of seriousness (however vital the latter may appear) 'belongs to the realm of death'.[5] The term 'tricky' does not function in exactly the same way. But it too has a freeing motion. Its lightness helps thinking rise above the petrifaction of previous thinking in these realms. The word works on us a little like an equally surprising term that Alain Badiou invokes to describe the necessary character of affirmative practice. In a quotation that bears strongly on design Badiou says this: when you decide no longer to behave as a critic, but to pluck up the courage to intervene 'with respect to a paradoxical situation, or … with regard to a relation that is not a relation', then you will be obliged 'to propose a new framework of thought, … you [will] have to affirm that it is possible to think this paradoxical situation, on condition, of course, that a certain number of parameters be abandoned, and a certain number of *novelties* introduced'.[6]

The surprise here is in the last term. Yet reflection shows us that the choice is not accident. It is the very lightness of the term, *almost* its frivolity, that permits the act of affirmation be, in the first instance, prospective, exploratory, prototypical – which is precisely as it should be. No 'paradoxical situation' for intervention is anything but (now to swop languages) a 'wicked problem'. It cannot be definitely answered, and certainly not at first go. Hence a space of slippage and possibility must be created. To accompany the definitive, reasoned, abandonment of one or more key parameters must be set the open space of the exploration of 'the novelty' that might take its place, that might compensate for its loss. For ethics, 'tricky' offers something of this kind of space. It frees thinking. It takes it out of the permitted language of 'thinking design' and that feeing in turn allows thought more space, more energy even, in which to move. The play and the flexibility of the term paradoxically throws into relief the seriousness of what is spoken about – infinitely more serious than was permitted within the discourse of design even twenty and certainly fifty years ago. Finally, it throws attention too onto what the book as a whole might be said to oppose, even strongly.

Three important oppositions seem to me to be at work in these texts.

1. The first, which takes place *without* generally falling over into the other side, is opposition to the *simple* assertion as to 'design's' affirmative character. One might say that, since Victor Papanek famously castigated the industrial design profession in the early 1970s, this has not been news. But I see these chapters as taking a more nuanced position: that there is never a simple neutrality for design. That design, ipso facto, is embroiled in relations and it cannot be other, no matter what degree of 'relative autonomy' it claims or used to claim. Latour has in effect maintained a similar point for a number of years now. The shift from 'matters of fact to matter of concern', from 'devices' to entities or situations understood as complex and contradictory assemblages, by definition places all things (situations, ensembles, moments) within the ethical. This means it places them in some relation to the question, 'What are the consequences, of this thing, for the living users of this thing?' and 'What are its implications?' This opposes, absolutely, the older ethos that design was sufficient as *only* its own reference, its own ethic.

2. The second opposition that can be felt in these chapters stands against ideas of the purity of design. By contrast, what emerges here, and radically so, is a view of design's necessary and inescapable *impurity*. Design, these chapters exemplify, is radically impure, complex, contingent, contradictory. As one of the authors who plays this theme the strongest – Jeremy Kidwell – puts it in his conclusion: 'One of the advantages of a design paradigm which places tricky hybridity at the centre is that it compels an appreciation of the necessary cohabitation of humans with other creatures.' In so doing it expands design to encompass 'a wider and more holistic range of liveliness'. This in itself will help take us further

> Away from the design paradigms which underwrote so much of the hygienic mass-death which was a result of modern manufacture in the 20th century and instead give way to more complex understandings of lively and tricky engagements that recognize complex systems … and the complex interplay of discourses such as hospitality, violence and cohabitation that lie at the heart of … design.[7]

3. The third tension, opposition or target of these chapters, is what we began with, namely the limits on speaking design. It is not that these have disappeared. A close reading would show in place after place remnants of these prohibitions. Design has by no means cast off these shackles, doubtless too it is busy elsewhere in inventing or asserting new ones. But there is no doubt that these chapters are spoken against limits that their authors feel permitted to try to think outside. There is little evidence here of writing that wishes to cover up the traces. If it is extremely difficult to face some of these issues within the lens of design, it nonetheless contains attempts to do so. These become indicative of a new level of possibility in talking about, in design and *through* design, so much of what, in fact has historically been excluded, not just 'as' design (though that too) but as the 'subject matter' of design; that – meaning those human moments – with which it necessarily dealt but wished, across most of the last century at least, not to speak about.

III

There is no need for me to repeat here what the chapters themselves explore, which are in any case both comprehensively introduced and reflected upon by the editors. The issue I will close on is simpler, it goes back to the theme I began with. There is, in a seminar by Badiou, which deals with the thought of the twentieth century, a line that has great pertinence I think for thinking today. He is talking about methodology and he asks, yes, but in 'thinking the century' what is important to think is what could *not* have been thought, what was literally *unthinkable*, in the previous century. This is a question that we, at the start of the twenty-first century, must also ask. What do the changed conditions under which we live, allow, permit, necessitate that we think that could not have been thought in the last century? What, objectively and subjectively, opens for us now? What do we *need* to think? What must we think? There is obviously a huge issue opened here: in effect, the question of thinking our times.[8] But in respect of the subject matter of this volume, the tricky, hybrid, ethics of things and making, of designing processes and social forms, it seems to me that these chapters are *beginning* this process: that they point towards things that must be thought and they do so by, obviously to varying degrees, both breaking with some of the norms and limits of the thought of last century and by introducing languages and ranges of concepts that help start this process. This is the book's value.

Notes

1 The famous opening sentence of *Design for the Real World* (London: Paladin, 1974) p. 1.
2 Eventually published by University of New South Wales press in Sydney, 1999.
3 See the essay 'Why Still Philosophy?' in Theodor Adorno, *Critical Models* (New York: Columbia University Press, 1998) pp. 5–17.
4 Italo Calvino, *Six Memos for the Next Millennium* (New York: Vintage, 1996) see pages 10, 4.
5 Ibid., p. 12.
6 Alain Badiou and Slavoj Žižek, *Philosophy in the Present* (Cambridge: Polity, 2009) p. 81. Badiou's formulation has complete resonance with design. It effectively describes the critically affirmative act of re-configuration.
7 Jeremy Kidwell, The Quest for Purity, 'Clean' Design and a New Ethics of 'Dirty Design', this volume, p. 204.
8 This really is the intellectual project of our century. But precisely because this a century of artificial design that cannot absent itself from this project without loss to both itself and to the understanding of what-could-be (and of how what-could-be can successfully be brought about). Again, recall Herbert Simon: 'The possibility of creating a science or sciences of the artificial is exactly as great as the possibility of creating any science of the artificial. The two possibilities stand and fall together.' *Sciences of the Artificial*, ibid., p. xi.

Introduction: Ways of Thinking Tricky Design

We don't have to disengage from the world ... because we may happen to think we will never be able to grasp it.

George Perec (2008: 265)

The purpose of this collection of chapters is to grasp (at) some of the ethical dimensions of Design. Perec wrote about the experience of Robert Antelme, deported to Buchenwald in 1944 – an event that remains hard to grasp, but was clearly the result of 'design'. He proposes that such events challenge us to really look at them, arguing that this necessary looking is made possible by art, by literature. While the subjects of the chapters in this book may not be as challenging as Antelme's experience, they cover some topics that we may find difficult to look at, and some we may find hard to grasp.

The scope of these examples, and the scope of the designed responses they in turn imply, may challenge the assumption that designers' ethical and political potency is limited to their responsibility to be competent by the standards of their discipline (Donahue 2004). Fenn and Hobbs (2015) point to the complexity, the *tricky difficulty* that characterizes the ethics of situations designers find themselves engaging with, and advocate a design process that eases the designer's task in such cases by accepting the 'problem ecologies' they are presented with. In contrast, Clive Dilnot has recently sought to shift our attention from design as a bounded, professional(ized) competence to design as 'mode of acting in the world', which is fundamentally about 'the negotiation of incommensurabilities' (2014: 68). This book is aimed at designers who like Fenn and Hobbs recognize that design offers no easy answers or solutions to the problems we face in our moment in history, but whose conscience means they cannot stop there. Like Dilnot, they are forced to consider the tricky nature of some of those problem ecologies, the interests that generate them and their political consequences.

By reviewing some of the challenges that particular contexts bring with them, the book intends to make a contribution to design debate that helps disentangle designers' desire to address problems from the conditions that define what such problems are and what might be valid solutions to them. The characterization of 'design' that is operative here is broader than the efforts of professional designers, but it includes them. It extends to encompass both the efforts of designers and the results of those efforts – the tools and techniques of designing, and the 'things' that result. It includes both the practices of designers and their social and commercial placement; both the material practices of design and their immaterial, social, effects. It demonstrates the degree to which design actions are ever entangled with their setting.

The book uses the idea of trickiness to inspect the ethical implications of these instances of design's entanglement. The word's common-sense usage is relevant. It indicates something that is difficult, requires care and skill because it is awkward to resolve. The wicked problems that design is argued to be good at addressing are tricky (Rittel and Webber 1973; Buchanan 1992). They present us with challenges that we know for their contradiction, uncertainty and ambiguity, but about which we have incomplete knowledge and with which we engage through unequal power relations. Here, the personification of trickiness in the trickster figure found in cultures across the world begins to become relevant – the problem fields we confront perhaps require such a figure; shape-shifting, dissembling, contradictory, mobile.

The chapters draw on this trickster archetype to cover topics that include the right of individuals to autonomy, the politics of representation, technological agency and government policy, all areas of concern that lie within the scope of design. They reflect on both the processes involved in designing and the consequences of those processes, discussing how design should be conducted, and in parallel considering the consequences of particular contexts for designing. The ethics of design processes connects to institutional concerns with the ethics of research processes in general, which seek to minimize risk of harm and ensure participant autonomy through informed consent. However, as Light and Akama's chapter shows, design research can involve principles that do not feature in institutional codes of research ethics, and such codes never cover the outcomes of research, or the uses to which it is put by those who commission it.

This is another dimension to the tricky – difficult – position a designer or design researcher is in who is concerned about the ethics of their practice, with only partial guidance on the ethics of their process and none on the ethics of its consequences, no control over the 'problem ecology' it is part of (Fenn and Hobbs 2015). This follows the logic of design's apparent *subaltern* status, serving rather than leading (Dilnot 2014: 59, 2015: 208). As the designer Milton Glaser put it:

> designers per se are usually in a very weak position in regard to what they do; they don't make the determinations, they don't decide what is to be sold, they don't decide on the strategy or the objectives very often. (quoted in Soar 2002)

However, the chapters in this book reflect efforts to push against this tendency, to use other types of trickery – which are perhaps design's special power – to bring about ethical consequences, ethical *things*. And the fluid, context-dependent nature of what we can identify as 'things', in this sense, is matched by the fluid trickiness of design itself. Design is defined by the fluid relationships between humans and matter that bring things into the world; it is a *practice* of 'thinging'. Archaeologist Michael Shanks proposes 'pragmatology' as a way to understand 'things':

Encompassing the richness of the old Greek meaning of the term, *pragmata* are 'things', but also 'deeds', 'acts' (things done), 'doings', 'circumstances' (encounters), 'contested matters', 'duties', or 'obligations'. The verb at the root of pragmata is *prattein* – to act in the material world, engaged with things. (2012: 69)

Put so, and extended to include the processes that bring 'things' about, design could appear to be beyond ethics, simply a practice, literally pragmatic, an instance of *prattein*. But this abstract view obscures the degree to which design is implicated in (and perhaps defined by) the where, when, why and how in which it takes place. Design's ethics are awkward – *tricky-difficult* – because they are always conditioned by and entangled in the setting in which the practice finds itself. The chapters in this volume both represent the range of those conditions, and exceed it.

Some of design's radical roots

There is another sense of trickiness that characterizes both design and the ethical dimensions of the conditions that affect it, in the gathering and re-gathering of the elements that make up the 'things' on which design works, and its relationship to the shifting 'social multiplicity' (Whitmore 2015: 43) that conditions it. Both are 'double', dissembling, contradictory; *slippery-tricky*. Currently, that social multiplicity is throwing up particular political challenges that take our attention beyond a discussion of design, as constrained by its apparently subaltern position. A *desire* to extend the scope of design beyond those constraints has long been evident and continues to be. Writing in 1970, Christopher Alexander drew the remit of design widely, ascribing to it an integrative purpose: 'Human feelings, climate, engineering, social problems, ecology, transportation, economics, must all be integrated' (Alexander 1970: n.p.). The association of design with 'human feelings' points towards a relationship to ethics; 'social problems' strongly implies politics – 'thinging' with ethical and political purposes.

Subsequent years have seen this call for integration answered through design's response to developments in technologies. Digital technologies have made demands at the broadest level on our understanding of the relationship between people and the world we make (Kimbell 2013). On a more practical level they have meant design research has developed rich connections with the other disciplines in the 'human sciences', to meet the methodological and conceptual challenges that these technologies have instigated. A significant contribution here has been the development of participative, action-based methods, drawing from a non-positivistic epistemology. While the Human Computer Interaction (HCI) research community is clear about the antecedents of these tendencies (see Kock 2011) in the 'cooperative enquiry' developed by John Heron and Peter Reason (1997, 2008) and Freire's participative approach to pedagogy for social change (Freire 1970), these roots are perhaps less evident in the design literature, with some notable exceptions. Victor Papanek invoked Freire when he called for a postgraduate design school 'for the southern half of the globe' in 1983, and recent years have seen a growing awareness of the connection between participative and social design, and particularly design methods and their radical roots (DiSalvo 2012, and see Koskinen 2016 for a review).

There are other current and recent symptoms of this awareness. The call to 'decolonize' design – reflected in Chapters 2, 5 and 6 – is one of them. Cinammon Janzer and Lauren Weinstein (2014) identify quite precisely the relationship between efforts to bring about social change through design – 'social design' – that are relatively embedded, or not, in the social systems they seek to change, warning against those that are not and appealing to Freire's precept of respect for those served by design. Eduardo Romeiro Filho (2013) uses Freire's work to construct an ethical frame to establish how best to use design to promote craft industries in Brazil. In Europe, Pelle Ehn and colleagues show how this radical orientation can be harnessed to an approach to design's role in bringing about 'things' in ways that go beyond an instrumental approach to 'users'. As they put it: 'In theory and in practice, users are much too often not only taken hostage by neo-liberal capitalism but also patronized by advocates of human-centered design' (2014: 8).

The origins and present of some aspects of design theory and practice that engage with the consequences of thinking about the ethics of things are at least critical, if not political.

Our political context and what tricky design might do about it

Design's progressive roots are especially relevant currently, given the character of our times, when liberal values seem under threat. In this respect, design has moved beyond its response to the opportunities presented by modernization and industrialization, which at the same time ameliorated some of modernity's negative consequences through design for better health and increased hygiene (Forty 1986; Lupton and Miller 1992). Since the 1960s, fear of existential threats from our own human activity has stimulated design that seeks to engage at a societal level with the consequences of new technologies and consumption (Koskinen 2016), using designs as social provocations (Ehn, Nilsson and Topgaard 2014), building on work motivated by concern for environmental sustainability (Charter 1998). Recent events have spurred calls directed at the HCI community to consider design's role in responding to existential crisis (Light, Shklovski and Powell 2017), along with war, migration, violent religious extremism and/or the impact on our communities of issues raised by technology, economic inequality, corporate greed, crime and intolerance.

Statements of dismay at the ethical consequences of design are not new. A list of eighty-five manifestos circulates on the internet from as far back as William Morris's 'The Arts and Crafts of Today' (including a couple of anti-manifestos).[1] The list includes the 1964 'First Things First' manifesto, attributed to Ken Garland and signed by twenty-one other designers, which gained notoriety for criticizing the application of graphic design to consumerism. It was re-launched in 2000, this time signed by thirty-three designers, Ken Garland among them. The distaste this manifesto expressed for the spectacle of consumerism, and disquiet at design's involvement in it, were amplified through the 'culture-jamming' phenomenon that appeared late in the twentieth century (see Soar 2002 for a summary) and it was again updated in 2014 by Cole Peters to reflect the influence of the internet on communication design. Garland's intervention continues to resonate. In 2015–16, the American design agency Mad*Pow developed a tool through which designers can generate a version of the medic's hippocratic oath that suits their situation (Dempsey and Taylor 2016) because they are 'sick of selling junk food' (Quito 2015).

Latterly, these expressions of distaste for consumerism, perhaps linked to what Armstrong and colleagues (2014: 1) discuss as a 'social design moment' have been joined by statements from thought leaders in design with a more explicitly political focus. Concerns about democracy have prompted Victor Margolin and Ezio Manzini to send an open letter to the design community containing a call to action, to 'take a stand, speak out, and act' against 'attacks on democracy' (2017: n.p.).[2] The year 2017 also saw a letter from the technology design community laying out some principles on the ethics of design that combine the distaste for low-brow, exploitative applications of design expressed in 1964, with a degree of engagement with the politics of these times. Calling for 'digital citizens, not mere consumers', the letter was generated by discussion at the Techfestival in Copenhagen,[3] gathering over 3,000 signatures online in the month after the festival. Later in 2017, the Montreal World Design Summit produced a declaration[4] intended to further the objective to develop 'an international action plan for harnessing the power of design to address pressing global challenges' rather than reinforcing consumerist values, that was signed by representatives of design associations from across the globe.

These interventions into the ethics of design practices point to the necessarily awkward (tricky) entanglement of design practices with Whitmore's 'social multiplicity', as well as the risk of hubris in practitioners who are necessarily in a subaltern position but take a high-minded view of the ethics of their work. By acknowledging the ethical and political discourse that has grown up round design over the last half century (see Margolin 2012), it is possible to set this contemporary discourse on design's ethics into an historical continuum in which the pragmata of design have a role in humans' relationships with each other, with Whitmore's 'social multiplicity', as much as with things. The idea that designers can stand up and make the case for democracy, as urged by Manzini and Margolin in 2017, reflects a background of contemporary uncertainty, including global problems of climate change and sustainability that may currently be overshadowed by immediate political tensions.

Design's engagement with these aspects of the 'social multiplicity' is implicated in design's trickiness in both the senses introduced so far. Responding to the challenges foreshadowed by Margolin and Manzini is 'tricky-difficult' and design often appears 'tricky-slippery' in its response. Sometimes design's engagements with the 'social multiplicity' seem diffident when measured against the scale of the challenges it throws in our path. Design always exists partly in imagination, and imagination is necessary to it. However, the speculative and critical design (SCD) subjected to critique in Chapter 6, by Luiza Prado and Pedro de Oliveira seems a slippery, albeit well-theorized, retreat to the gallery from the bizarre consequences of new technologies and circumstances, and consequently is perhaps an inadequate response to those challenges. And this (tricky) difficulty with dealing with future 'things' that goes beyond speculation and critique confounds philosophers as well as designers – as a 2013 interview with Graham Harman demonstrates. Harman implies that the speculative 'counterfactual' is design's only recourse to responding to the future as it arrives (Kimbell 2013).

Along with the description of the trickster figure that features in Latin American mythology to be found in Chapter 6, the concluding remarks at the end of this book explore the history of the trickster concept, and the ways it has been related to design by Vilem Flusser among others. Some threads of the trickster's history are particularly relevant here so worth pre-figuring. There is a useful distinction to be made between the trickster *character* that appears in cultures across the globe and trickster *characteristics*. This distinction, between the 'trickster figure' and the 'trickster mind', could equate to the difference between 'design', as a professional category, and 'design thinking' (see Kimbell 2011, 2012; McDonnell 2015), as the special ability that design brings to situations (see Kimbell 2011, 2012).

Returning to the problematic set out above – how design can engage with challenges such as that set by Manzini and Margolin – it is useful to note another aspect of the trickster character in global cultural traditions. This figure appears to be transgressive – they break the rules – but is actually normative. The trickster doesn't alter the rules, they only make them more evident by challenging them, always to be co-opted. We have seen above that aspects of design have roots in participative and political pedagogic practice that challenges rules and seeks to change assumptions, such as the conventional lack of power of those at the bottom of the economic heap. As Fisher sets out in Chapter 1, historically, design has been seen as a force for good, and continues to be. It is figured as an agentive, purposeful pursuit, exemplified in Hebert Simon's oft-cited comment 'everyone designs who devises courses of action aimed at changing existing situations into preferred ones' (1996 [1969]). However, design's tendency to diffidence, being the slippery trickster who exposes power but does not seek to change it, leads some commentary on Manzini and Margolin's letter to acknowledge an obvious and simple corrective to Simon's dictum, which is both ethical and political. Writing on the DESIS website, which focuses on design for social innovation and sustainability, Carla Cipolla insists that 'to be transformative, social innovation has to consider the *direction* of the desired transformation' (Carla Cipolla 2017, emphasis in original). Her call addresses the question of 'whose preference' should prevail, and can be laid over the topics addressed by all the chapters.

Relational tricks with things

'We are mingled with the things of the world in such a way that we are *ontologically indivisible*'. (Webmoor and Whitmore 2008: 59; emphasis in original)

The discussion above has drawn from the academic attention to *things* seen in the last few decades. This move has seen a shift away from an obsession with symbolic meaning, interpretation and a privileging of human rationality in understanding our relationship to our material surroundings. Instead, recent work has acknowledged that agency is distributed through networks of relationship that encompass humans and non-humans, which touch each other socially, materially and aesthetically, are contingent and time-bound (Appadurai 1986, 2006; Kopytoff 1986; Brown 2001; Fisher 2004; Latour 2005). This is deep relationality; contemporary philosophy deals with material agency at the level of particulate matter (Bennett 2010; Barad 2012), and our relationship with, and definition by, technologies (Harman 2002).

This 'move to things' can be positioned in the history of design theory through a brief digression into the systems-orientated approach that was prevalent in the mid-twentieth century. In his early work, Christopher Alexander's focus on the identification of patterns of 'fit' between 'form and context' led him to propose a systems-orientated approach to correcting misfits, to compensate for the inadequacies of the individual designer. This 'bewildered' (1964: 4) figure was to be assisted by the systematic approach that Alexander proposed. While he later much revised this conception of a solitary designer, it has a family resemblance to persistent ideas of designers who are relatively cut off from the context in which they operate, perhaps occupied mostly with manipulating meaning, isolated from the consequences of their practice. Isolated in a sense from its ethics. The correctives to such isolation found in 'social design' approaches range from Margolin and Margolin's practical overview of 'what a designer can contribute to human welfare' (2012: 28), orientated towards the needs of clearly delineated groups, such as the elderly, to more recent and arguably more systemic work discussed below (Ehn et al. 2015).

On the face of it, this move is welcome. Understanding design as a practice restricted to playing in the symbolic realm downplays both the relational material and human engagement that characterize it (drawing, making, representing) and the connectedness to its setting that may motivate it. From the perspective of design, there is a sense that in this move towards materiality the rest of the human sciences have been catching up with insights that design may have been unable to articulate, but always necessarily operates with. The move to materiality makes available for analysis matters that design has worked with intuitively. In an equivalent way, the ethical dimensions of design have necessarily been present, but relatively unarticulated. Exploring the ramifications of the relational principle may help us to bring them into the open too.

The relational principle has expressed itself in recent work that develops ways of designing with the 'social multiplicity' through a focus on 'things' in a series of publications by Pelle Ehn and colleagues, coming from HCI towards social design (Ehn 2008; Binder et al. 2011; Björgvinsson, Ehn and Hillgren 2012; Ehn, Nilsson and Topgaard 2015). In *Design Things* (2011), Thomas Binder and colleagues describe design and designing as a mode of inquiry rather than as professional competency in a particular domain of expertise. Their purpose is to move from 'designing "things" (objects) to designing Things (socio-material assemblies)' (Björgvissen, Ehn and Hillgren 2012: 102). Their reference point for this re-assessment of design's relationship to the 'social multiplicity' by introducing the 'Thing' concept is the ancient Nordic sense of the word to mean a place of meeting or assembly, as well as matters of concern and inanimate objects, preserved in the name of the Icelandic parliament, the 'Althing'. This 'reinvention of the Nordic thing' has put in the foreground the potential for design's capacity for making to mean it engages with governance, and consequently with ethics (Ehn, Nilsson and Topgaard 2015: 8).

Setting this formulation in the participatory design tradition, with its roots in the Scandinavian movements for democracy at work, Ehn's 2008 essay and his later work propose that an orientation to 'things' allows design to engage with Latour's enfolding of humans and non-humans, in 'constantly changing collectives' (1999: 16, 174ff) to construct a 'socio-material *design thing*, a meaningful potentially controversial assembly' (Ehn 2008: 94). This offers a more sophisticated way of talking about design than an object-based or professionalized account can offer and is developed further in *Design Things*, which explores how *design things* can 'modify the space of interaction and performances … as sociomaterial frames for controversies, ready for unexpected use and opening up new ways of thinking and behaving' (Binder et al. 2011: 1).

Among the roots and antecedents of this work in design, and of the broader ethical concern with things of which it is part, are some strands of the sense of 'thinging' that Heidegger developed. It is possible to extract from the complexities of his phenomenological approach to the essence of things a simple (and perhaps obvious) principle, into which the ethical consequences of 'thinging' are bound – that things act back on their makers. So his jug is 'an object which a process of making has set up before and *against* us' (1971: 165, emphasis added). This principle (admittedly rather crudely extracted from Heidegger's work) points to relationality and engagement as the necessary factors to help design articulate its connection to technologies, 'problems' and societies, and the consequences *for design* of doing so.

Designs acting back on design

A recent (and ongoing) project in London, strongly informed by the ideas outlined above, clearly reveals the potency in this relationality. Using 'hacked' air quality sensing technology with a group of 'citizen scientists' to generate air quality data through 'citizen sensing', Jennifer Gabrys has deployed experimental tactics in a domain normally dominated by institutional (governmentally controlled) technology. Her tactics trouble normal relationships between air, sensing technology, data and citizens. Gabrys frames what she is doing through a set of ideas drawn from A. N. Whitehead and Gilbert Simondon, which complement the 'thing' orientation described above. For Whitehead, 'the actual world is a process', a process that populates the world with 'creatures' that may be human, or non-human (Whitehead 1929: 22). The work of Gabrys's citizen scientists – gathering air quality data – produces citizen scientist creatures, at the same time as it produces data 'creatures'. As Gabrys puts it: 'Environments, as understood within Citizen Sense research … are then at once an "object" of study as well as a mutually in-formed and coproduced relation through which monitoring practices and gathered data take hold and gain relevance' (2017: 16).

It is appropriate to wonder what are the ethical consequences of this 'acting back' of the creatures of the world (in Whitehead's sense) on designers and on our understanding of design. Clearly, this effect might be restricted to work undertaken in the spirit of 'thinging' with the relational principle to the fore such as that touched on above, and more conventional design and designers may be unaffected by the consequences of and context for their work; it may not act back on them. As editors, however, we bring our particular inflections on this question, modulated through our work on design in the context of social transgression (Lorraine) and in armaments (Tom) and it runs through many of the chapters below.

Graham Harman notes that material agency, and the relationality that is its consequence, is not much considered in design (Kimbell 2013: 109). However, it takes little imagination to accord independent agency to weapons – drones are at least semi-autonomous (Chamayou 2015) – and it is not difficult to impute to weapons what can seem to be a will to act, that affects their human creators, including their designers. Mieches's (2017) account of weapons acting on us through our desire for control is perhaps only a particular, and particularly obvious, case of a mechanism through which the qualities of all designed things act back on us. Noting that 'as weapons become, so do their users' we may simply be pointing to things with agency that are not in principle different from any other designs in their effect on the humans involved in their 'thinging' (Bousquet et al. 2017: 4). Weapons are just a particularly clear case of the premise that 'what we make changes us', in which arguments for controlling the design, production and exchange of the material artefact have strong ethical validity.

Design is often characterized as a positive force, the practice that brings us new things that are going to solve problems, give us pleasure, make us feel good. But reflecting on the entanglement between our changing, mutable human being and what we make throws up many instances, apparently less charged than our relationship with weapons, where that entanglement produces questionable results. Technologies of communication produce social isolation, while 'connecting' us. Systems of provision of cheap food produce ill health. Collective/commercial responses to environmental crisis design 'solutions' that load responsibility for action disproportionately on individuals. As Light and colleagues put it: 'Our tools shape us, so what we make affects how we handle uncertainty in constructive ways' (2017: n.p.). This is not a matter of what we make failing, or 'going wrong', or a matter of the actions of people using them; it is a systemic matter, a matter of relationships, with things.

Another obvious question that arises is whether there are boundaries to this relationality, or if there are not, whether there are different complexions on it as it plays out in different aspects of human–thing entanglement. It is tempting to describe technologies as if they were independent of us. This is evident, for instance, in the writing of Gilbert Simondon (1958: 17), who talks of technical objects evolving 'by virtue of internal necessity', in a discussion of the 'evolution' of the internal combustion engine, where the necessity is clearly brought about by relationships between non-human elements that have the characteristic of Latourean 'actants'. Academics and practitioners interested in 'things', from designers to archaeologists, have previously thought in terms of a dichotomy between the functional and the symbolic – one material, the other not – and such a view would position Simondon's engine components in the 'functional' domain. Paul Graves-Brown (2000) seeks to dispense with this division, suggesting they both demonstrate in their different ways the degree to which the function that we ascribe to objects is in a sense the 'materiality' of human culture, because of the fundamentally relational nature of function.

The unpredictable, tricky, consequences of interventions into sociomaterial entanglements are a consequence of this relationality, with weapons again being a clear example. Benjamin Mieches discusses the becoming of weapons in terms of the object-orientated philosophy developed by Graham Harman and others. As he puts it: 'According to these theories, objects of all kinds resist the categories, representations, and strategies applied to them while producing unintended or unanticipated changes in politics' (2017: 12). If we distinguish between designers who occupy the group identified above who have relatively little autonomy and designer-researchers who undertake design as a knowledge generating process, perhaps a lack of predictability in the way that designs play out in the world may make it *easier* for the former to wash their hands of the ethical consequences of what they are employed to do. But it doesn't let the latter group off the ethical hook and even for the former group, working in the mainstream, weapons may provide an analogy to the effects of their efforts in apparently less charged settings. Our discussions on these matters led to the creation of twelve new chapters by authors herein, either as part of conference stream engagements or from conversations that we as editors continued with other scholars who also agreed to write about tricky issues for this book. These accounts are located and grouped within three main themes which clearly emerged from the focus different authors took: they provide accounts of (i) **tricky thinging**, (ii) **tricky processes and tricky principles**, and/or the potential of design to address them, and (iii) **tricky policy** issues, as we summarize below.

Chapters introduction

The variety in the way they use the trickster theme matches the variety of the topics the chapters cover. The trickster is itself a slippery character – simultaneously inside and outside institutions; simultaneously truth-telling and deceitful; simultaneously powerful in its trickery and powerless; simultaneously wise and foolish. But a common feature of these manifestations of the trickster is an engagement with ethics, in some form or other, very often bound up with articulations of power. Till Eulenspiegel delights in tricking the powerful into debasing themselves with scatological deceits – because Till tricks him, the holy priest ends up in the shit (Oppenheimer 2001: 185).

Many of the chapters engage with an ethics of 'might' – power – and its resistance. In the first, Tom **Fisher** engages with what is perhaps the clearest materialization of might, weapons, which seem perhaps an odd focus for a discussion of ethics and design, since they are not characteristic of most of the work that design does. They are relatively hidden and have more in common perhaps with industrial equipment than with the consumer goods familiar from everyday life. But one of his chapter's purposes is to trouble the assumption that the world of weapons is so separate from everyday experience. To achieve this, Fisher is in a sense playing tricks on himself – trying to get a view that is outside what he (and the rest of us) are inside, a militarized culture. And vision is the theme he uses to unify his discussion of design as a particular instance of the generalized desire for action at a distance that underlies weapons. The destructive potential in this desire, a desire for control (Mieches 2017) which acts back on us, is realized routinely in the fearsome consequences of military designs that are taken to be at least ethically neutral, if not as a positive good for their economic benefit.

Discussing products that cross over between the civilian and military worlds, their presence in both making obvious the close relationship between the two, Fisher draws out a question about our assumptions about design as an inherently beneficent practice. Part of design's tricky duplicity is exposed in its capacity to be both world improving and world destroying. Certain aspects of modern warfare are reflected in some of the other chapters. 'Defence' has changed from conventional conflict to policing, from counterinsurgency to antiterrorism, from battle to assassination using drone technology, predicated on the assumption that bad outsiders can be identified and 'taken out'. There are echoes here of the prison industrial complex approach to crime that is the topic of Chapter 7 by Shana **Agid**, and clear relationships to Mahmoud **Keshavarz's** discussion of passporting and borders.

In Chapter 2, Keshavarz lays out a 'critical trickification' of design by levering open the conventional coupling of design practices with practices of power. He uses the trickster as a figure from which to build a criticality into a discussion of designed regimes of control and exclusion through passports, and their subversion through carefully designed forgery. His proposition is that the subversive 're-design' of passports by forgery and of the border system by migration brokers exposes the constructed nature of the mobility regime and is a critique of it, showing up the workings of the legal control of mobility. It works that classic trickster trick of exposing what it reflects, and what generates it. The transgressive act of forgery challenges the 'things relations and environments' of the bordering system that make up the 'material articulations' of the prevailing Foucauldian 'mobility regime'.

Keshavarz discusses a particular context for what he suggests is design's 'inherent violence' – its conventional alliance with power that in the case of bordering renders some secure at the expense of the insecurity of others. Passports clearly project power, they act at a distance in time and space, but as Keshavarz indicates, they are themselves 'tricky, shape-shifting artefacts'. Their systematization of control – what he names an 'affirmative material practice' – can be subjected to a 'critical material practice' through forgery.

But this is not a distanced, academic critique, it is critique through an 'act of refusal', more pointed, and more significant, than the critique practised in the seminar room or the art gallery – the critical design that is all about 'fetishising critique in the skin of commodity' as Keshavarz puts it. But neither is it pure – migration broking can be a moneymaking venture that might take advantage of vulnerable people. The generalizable point contained in Chapter 2 draws from Walter Benjamin's essay 'Critique of Violence', giving a tricky reading of the opposition of the violence of law-making with the 'non-violent violence' of resistance, promoting the resistance inherent in forgery, while refusing its exploitation of the vulnerable.

In contrast to the engagement with the systems designed by states that is the focus of Keshavarz's criticality, Nidhi **Srinivas** and Eduardo **Staszowski's** chapter describes the tricky features of processes of socially engaged designing that provide 'moments of contestation' in particular urban locations. Setting their discussion in the context of civic design, they discuss the designer–client relationship in terms of trickery and guile, to resolve tensions between designers and public clients. Maintaining that it is through the complexity of such relations that designed things come about, they seek to move their discussion beyond the established function of design processes to manipulate meanings to address well-articulated problems. Instead, they acknowledge the degree to which design engagements are ever mixed and entangled with social relations, offering a more complex reading of the relationship between design(ers') actions and their consequences.

Srinivas and Staszowski's view interrogates the relationships that prevail in design processes. They point towards the principle of entanglement/mixture by drawing from the elements of design through two case studies, of the modernist development of Brasilia and a project in the Public and Collaborative programme in the Parsons DESIS Lab. They conclude by identifying three forms of trickery, taking the slippery trickster as a force that can 'make novelty fall in line with latent expectation'. They focus on relationships in the design process, between the roles of designer and client, which vary according to the type of design process, and its setting. Their discussion reaches towards the consequences of the entanglement that they set out, translating it into language relevant to the practice of design, where tricks are a 'form of social cunning' in a process that constantly throws up effects that defeat intentions.

Chapter 4 takes a phenomenological view on a type of object that exemplifies the gap between material facts, and the ethical consequences of the ways that objects play out in actuality – guns. Discussing hand guns specifically, and pointing up their significance for discussions of human and material agency, Tim **Dant** takes the reader through a carefully inflected discussion to argue for the primacy of collective human responsibility for their effects. Stressing a point that relates this chapter to Fisher's discussion of (other) weapons of war, for Dant it is guns' symbolic potency that is at the heart of their ethical consequences, which being an aesthetic matter is the link to the discussions of design elsewhere in this volume.

To establish his position on our collective rather than individual responsibility for the moral power of guns, Dant discusses relevant aspects of the philosophy of technology. He argues that our collective responsibility is compromised by the human-object symmetry found in Latour's Actor Network Theory and Peter Paul Verbeek's postphenomenology. Instead, Dant appeals to ideas from Hans Jonas to position guns as a problem for 'collective cultural responsibility', contrasting Heidegger's 'framing' of technologies which accords agency to humans with Latour/Verbeek's idea of 'mediation'.

Dant's position hinges on the proposition that guns are morally *relevant* but do not have moral *agency*, which is 'ultimately human, however morally relevant the technology is'. While this is clearly true of a gun, or other technology once it exists as a separate thing from humans and all other things, it does not account for the considerations that enter into a process of design that might bring an as-yet non-existent gun about. Dant's discussion is therefore restricted to considerations that affect designs, rather than design(ing), aligning with the point referred to above in respect of the power of object-orientated theory to account for processes of design.

However, it is clear that in practical terms, a challenge does exist to design a world where the destructive potential of guns is appropriately constrained by the *dispositif* within which they exist. Dant's chapter ends on the potential for guns to have *decivilizing* effects that threaten social relations, emphasizing the moral agency of their possessor, which is the locus of the threat. This points to the relevance of his emphasis on the importance of changing their cultural and symbolic status as a way of controlling their inherently anti-life quality.

Changing the *dispositif* in this respect presents a tricky challenge and while there are various 'takes' on the trickster theme in the following chapters, Cameron **Tonkinwise** is the only author to pick up on the befuddling sleight of hand that is one speciality of trickster figures. However, he distinguishes between 'trickery' and 'magic', arguing that because design's process (abductive synthesis) is invisible and the workings of the technologies that it brings into the everyday world also obscure, it functions as magic, in the sense that Arthur C. Clarke set out:

Any sufficiently advanced technology is indistinguishable from magic. (1973: 38)

He contrasts what he argues are the properly 'magical' properties of the designed world, which appears to have no limits in extent or scope, to enlightenment assumptions of the power of reason, and the colonialist othering of those who remain influenced by magical thinking, noting that if we accept that design's trickery is indeed magical, we accept that the distinction involved in that othering is untenable. In an apparently determinist – non-relational – argument that aligns with Dant's analysis of guns, he holds design responsible for turning

materials into forms that can act at a distance on groups of people in lasting ways that those people find difficult to resist and that consequently become predictive of their future habits.

This stands in contrast to Fisher's chapter, which acknowledges the *desire* to act at a distance, but sets this in systems of relationality and Tonkinwise's reading of fetishism actually seems neatly circular, and therefore relational. He identifies that fetishism 'has the very power it wishes to dispel', and that magical *value* persists. He also proposes a circular notion of use – material is defined by person as thing, thing defines person as user. His discussion holds to a view of design as beneficent, which it clearly is not always, though the elements of the beneficence of the design process that he identifies – empathy for instance – can be understood independently from their application to any particular end, with attendant moral consequences. However, even empathy with an other does not require care for that other.

While Tonkinwise points to the entanglement of design with actor networks, and the necessary ethical dimensions of the things that result, Pedro **de Oliveira** and Luiza **Prado** take a view of the recent phenomenon of Speculative and Critical Design (SCD) from the perspective of theories of coloniality. They inspect two pieces of SCD work, by Burton and Nitta and by Montgomery and Brillatz, finding in them clear evidence of the persistence of coloniality in relation to people and places, through their characterization of non first-world 'others' and 'other places'. Their reading of this work, strongly informed by their citizenship of the global south, is a convincing basis for their argument that by acting as a 'mildly dystopian wing of the status quo', SCD, and potentially design as a whole, reproduces coloniality.

Their discussion of the origins of this contemporary coloniality in an uncritical inheritance of colonial assumptions bears out Clive Dilnot's observation of 'the almost complete lack of historical perspective in design research that renders [it] all but null-and-void as genuine understanding' (2014: 59). However, by recommending a 'tricky' design that is located in both past and future, Prado and de Oliveira develop a position that can amount to practical steps for doing design that address this nullity. They offer this proposition as an outcome of their analysis of SCD rooted firmly in the Latin American mythology of the shape-shifting trickster, perhaps making a richer use of the concept than any of the other chapters. As they put it, this 'requires designers to act as trickster figures: debating, listening, and crafting possible, speculative worldviews' that challenge coloniality, instead of reproducing it.

As a route to this decolonization, they offer a practice based in two principles: 'yarning' and 'siting'. The first is devoted to a dialogic untangling of the one-dimensional representation offered by SCD, by bringing into design discourse 'discussions initiated by decolonial and feminist thinking'. The second, which is a component and consequence of yarning, draws from Haraway, bringing to the foreground the position that the researcher occupies and the need for awareness of it against the Eurocentric approaches to knowledge which design inherits. This brings them back to the shape-shifting trickster that allows divergent thinking by allowing navigation between world views.

Prado and De Oliveira's critique of fictional(ized) design engagements with an abstracted, and ideologically loaded, 'social' is answered by Shana **Agid**'s chapter, with its focus on crime and safety. In contrast to the SCD cases just covered, this discussion is structured round design engagements with actual social and political matters, in a specific location, working collaboratively with people directly affected by the reality of the prison industrial complex. The theoretical focus of Agid's discussion brings Donald Schon's principle of 'problem setting' into a critical relationship with Paulo Freire's concept of 'problem posing'. In this, Agid identifies the potential to expose the implicitly political dimensions of the designer-centric aspects of Schon's formulation through the explicit politics of a 'collective and dialectical' process that draws on Freire.

Agid situates the discussion of the systemic conditions that affect the politics of policing and incarceration in the United States, and their effects on people in Oakland, California. Relating it to the design process in the participative design literature, Agid places the case study in the literature on crime and policing. Here, the chapter's argument finds strong support for its historicized, politically inflected approach to participation, in which its design approach can seek to answer fundamental questions, such as 'What might it mean to design *for* "freedom" or "well-being" instead of *against* crime?' in imagined futures that are politically intelligent.

Moving from an account of social design methods in a particular setting, and the ethical dimensions of problem setting, Ann **Light** and Yoko **Akama's** chapter takes a broader view of the ethics of design research processes tied into cases of design research in the UK, Ghana, Chile, South India and New South Wales in Australia. At the centre of the chapter is a discussion of what characterizes the ethics of working with participant groups in these settings, which extends the focus of Agid's chapter.

Whereas the ethics of research *processes* are heavily codified to ensure the rights of participants, and researchers' obligations to them, Light and Akama propose instead an ethics of care. Through the range of the examples of research that they cover they are able to bring the challenge that they present into relief – it is ethically tricky to work with diffuse and 'nebulous' groups of people, when the unboundedness of the groups of participants is matched by that of the design process itself. The chapter proposes that this unboundedness implies an evolving ethics of trust, as an efficient replacement for the constant negotiation necessary in an ethics of rights and obligations. Trust in the particular and the personal acknowledges our 'primordial interrelatedness'.

As the first chapter in the book's final part, 'Tricky Policy', Lucy **Kimbell**'s chapter turns the focus from Light and Akama's account of the ethics of research processes, towards design and policy, drawing from her extensive experience of working closely with government as part of the UK Cabinet Office Policy Lab. She notes that this experience, embedding design process in government, can be seen as a result of a move away from top-down technical rationalist approaches to policy development. Her chapter develops a rich exploration of the implications of this move, which amounts to an acknowledgement of the value of design as an *aesthetic* method, which is paralleled by moves in other disciplines, for instance international relations (see Gibbon and Sylvester 2017), but in this case is for the development of 'socio-material policy objects'.

Kimbell draws on Agamben's (2009) characterization of Foucault's concept of the 'apparatus', the force that in the context of public policy development subjectifies both citizens and public servants. She points to design's capacity for the 'manipulative gamble', a characteristic of the quality that the ancient Greeks named *metis*, as an element in an 'anti-heroic' revision to design, and its role in what Agamben called the 'profanation' of apparatus through feeling, through the aesthetic. There is a counter argument here, and in the other chapters in this part of the book, to the assumption that design necessarily occupies a subaltern position (Dilnot 2014). However, Kimbell's own assertion that such an anti-heroic design engages with a problem field such that its contributions are 'co-emergent with their context' suggests that this design is by definition what its context makes it. Nonetheless, the built-in trickery of her anti-heroic design makes it an attractive proposition.

Kimbell's focus on policy pre-figures a move to the tricky situations that design finds itself in when its potential for engineering change is applied to innovation in public service *provision*, which is unpicked in Adam **Thorpe**'s chapter. He builds from a reading of Rittel and Webber's foundational text that identified the 'wicked' nature of problems in planning, and therefore in design, but rendered this wickedness as simply difficult, rather than ethically negative. The case studies of the design of public service innovation that Thorpe discusses are defined by the contemporary politics of neo-liberal austerity, which he identifies as both 'wicked', and 'tricky' in the sense of 'deceitful and crafty'. He identifies the ethically tricky consequences of austerity politics for public service innovation through detailed case studies from the 'Public Collaboration Lab' at Central St Martins, University of the Arts, London. From these, he draws out what are examples of the 'molecular' social design that Koskinen and Hush (2016) identify. In the re-design of a home library service; youth club services; home over-crowding, he makes a strong case for the potential for design to responsively make space, openings for action – a political design that can address the 'problem with politics' (DiSalvo 2010).

From Adam Thorpe's discussion of the design of public services in what it is to be hoped are temporary conditions of austerity, Lorraine **Gamman** and Pras **Gunasekera** discuss design's potential to engage with the permanence of voluntary death: suicide; ethically tricky and potentially crushing in its effects on those left living. Reviewing current debates, and drawing on work with postgraduate students, their chapter covers potential design interventions in public spaces that might discourage suicide as a result of mental illness, and the possibility for design to work with assisted suicide systems to help terminally ill individuals to end their own lives. While the former covers matters that relate closely to the situational crime prevention on which Gamman has published extensively, the latter takes their work into new territory. In this, they draw on principles close to the centre of design practice – its capacity to pre-figure situations through processes of enactment and visualization, to offer new ways to understand design for death. They propose using designs for assisted suicide to test what could work and what might work less well to both engender debate and engage policy makers by bringing the ethical/political dimensions of a future situation into the present. In this, they draw on Mouffe's (2013) principle of agonistic democracy, applying this to design that can produce 'positive conflict' over assisted dying.

Through case studies in art and architecture that have strong connections to the theme of hygiene, and by implication to death, Jeremy **Kidwell** develops a different take on the conundrums for design that arise in the light of recent thinking on human/non-human engagements. These cases focus on the variety of design ethics that have emerged in response to changing ideas about the agency of microscopic life. His discussion links the human/material through the effect of 'hygienic' modernism on the sense of self – proposing that there we are made up of 'tricky substances' that were hitherto thought of as 'dirty'. As well as confounding modernist assumptions, he connects his discussion to the ethics of personal spaces and a move from a conception of the self as bounded, to one that acknowledges its porosity.

Kidwell reviews design's engagement with dirt, and fear of disease, and therefore death, in an obverse to the connection Gamman and Gunasekera's chapter makes to the voluntary management of the end of life. Both reach for elements of the significance of life itself for designing, Kidwell's focusing on the relationship of design to a pathological pursuit of hygiene, which at its extreme invokes the 'hygiene' of collectives expressed as racial 'cleanliness'. His account of the hygiene ethics of modernist purity can be supplemented by the link recently established between Le Corbusier's political activity before the Second World War, and his relationship to the collaborationist Vichy government during it (de Jarcy 2015).

From identifying modernist forms motivated by the avoidance of death through prohibiting the contamination of individual bodies, Kidwell moves to examples that illustrate his argument for design that acknowledges a 'liveliness' that *includes death* – of objects and materials – in unfolding cycles in which design can engage. Here, there is perhaps a way to move beyond the concern expressed by Lucy Kimbell (2013) that contemporary thinking on lively human–material engagements is limited to a retrospective view. Design can engage in the cyclical vibrant relationships that Kidwell sketches in his concern to help design to 'express a wider and more holistic range of liveliness'.

Notes

1   See the 'Social Design Notes' blog, hosted by the design and technology consultancy *Backspace*: https://backspace.com/notes/2009/07/design-manifestos.php
2   'We are in difficult and dangerous times. For many years, we lived in a world that, despite its problems, was nevertheless committed to principles of democracy in which human rights, fundamental freedoms, and opportunities for personal development, were increasing. Today, this picture has changed profoundly. There are attacks on democracy in several countries – including those where democracy had seemed to be unshakable. Faced by these developments, we believe the design community should take a stand, speak out, and act: practitioners, researchers, theorists, students, journalists, publishers and curators – all who are professionally involved in design-related activities.'
3   The text of the letter can be found at https://copenhagenletter.org
4   The declaration can be found here: https://worlddesignsummit.com/wp-content/uploads/2017/10/20171004_WDSM2017_Brochure_declaration_65X9_AN.pdf

Bibliography

Agamben, Giorgio (2009) *What Is an Apparatus? And Other Essays*, Stanford, CA: Stanford University Press.

Alexander, Christopher (1964) *Notes on the Synthesis of Form*, Cambridge, MA: Harvard University Press.

Alexander, Christopher (1970) 'An Early Draft of *The Timeless Way of Building*'. Available at: https://www.patternlanguage.com/archive/timeless.html#, accessed February 2017.

Anslow, James Alan (2011) *The Tabloid Trickster: A Post-Jungian Evaluation of Early 21st Century Popular British Newspaper Journalism Characterised by That of The Sun*, Unpublished PhD thesis, University of Essex.

Appadurai, A. (ed.) (1986) *The Social Life of Things Commodities in Cultural Perspective*, Cambridge, MA: Cambridge University Press, pp. 64–91.

Appadurai, Arjun (2006) 'The Thing Itself', *Public Culture*, 18, 1: 15–21.

Armstrong, Leah, Bailey, Jocelyn, Julier, Guyand and Kimbell, Lucy (2014) *Social Design Futures: HEI Research and the AHRC*, Brighton: University of Brighton.

Barad, Karen (2012) 'On Touching – The Inhuman That Therefore I Am', *Differences, a Journal of Feminist Cultural Studies*, 23, 3: 207–223.

Bennett, Jane (2010) *Vibrant Matter: A Political Ecology of Things*, Durham, NC: Duke University Press.

Binder, Thomas, Ehn, Pelle, De Michelis, Giorgio and Jacucci, Giulio (2011) *Design Things (Design Thinking, Design Theory)*, Cambridge, MA: MIT Press.

Björgvinsson, Erling, Ehn, Pelle and Hillgren, Per-Anders (2012) 'Design Things and Design Thinking: Contemporary Participatory Design Challenges', *Design Issues*, 28, 3: 101–116.

Bousquet, Antoine, Grove, Jairus and Shah, Nisha (2017) 'Becoming Weapon: An Opening Call to Arms', *Critical Studies on Security*, 5, 1: 1–8, doi:10.1080/21624887.2017.1343010

Brown, Bruce (2001) 'Thing Theory', *Critical Inquiry*, 28, 1: 1–22.

Buchanan, Richard (1992) 'Wicked Problems in Design Thinking', *Design Issues*, 8, 2: 5–21.

Chamayou, Gregoire (2015) *A Theory of the Drone*, Translated by J. Lloyd, New York: New Press.

Charter M. (1998) 'Sustainable Product Design', in M. Kostecki (ed.), *The Durable Use of Consumer Products*, Boston, MA: Springer.

Cipolla, Carla (2017) 'DESIS Supports the Open Letter to the Design Community Stand up for Democracy'. Available at: http://www.desisnetwork.org/2017/04/11/open-letter/, accessed June 2017.

Clarke, Arthur C. (1973) Profiles of the Future: An Inquiry into the Limits of the Possible, New York: Harper & Row.

De Jarcy, Xavier (2015) *Le Corbusier, Un Fascisme Français*, Paris: Albin Michel.

Dempsey, Samantha and Taylor, Ciara (2016) *Designer's Oath*, Mad*Pow. Available at http://designersoath.com/index.html, accessed June 2017.

Dilnot, Clive (2014) 'Is There an Ethical Role for the History of Design? Redeeming through History the Possibility of a Humane World', Keynote address, 9th International Committee Design History and Design Studies, 8–11 July, Aveiro Portugal, *Blucher Proceedings*, 1, 5: 57–81. Available at: http://www.proceedings.blucher.com.br/article-list/icdhs2014-238/list#articles.

Dilnot, Clive (2015) 'History, Design, Futures: Contenting with What We Have Made', in Tony Fry, Clive Dilnot and Susan Stewart (eds), *Design and the Question of History*, London: Bloomsbury, pp. 133–243.

DiSalvo, Carl (2010) 'Design, Democracy and Agonistic Pluralism', in David Durling, Rabah Bousbaci, Lin-Lin Chen, Philippe Gauthier, Tiiu Poldma, Seymour Roworth-Stokes and Erik Stolterman (eds), *Design and Complexity*, Proceedings of DRS2010, 7–9 July, 366–371.

DiSalvo, Carl (2012) *Adversarial Design*, Cambridge, MA: MIT Press.

Donahue, Sean (2004) 'Discipline Specific Ethics', *Design Philosophy Papers*, 2, 2: 95–101.

Ehn, Pelle (2008) 'Participation in Design Things', *PDCd'08 Proceedings of the Tenth Anniversary Conference on Participatory Design*, Bloomington, Indiana, 1–4 October: 92–101.

Ehn, Pelle, Nilsson, Elisabet M. and Topgaard, Richard (2014) *Making Futures: Marginal Notes on Innovation, Design and Democracy*, Cambridge, MA: MIT Press.

Ehn, Pelle, Nilsson, Elisabeth M. and Topgaard, Richard (eds) (2015) *Making Futures. Marginal Notes on Innovation, Design, and Democracy*, Cambridge, MA: MIT Press.

Fenn, Terence and Hobbs, Jason (2015) 'Wicked Ethics in Design', *Proceedings of 7th DEFSA Conference, Design Education Forum of Southern Africa*, 127–135.

Fisher, Tom (2004) 'What We Touch, Touches Us: Materials, Affects and Affordances', *Design Issues*, 20, 4: 20–31.

Forty, Adrian (1986) *Objects of Desire: Design and Society since 1750*, London: Thames and Hudson.

Freire, Paulo (1970) *Pedagogy of the Oppressed*, New York: Continuum.

Fuller, J. F. C. (1998) *Armament and History: The Influence of Armament on History from the Dawn of Classical Warfare to the End of the Second World War*, New York: Da Capo Press.

Gabrys, J. (2017) 'The Becoming Environmental of Computation. From Citizen Sensing to Planetary Computerization', *Tecnoscienzia: The Italian Journal of Science and Technology Studies*, 8, 1: 5–21.

Garland, Ken et al. (1964) 'First Things First: A Manifesto', *The Guardian*, April 1964.

Gibbon, Jill and Sylvester, Christine (2017) 'Thinking Like an Artist-Researcher about War', *Millennium: Journal of International Studies*, 45, 2: 249–257.

Graves-Brown, P. M. (1995) 'Fearful Symmetry', *World Archaeology*, 27, 1: 88–99.

Graves-Brown, P. M. (2000) 'Introduction', in *Matter, Materiality and Modern Culture*, London: Routledge.

Harman, Graham (2002) *Tool Being: Heidegger and the Metaphysics of Objects*, Chicago, IL: Open Court.

Heidegger, Martin (1971) 'The Thing', in *Poetry, Language, Thought*, London: Harper Collins.

Heron, John and Reason, Peter (1997) 'A Participative Inquiry Paradigm', *Qualitative Inquiry*, 3, 3: 274–294.

Heron, John and Reason, Peter (2008) 'The Practice of Co-Operative Inquiry: Research "with" rather Than "on" People', in Peter Reason and Hilary Bradbury (eds), *Handbook of Action Research: Participative Inquiry and Practice*, London: Sage, pp. 179–188.

Janzer, Cinnamon, L. and Weinstein, Lauren S. (2014) 'Social Design and Neocolonialism', *Design and Culture*, 6, 3: 327–344.

Kimbell, Lucy (2011) 'Rethinking Design Thinking: Part 1', *Design and Culture*, 3, 3: 285–306.

Kimbell, Lucy (2012) 'Rethinking Design Thinking: Part 2', *Design and Culture*, 4, 2: 129–148.

Kimbell, Lucy (2013) 'The Object Strikes back: An Interview with Graham Harman', *Design and Culture*, 5, 1: 103–117.

Kock, Ned (2011) 'Action Research: Its Nature and Relationship to Human-Computer Interaction', in Soegaard, Mads and Rikke Friis Dam (eds), *Encyclopedia of Human-Computer Interaction*, Aarhus, Denmark: The Interaction Design Foundation.

Kopytoff, Igor (1986) 'The Cultural Biography of Things: Commoditization as Process', in A. Appadurai (ed.), *The Social Life of Things Commodities in Cultural Perspective*, Cambridge, MA: Cambridge University Press, pp. 64–91.

Koskinen, Ilpo (2016) 'Agonistic, Convivial, and Conceptual Aesthetics in New Social Design', *Design Issues*, 32, 3: 18–29.

Koskinen, Ilpo and Hush, Gordon (2016) 'Utopian, Molecular and Sociological Social Design', *International Journal of Design*, 10, 1: 65–71.

Latour, Bruno (1999) *Pandora's Hope: Essays on the Reality of Science Studies*, Cambridge, MA: Harvard University Press.

Latour, Bruno (2005) *Reassembling the Social: An introduction to Actor Network Theory*, Oxford: Oxford University Press.

Light, Ann, Shklovski, Irina and Powell, Alison (2017) 'Design for Existential Crisis (or Avoiding Bovine Design*)'. *Proceedings of the 2017 CHI Conference Extended Abstracts on Human Factors in Computing Systems*, pp. 722–734. ACM Digital Library.

Lupton, Ellen and Abott Miller, J. (1992) *The Bathroom, the Kitchen and the Aesthetics of Waste (A Process of Elimination)*, New York: Kiosk.

McDonnell, Janet (2015) 'Gifts to the Future: Design Reasoning, Design Research, and Critical Design Practitioners', *She Ji: The Journal of Design, Economics, and Innovation*, 1, 2: 107–117.

Manzini, Ezio and Margolin, Victor (2017) 'Democracy and Design – What Do You Think?' Available at http://www.desisnetwork.org/2017/04/11/democracy-and-design-what-do-you-think/, accessed June 2017.

Margolin, Victor (2012) 'Design and Democracy in a Troubled World', Lecture to School of Design, Carnegie Mellon University, 11 April 2012.

Margolin, Victor and Margolin, Sylvia (2002) 'A "Social Model" of Design: Issues of Practice and Research', *Design Issues*, 18, 4: 24–30.

Meiches, Benjamin (2017) 'Weapons, Desire, and the Making of War', *Critical Studies on Security*, 5, 1, 9–27.

Mouffe, Chantal (2013) *Agonistics: Thinking the World Politically*, London: Verso Books.

Oppenheimer, Paul (tr.) (2001) *Till Eulenspiegel: His Adventures*, London: Routledge.

Papanek, Victor (1983) 'Proposal: For the Southern Half of the Globe', *Design Studies*, 4, 1: 61–64.

Perec, Georges (2008), 'Robert Antelme or the Truth of Literature', in *Georges Perec: Species of Spaces and Other Pieces*, London: Penguin Classics.

Quito, Anne (2015) 'Sick of Selling Junk Food and False Promises, Designers Declare their Own "Hippocratic Oath"', *Quartz*. Available at https://qz.com/456845/sick-of-selling-junk-food-and-false-promises-designers-declare-their-own-hippocratic-oath/, accessed June 2017.

Rittel, Horst W. J. and Webber, Melvin M. (1973) 'Dilemmas in a General Theory of Planning' *Policy Sciences*, 4: 155–169.

Romeiro Filho, Eduardo (2013) 'Design and Craftsmanship: The Brazilian Experience', *Design Issues*, 29, 3: 64–74.

Shanks, Michael (2012) 'Let Me Tell You about Hadrian's Wall: Heritage, Performance, Design', *Reinwardt Memorial Lecture*, 11 May 2012, Reinwardt Academy. Available at http://www.mshanks.com/wp-content/uploads/Shanks-Heritage-Performance-Design.pdf, accessed February 2017.

Simon, Herbert (1996 [1969]) *The Sciences of the Artificial*, Cambridge, MA: MIT Press.

Simondon, Gilbert (1958) *On the Existence of Technical Objects*, Mellamphy, London, ON: University of Western Ontario.

Soar, Matthew (2002) 'The First Things First Manifesto and the Politics of Culture Jamming: Towards a Cultural Economy of Graphic Design and Advertising', *Cultural Studies*, 16, 4: 570–592.

Webmoor, Timothy and Whitmore, Christopher (2008) 'Things Are Us! A Commentary on Human/Things Relations under the Banner of a "Social" Archaeology', *Norwegian Archaeological Review*, 41, 1: 53–70.

Whitehead, Alfred North (1929 [1985]) *Process and Reality*, New York: The Free Press.

Whitmore, Christopher (2015) 'Archaeology and the Second Empiricism', in Charlotta Hillerdal and Johannes Siapkas (eds), *Debating Archaeological Empiricism*, Abingdon: Routledge, pp. 37–56.

Part One

Tricky Thinging

1

Concealed Trickery:
Design and the Arms Industry

Tom Fisher

It is strange to think that the same type of machine can carry a love letter or tons of concentrated death.

Fuller (1934)

Eurosatory

I am sitting on a stool, at a high café table. The table is near the entrance to an enormous exhibition space, stretching much further than I can see. The café is slightly above the level of the exhibition space, so I have a broader view of the exhibits than do the people moving among them. If I were setting the scene for a certain sort of narrative, I might call this a 'commanding' view. Who can I see? The scene is busy with people, most of whom are male. A lot of these men are wearing dark business suits, some, military uniform. There are females here too, some dressed in a dark suit with a skirt, some wearing more flamboyant outfits. I am wearing a dark business suit. I intend to blend in.

What can I see? A succession of exhibition stands run away into the distance, each designed to create as strong a visual impression as possible, competing with each other in this respect. Some of the products they display are large, some enormous, leading the eye upwards towards the space-frame roof of this vast hangar. The roof belongs to the Parc des Expositions, Paris Nord, Villepinte and while I drink my coffee I am observing the goings on at one of the world's three largest international arms fairs, Eurosatory. The exhibits that jostle with each other for my attention are showing all the conceivable products of the arms industry. Beyond the brutish outline of military vehicles I can see howitzers, missiles, bombs and drones, with motion provided by film-loops showing warplanes and vehicles in action, soaring over and plunging through desert terrain, accompanied by spectacular explosions.

Introduction

The narrative above summarizes impressions gained from visiting four international arms fairs between 2014 and 2017 in Europe and the Middle East. I have visited these events as a design research academic troubled by an awareness that design is entangled with the arms manufacturing industry, and by extension with the trade in weapons that is the raison d'être of the trade fairs for military and security equipment that take place in many parts of the world every year.[1] This chapter unpacks three elements that make the extent and nature of this entanglement relatively obscure: an assumption that design has a moral purpose; the relative secrecy that surrounds the arms industry and trade; design's role in rendering the industry a 'normal' and acceptable part of our culture.

This chapter uses my subjective experience of arms fairs to explore connections between design as we encounter it in everyday, civilian, life and the relatively obscure, but no less designed, world of armaments and military equipment. My intention is to use the experience to help me to show how design's potential to make a more caring world exists alongside its capacity to make matters that are arguably unreasonable and unacceptable appear normal. Being based on my experience, a sample of one, the chapter relates to qualitative work in the humanities, such as Brewster's discussion of her use of beach walks to help her to take a critical position on white Australian identity (2009). She is a white Australian trying to see white Australian identity, I am a design academic trying to take a critical position on design.

Weapons raise ethical concerns, and are met with protest based on the fact that both the manufacture and the trade in arms have at least a facilitating and potentially a causative role in armed conflict (Wezeman 2010: 195).[2] Weapons require the creative application of technologies through design, and design is also implicated in rendering them 'normal' – their aesthetics and the applications of the technologies in question bleed into everyday life. Although we perhaps prefer not to think too hard about this application of creativity through design, this chapter uses my first-hand experience to do so, following work by Arthur Cropley (2005, 2010) on the 'dark side' of creativity. The discussion places the moral tone of design historically and draws on some ideas from science and technology studies and the philosophy of technology to think about some examples of designs that cross over between civilian and military applications.

Anecdotal evidence for the entanglement of design with the arms industry includes the number of my engineer and designer colleagues who have worked for it, as well as its scale.[3] When its morals are questioned, the arms industry is often justified in political discourse by the employment it generates. Arguments against it focus on the role of the trade in arms in fuelling conflict and diverting resources away from more socially useful purposes, such as healthcare and housing (Holden 2017). The industry, and the moral implications of trade in arms, surfaces in the media occasionally, but mostly it is not news – the arms trade is kept in a conveniently shadowy world (Feinstein 2011).[4] The arguments *for* the arms industry hinging as they do on its role in providing manufacturing jobs[5] that use and develop advanced technology, necessarily connect it to design.

Is design beneficent? Does it promise better futures?

Design is all around you, everything man-made has been designed, whether consciously or not. (Hunter 2014)

So says Mat Hunter, former Chief Design Officer at the UK's Design Council. The weapons and equipment that surrounded me at Eurosatory were all designed. Design was all I could see. On the same web page as the quote above, the Design Council invites its readers to ask 'how can I use good design to make the world around me better?', strongly implying that the purpose of design is to do just that. Clearly, 'good' here is intended to differentiate design that is 'good' because it is effective, from design which is not effective, and therefore 'bad design'. While 'good design' does not in itself point to a moral purpose for design, the quotation connects design with a 'better world' – a good that extends beyond effectiveness, perhaps underlying it. The Design Council frames design's contribution both in terms of making a world that performs better, helping people by providing goods and services that work well, and in terms of adding value that benefits economic performance and makes profit. It is fitting that the Design Council espouses such an ethic, given its history, set up near the end of the Second World War to contribute to physical and economic reconstruction, promoting industrial design to improve human life. However, much of the design I can see at Eurosatory has been carefully thought out and produced to control human life, and a good deal is designed solely to end it. All of it is for sale. In the context of global capitalism, this is the emphasis – arms are for trading and design is about making a sale. All other considerations are subsidiary.

Clearly, we are in a tricky situation if the same way of organizing human capacities – design – can be justly described as both life-improving and life-terminating, able to reshape the world for good and implicated in a destructive global trade in weapons. It is therefore appropriate to indicate what conception of design is in play in this chapter. Rather than seeking its universal properties, it is more useful to think about design as a phenomenon, what it is taken to be, how its properties are invoked and how it works in relationship with other social and cultural phenomena. Apparently defining features of design, processes such as 'design thinking', are not relevant. It is sufficient to acknowledge that design has both aesthetic and functional aspects as Cropley and Cropley (2005: 169) recognize, the former of which tends to prioritize imagination and to emphasize visuality. Indeed, efforts to elucidate a 'design thinking' that retains the same character independent of its application are problematic in themselves as Kimbell (2011, 2012) has shown, tending to ignore the relationality that is necessary to any particular design process. Design is, in Suchman and Weber's (2016) science and technology studies terms, a 'world making practice' and its manifestation in the arms industry brings into sharp relief their call for critical interventions into that practice.

While design may have no inherent moral character, a progressive purpose is often assumed to be one of its characteristics. In a 2004 article that criticizes design for the lack of a positive ethos, although it sometimes espouses virtuous ethics, Cameron Tonkinwise still asserts that:

Design is the process of trying to make the world friendlier to us clumsy humans; it is the effort to make the world more caring toward us, more accepting of us and so more morally acceptable to us. (2004: 142)

Design may sometimes do this, but it clearly does not always and there has been a tension between its progressive and destructive characteristics through the history of design discourse. Early modernist architecture was associated with direct benefit to human bodies and improved individual and collective health, through hygiene summed up in Alvar Aalto's tuberculosis sanatorium at Paimio, Finland, of 1933, and Berthold Lubetkin's 1938 health centre at Finsbury, London. The design of domestic devices was bound up in creating what Hand, Shove and Southerton (2005) call 'moral technologies' that relate conceptions of cleanliness to social demarcation. Design historical research (Forty 1986, Lupton and Miller 1992) shows that being embodied in designs these ideas share their somewhat moralizing character with more ambitious twentieth-century urban future fantasies, such as those of the Italian Futurists Sant'Elia and Marinetti of 1914 or the dystopian fantasy architecture of Superstudio in the 1970s (1972). This history complicates a sense we might wish to construct of modernist design as a benign way to envision the future, let alone construct it.

However, design *is* a powerful means to envision futures, encapsulating our hopes in forms that are buildable, even if not (yet) built. That was the function of futurist fantasy architecture, and continues, much enhanced by computer graphics in the design fantasies that circulate online, such as a proposal for an 'Urban Skyfarm' in Seoul, by Aprilli Design Studio (World Architecture News 2014) and the Ring Garden project in Santa Monica, by Alexandru Predonu – a finalist of 2016 Land Art Generator Initiative competition. Beyond providing visions of the future, Design helps construct *expectations* about those futures, expectations which themselves have agency. These expectations are 'performative', both 'the cause and consequence of material, scientific and technological activity', as Mads Borup puts it (2006: 286).

Positive visions of the future coexist with themes that reflect perverse expectations of pain and destruction, rather than care. Marshall Berman's reading of Marx's account of capitalist political philosophy points to the 'creative destruction' that is a defining feature of modernization – 'all that is solid melts into air', confounding any sense of care (1982). This sentiment was twisted in the Futurist Manifesto into Marinetti's famous statement: 'We will glorify war – the world's only hygiene – militarism, patriotism, the destructive gesture of freedom-bringers, beautiful ideas worth dying for, and scorn for woman.' It persisted through the twentieth century and was evident in mid-century discourse that celebrated the 'cleansing' potential in nuclear weapons (Hecht: 76).

Of course, design can be used to resist 'militarism, patriotism etc.' just as it can serve them, shown by the inventiveness, the design, that goes along with protest (Fisher 2008; Abrams 2014), but we would perhaps prefer not to see clear evidence of design's implication in its morally problematic consequences, or to not see it clearly. To witness an arms fair is to open up a world that is usually kept out of sight. That concealment perhaps helps us preserve the idea that design places technologies in the world to make the world more caring. Being in an arms fair I can see more than I should, given that I am here under false pretences. I am not here on business, but to observe.

Dassault Designs the Future

I can see the Dassault Aviation stand from where I sit, with two scale model jet fighters the prominent products. I am looking past a couple, a man and a woman sitting on steel framed stools with pink vinyl seats, at a tall table with a pink laminate top that matches the stools. She is wearing a pale pink blouse, with pearls, a heavy silvery watch loose on her wrist, a Eurosatory security pass hangs from a lanyard round her neck.

On the back wall of the Dassault stand is a very large plasma screen showing a continuous video. Warplanes are being made by skilled technicians in a modern factory. They are being flown, refuelled in flight over desert terrain. There are night vision shots from a UAV of a 'target' in an active war zone. The target disappears in a huge explosion. Warplanes take off from an aircraft carrier and words appear: 'Designing the Future', then a quote from M. Dassault himself 'every time a plane is beautiful, it flies well' – 'we are proud of our DNA to design the future'.

Then comes a segment about an agreement between Italy, Germany and France to collaborate to produce an Unmanned Aerial Vehicle – a drone – illustrated with shots of Computer Aided Design (CAD) stations showing progress in the design studio, with a female CAD operator prominent.

To imply that design is inherently beneficent, or to assert that its purpose is to 'care', or to emphasize its progressive history, clearly requires that we ignore its arguably negative manifestations, such as in the arms industry.

This is relatively easy to do, for two reasons. First, the arms industry 'proper' keeps itself relatively secret. Second, design as an element in consumption normalizes defence-related motifs and technologies, meaning that when they bleed into everyday life they are rendered as 'empty signifiers' (Chandler 2002: 78), without clear connection to their referent in armaments and defence equipment. Everyday motifs such as the ubiquitous camouflage, rendered sweetly as 'camo', divert our attention from their referent in the actual arms industry, which keeps a low profile. It is not easy to get access to international arms fairs. A security pass is needed, to exclude individuals who might protest against the connection between arms sales and their effects in what is now a globalized trade, relatively free of governmental control.

As I write this, British-made weapons, such as the 'Paveway 4' guided bomb (Figure 1.1), are being used by the Saudi Arabian government against Houthis in Yemen, leading to well-documented civilian casualties (CAAT 2017). Among these British-made weapons are cluster munitions sold to Saudi Arabia before an international treaty banning them was signed by the UK, but not by Saudi Arabia. The use of such weapons is grounds for protest, but given the secrecy that surrounds the arms industry it took a good deal of campaigning before the UK government was forced by the evidence to send Defence Secretary Michael Fallon to the House of Commons to admit these illegal, UK-made, weapons have been used by Saudi Arabia in Yemen (HC Deb 19 December 2016). Saudi Arabia is the second biggest market for armaments in the world (Blanchfield, Wezeman and Wezeman 2017) and its role as a customer for our arms is therefore economically as well as geopolitically important.

Figure 1.1 'Paveway 4' guided bomb, manufactured by Raytheon in the UK, DSEI2017 (Author's photograph).

Weapons such as those currently in use in Yemen confound the long-embedded progressive connotation of design evident in the Design Council's narrative. But both design's morally progressive and its morally dubious manifestations resonate strongly with its role as a component (and product) of a modernization evident through the twentieth century. Given that all the arms that are traded at events like Eurosatory are the outcome of processes of design, faced with the spectacle of an arms fair it is clear that design is not inherently a force for good, and it even becomes difficult to hold on to the sense that it *can* be such.

The arms trade's relative secrecy makes it possible to separate the commercial/ political purposes of the arms industry from its material facts. Arms fairs are closed events, part of a discrete 'world'; difficult for outsiders to enter. This separation from the everyday makes it easy to see the things they contain simply as products to be traded. Mental effort is required to project these technologies to their logical, destructive, conclusion. The representations of their explosive potential that are on show tend to be distanced, placed at a technologically enabled remove from direct experience, through the same imaging technologies that enable remote offensive operations. In contrast to the secrecy of the arms fair, public displays of military technology demonstrate political power. At a more mundane level, while conflict is a common theme in popular culture it is not necessarily connected to the military or to the defence industry, or to defence technology. Design colludes in preserving these distinctions, by normalizing the many technologies, motifs, styles and attitudes that bleed from one world to the other. In visual culture these include fashion motifs – the ubiquitous 'camo' pattern – as well as generalized ethics, or approaches to life.

Survivalism, one such ethic that sees people arming themselves for an imagined apocalypse adopts many visual motifs borrowed from the military (Mitchell 2002). Here, the visual rhetoric of defence expresses a desire for mastery that aligns with the version of masculinity that survivalism espouses. There is a connection in this visual rhetoric to a more abstract notion of 'technology', to human efforts to master nature through material, with its connections to a Baconian frame for science and technology (Montuschi 2010). At the same abstract level it is possible to make a connection between design and ideas of mastery.

Mastery, visuality and action at a distance

Although in this narrative the theme of mastery emerges from a rather obvious source in armaments, it connects directly to the ways in which the imaginative potential of design has been represented as an aspect of modern culture. The imagination that is evident at the arms fair is a work of imagined mastery, of both human and non-human nature, through action at a distance. Weapons quite obviously embody the principle of action at a distance, claimed in discussions of weaponry as the 'impulse to master and dominate space and the bodies within it' (Bousquet et al. 2017: 5). Any permutation of this mastery is possible in the arms fair, addressing imagined but unspecific threats, providing imagined omnipotence. There is almost no reference either to the effect of the weapons and weapon systems or to the political context of their production and use – images of explosions are rare and there are no pictures of dead bodies.[6] Similarly rare are references to the global power play that the arms fair connects to, and is an aspect of. The Russian stand plays a video of a weapons parade in Red Square, but this says more about Russia's current (2017) military bravado than the character of the event.

The reason these images stand out is because the arms fair is largely an aesthetic event. The sense of sight is prominent – the visuality of the spectacle that I witness is part of a 'scopic regime', what Gregory calls 'a mode of visual apprehension that is culturally constructed and prescriptive, socially structured and shared' (2011). Using the concept, borrowed from Metz (1982: 61–62), to connect art to modes of human knowledge of the world, Martin Jay notes how scopic regimes position subjectivity in relation to what is pictured, or observed. He contrasts renaissance Cartesian perspectivalism, a singular, masculine gaze, a 'disincarnated, absolute eye' (1988: 8) with the 'objectively orientated Baconian empiricism' of 'descriptive' Dutch art (1988: 11). This analysis of premodern art implies a connection to design, which is both a product of modernity and retains a strong cultural connection to art. Gregory's focus on visuality in a discussion of drone warfare confirms its significance in this discussion. The arms fair's visual spectacle points towards the particular scopic regimes embodied in the designed technologies that are for sale.

The few explosions that are depicted on screens and the tableaux that are acted out on the back lot are intended to stir the emotions and play into scenarios of imagined dominance, rather than to provide hard facts about the merchandise. We can see them but we know we will never feel them. They are part of the aesthetic power of the arms fair (Gibbon and Sylvester 2017), producing the sublime awe that is invoked by the sense-confounding spectacle that the arms fair provides, a spectacle of dominance through designed action at a distance.

It is possible to relate the desire for dominance through action at a distance underlying this spectacle to a drive that exists in in design to shape the world at the expense of individual human subjects. It is reminiscent of a scene from novelist Ayn Rand's characterization of the dominating libidinal aesthetic power of architect Howard Roarke, the central character of her novel *The Fountainhead*. Interpreted through the eyes of one of the female characters in the book, Dominique Francon, Roarke's capacity as a designer is characterized simultaneously by vision, domination and action at a distance. Although these are qualities that would be at home in an arms fair, as would Rand herself, the novel places Dominique in Roarke's design studio where:

> She rose and walked to the window. The buildings of the city far below looked no bigger than the model on his table. It seemed to her that she could see his hands shaping the setbacks, the corners, the roofs of all the structures below, smashing and molding again. Her hand moved absently, following the form of a distant building in rising steps, feeling a physical sense of possession, feeling it for him. (Rand 2007 [1943]: 332–333)

These feelings of imaginary possession, of control, of the ability to manipulate what you can see, even though you can't touch it, connect with the sense of action at a distance that originates in a particular way of looking that characterizes both the experience of the arms fair and the purpose of many of the technologies it contains. While for Rand's Dominique, and for designers, these are imaginary actions, the capacity to act at a distance of time or space is what the technology of arms adds to human capacities in reality – whether that is through projectiles that travel through space, technologies that provide vision at a distance such as those discussed below or the projection of indiscriminate destructive agency into the future through landmines.

The following discussion of products that cross over from the arms industry to civilian life develops the theme of visuality, selecting designed technologies that emerge into public discourse and everyday life as technologies that extend human agency by supplementing vision.

Lethal agency and relationality

Defence is not the only market that many of Eurosatory's exhibiting companies address. The fair is full of companies that have some technology for sale that can be applied in either civilian or military applications, and see defence as a useful market. Among the displays of guns and bombs at Eurosatory is the stand of a French precision machining company that happens also to make components for a saxophone manufacturer. If, as anthropologist Pierre Lemonnier puts it, 'technology embraces all aspects of the process of action upon matter' (Lemonnier 1992: 1) then perhaps there is in principle no valid distinction between the design of technology by an explosives manufacturer offering 'insensitive munitions',[7] by a company offering technologies to precisely guide bombs or drones, by the manufacturer of surveillance equipment and by a company offering a technology that can be used to make saxophones, as well as components for armaments. But the idea of designing and making saxophones certainly feels different to the idea of designing armaments – feelings, aesthetic matters, point to the moral implications of both.

These 'processes of action on matter' are clearly multi-determined and one factor that bears on their moral implications is how close are the designed technologies that I can see in the arms fair to the effects of armaments when they are used; the closer the more problematic, perhaps. This varies by the type of artefact in question and some of the designs are clearly protective rather than offensive. However, the closer they are to a clearly offensive use, the more difficult it is to ignore the moral power of what seem to be their essential physical properties, rather than the symbolic properties that are to the fore in, for example, the use of weapons to display of political power or in the use in a military band of a saxophone made with machinery that can also make weapons.

In the arms fair, the gap left by the scarcity of direct references to the fatal consequences of using arms is filled by a liberal use of the word 'lethality' as the key criterion of performance. Taking the place of references to the actual physical propensity of weapons to destroy people and places, 'lethality' becomes a slogan, a piece of marketing jargon, a USP that stands in for the power and capability of weapons at the same time obscuring the consequences of their use (Figure 1.2). This evacuation of the material referent of 'lethality' from even this apparently explicit word is part of the commodification of the destructive agency that is designed into the products on display, inviting visitors to the arms fair to construct a view of the end-purpose of these designs that is conveniently obscured by their status as commodities, their lethal agency transformed, by design, into seductive action at a distance.

The multi-determined nature of the designs I can see in the commodified spectacle of the arms fair, which means that many of the companies do both civilian and military work, also means I don't see clear delineations between different products and technologies. This is an instance of the relationality behind Pierre Lemonnier's observation that 'technologies are social phenomena; they are composed of … elements related in a systemic way to each other and to other social phenomena' (1992: 11). The position I can take in relation to a particular design that I might observe in an arms fair is conditioned by my understanding of its context, which is defined by 'international relations' that are mixed up with globalized trade within a neo-liberal hegemony. This is Lemonnier's point about the relationality of technologies incarnate, and is reminiscent of Peter-Paul Verbeek's observation that technological artefacts are constructed from 'networks of relations' (2015: 190), as well as my understanding of Latour's concept of the actor-network. Latour's ideas are particularly relevant, and potentially useful, as he applies them to the relationship of humans to the particular

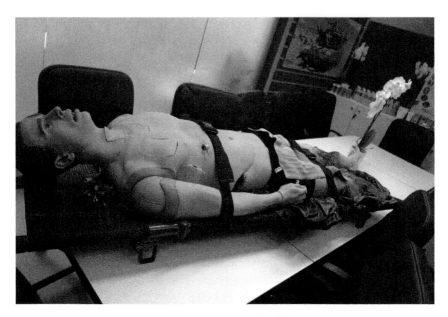

Figure 1.2 Battle injury simulator, Eurosatory 2016 (Author's photograph).

'non-humans' that are potentially offensive weapons (1999: 179–180), which is the focus of Dant's chapter in this volume.

As the saxophone example shows, the technologies evident in the arms fair are no more inherently moral than is the activity of designing them. The challenge for determining the moral status of what I can see at the arms fair is evident in the complex relationality behind both. Even to attempt to untangle these relationships is to define the terms on which their ethics can be considered and such attempts are therefore themselves ethically loaded. This point is not lost on Suchman and Weber in their discussion of autonomous military systems. Here they point out that arguments for and against the ethical validity of these systems depend on creating discrete 'objects of analysis' that either distinguish between human and technological agency or appeal to their combination:

> Beginning with the premise that discrete units of analysis are not given but made, we need to ask how any object of analysis – human or machine or combination of the two – is called out as separate from the more extended networks of which it is part. (2016: 21)

In a parallel of the interrelatedness of Lemonnier's 'technological elements', Suchman and Weber confirm that identifying a discrete *designed technology* is a significant act in a discussion of morals in the context of particular types of arms. In this discussion, their point is extended to an equivalent difficulty – distinguishing between types of technology design that might be considered 'military' or 'civilian'.

The arms fair includes a mess of technologies, all interrelated and some quite ancient in their origin. Complicating the event's moral implications, many of these designed technologies can have both offensive and constructive applications – even explosives – and the 'social and political milieu' in which they exist might provide moral justification for their use as offensive weapons. Clearly these designed technologies are in the language of the philosophy of technology 'multistable' (Ihde 2009). But in the setting of an arms fair you can't avoid seeing explosives and the systems that deliver them represented for their offensive *potential*, with graphic designers, art directors and copywriters using exquisite design to represent them as such, by selling a 'lethality' that at the same time distances them from their material effects, placing them firmly in the sphere of trade. This representation of explosives is appropriate, in an arms fair. It is an appropriately designed mediation between their engineered physical propensity to explode and their social and political milieu. The engineering design and the communication design involved are valid in that setting, but this validity requires that they are cut off from any 'extended network', made into a 'discrete object of analysis', an object of design.

Seeing the familiar through militarized eyes

Their mediation *by* design may also explain why the technologies in arms fairs are hard to see for what they are. While their multistable identity in many cases includes the most extreme 'offensiveness', propensity to kill, they are also ubiquitous, strangely familiar, normalized by this designed mediation. As a whole phenomenon the arms fair also has a normalizing effect – the initial shock that the spectacle elicits is soon dulled by familiarity. This bizarre event quite quickly comes to seem normal. Revulsion quite quickly turns into fascination with odd details, or boredom. To explore the broader phenomenon of the normalization of arms and arms trade in our culture, this chapter will conclude by considering some products that 'cross-over' from the military to the civilian worlds – associated with 'lethality' in the military setting but taking on other, placid, connotations in civilian life. There are many examples of this cross-over in the arms fair – I recognize brand names from the civilian world. I find Berghaus rucksacks, but where are their associations with a healthy outdoor life in nature? Here the mild and benign civilian association with nature that accompanies their use for hiking is transformed into the capacity to support the military domination of space as part of a soldier's survival equipment.

There are other firms here whose products we might not buy, but which we use in civilian life, as we ride in a Boeing airliner, or drive a car painted with DuPont paint,[8] but the example I want to discuss involves material technologies applied to optics, and physically impinges on the body of their users – eyewear. These products, made by Oakley, are sold in both arms fairs and specialist outlets that serve the climbing/outdoor market, as well as online.[9] You may know the products for their rakish and somewhat futuristic styling, and their high cost (Figures 1.3 and 1.4). While civilians can buy Oakley products and soldiers use them as part of their issued equipment, the

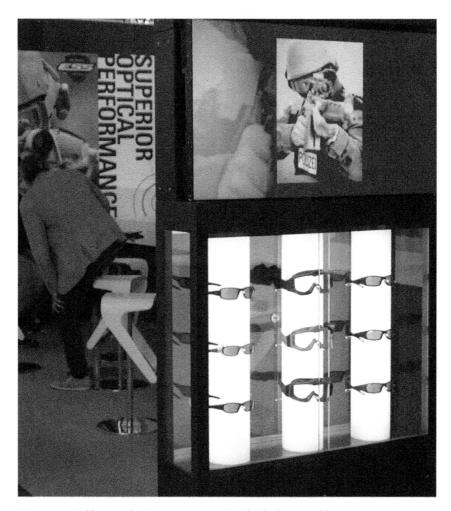

Figure 1.3 Oakley stand at Eurosatory 2014 (Author's photograph).

sales material directed at civilian markets is different to that which addresses military, or wannabe military, customers. However, the presence of a link to the military site through the civilian one shows that the company knows that the two worlds are not distinct.

Some elements of Oakley's visual and narrative design rhetoric have remained stable over the past twenty years. Then, as now, they emphasized their use of trademarked technology: 'Plutonite' lenses and components made of 'unobtainium', with frames made of '0-matter'. This sort of fantasy spinning, carried through into the 3D design of the products is the stock-in-trade of product design and marketing, and has a strong relationship to the tradition of future visions explored briefly above. Although eyewear is not capable of 'lethality' in any sense whether in a civilian or a military setting, the

Figure 1.4 Oakley display at a UK outdoor shop (Author's photograph).

presence of this design rhetoric in both Oakley's civilian and military ranges brings into relief the ways in which design mediates the other technologies that we do encounter only inside the arms fair.

As with Oakley's fantastical eyewear, design gives these 'lethal' products form and substance and the argument here is that at the same time design normalizes their purpose. In the case of Oakley products, so confident is this normalization that it can bear self-subverting 'material irony'; unobtainium is a designer's joke. This humour emphasizes the art involved in normalizing these 'cross-over' products and obscures the technology for which it provides a visual and poetic language, behind a cloak of secrecy, of 'high design'. To identify these aspects of Oakley's 'military capable' designs aligns with Verbeek's recommendation that when studying how design mediates technologies, 'we should not only study *what things do*, but also how *humans* give meaning to these mediations' (Verbeek 2016: 190). Humour keeps the technology and its effects close to human subjectivity and in a benign space. Design humour normalizes the mastery it provides as equipment for leisure, and as part of an array of military hardware.

On the face of it, Oakley's eyewear products comprise literally inoffensive design; protective rather than offensive, whether worn by a soldier or a skier. While Oakley offers a line in 'ballistic eyewear', ballistic here means *protection from* ballistic objects, not their projection through space. However, there is a clear connection between the technologies of flying and driving that are much in evidence at the arms fair, and particular ways of distancing the human body from its surroundings, providing it with a second skin through which to act, such as eyewear. Gabriele Mentges explores this connection in her writing on the accoutrements of early flyers, making clear the necessary relationship between these technologies and action at a distance, mastery and vision (2000). So the fact that Oakley's 'cross-over' products use the design of technology to enhance *vision* is telling, and connects them to (but does not implicate them in) the more obviously contentious aspects of what is to be seen at arms fairs. Oakley's products are about preserving sight, the sense necessary to physical action at a distance. This means they are connected to a clearly morally charged aspect of contemporary military technology – that which gives agency to military hardware in autonomous weapons systems – albeit that this connection is only in principle, and relatively remote.

In the process of working out the ethics of autonomous weapons systems (Bhuta et al. 2016), a good deal of resistance has been expressed to the principles on which they are based (Suchman and Weber 2016). Action at a distance through remotely controlled weapons has a long history, with autonomous weapons its latest manifestation and as soon as the active remote control of weapons began to be technically feasible, commentators recognized its moral implications. Writing in the journal of the Royal United Services Institution in 1924, Lieutenant-Commander G. C. Steele noted that 'the novelty and inevitable moral effect of distant controlled weapons must not be lost sight of' (1924: 552). There is a coincidence between the visuality necessary to remotely controlled weapons, made possible by devices like the one in Figure 1.6, and the nature of Oakley's cross-over products. This coincidence may activate our sense of morality both in relation to the 'distant control' involved in military drone technology and the aesthetic normalization of action at a distance through design that Oakley's products achieve.

This is of course not a matter of causal connection – it would be nonsense to propose that sunglasses are responsible for drones – but is made at the level of

Figure 1.5 Male and female selves projected through gun-sights at Eurosatory 2016 (Author's photograph).

the designed aesthetics of the arms fair, which connects the projection of agency through gun-sights (Figure 1.5) and remote imaging technologies (Figure 1.6), with the protection of (some) selves through eyewear and the remote control of UAVs (Chamayou 2015). These connections are not lost on other commentators. Writing on the nature of weapons, Bousquet and colleagues suggest that it is not so much that 'the weapon that has come to serve as a prosthetic extension of the eye than perception itself which has been caught up in an unrelenting process of becoming-weapon' (2017: 6). Design is clearly not a *causal* factor in these connections, but it is certainly implicated, connected to the technical–human nexus of visuality that is involved, bringing it into everyday life through humour and forms that can give purchase to imaginative consumption (Campbell 1987). Oakley's protective 'ballistic' eyewear is made using 'unobtainium' both to make it perform better and to be the focus for a projective fantasy that is part of the product that is traded. In the context of the arms fair at least, if not of its use, this feels like a suitable material for the device in Figure 1.6. This connection might trouble design researchers who wish to retain a sense of design as 'caring'.

Figure 1.6 Remote sight head ball, Eurosatory 2017 (Author's photograph).

Conclusion

This chapter has made connections between ways of thinking about design as a positive, caring, progressive way to configure matter, and less appealing applications of human intelligence through design, that serve conflict and destruction in military technologies. By tracing the connection between the civilian and military markets for Oakley eyewear, it demonstrates that there is no clear distinction between military and civilian applications of design to technologies. This type of product was chosen deliberately for its potential to point up the significance of imaginative vision both for design and for particular types of military technology.

As its empirical basis the chapter has used the visual experience of attending arms fairs, an experience that is filled with particulars: brands, products and spectacle. Citing discussions of autonomous weaponry in science and technology studies, it has shown that to focus on the particulars of a designed technology requires a value-laden choice, and is a way to avoid the moral power of the arms fair as a whole. This is tricky for designers, used as we are to attending to particulars, or the 'job in hand', and, perhaps, to avoiding the moral implications of the consequences of our work. Consequently, the chapter's contribution to this volume includes noting the connection between certain particulars, between details in design language and themes that connect them to broader, geopolitical questions. Such connections are often underplayed, and the ethical difficulties they present to actual designers and design researchers skated over, to get the job done.

This tendency exposes a dimension of design's subaltern status (Dilnot 2014, 2015: 208). Design 'serves'. Its capacity to render matter into forms that play aesthetic as well as functional roles means that it can serve the normalization of military technology. Its thorough entanglement in this 'world making' includes the 'hard' technologies with which it works, and their cultural meaning. It may seem counter-intuitive to stress the 'cultural' meaning of armaments, but they feature in culture as active agents. The most extreme weapons rely on technology that bleeds across the military–civilian divide – as Hecht notes in reference to nuclear technology: 'The nature of a discovery might shape but does not determine its cultural meaning' (2010: 78). Design is as implicated in the enculturation of military technologies as it is with all others, with its 'tricky' persona, balanced between reason and play, between reason and fantasy. Design contributes to the way an arms fair takes the nonsense, the un-reason of the arms industry and gives it a veneer of regularity and reason. Design makes sense in/of the arms industry.

Notes

1 In years when there is no arms fair in Paris, there is one in London – DSEI; Defence and Security Equipment International. There are others, round the world in Czech Republic, Germany, Indonesia, Israel, Kuwait, Malaysia, Pakistan, Singapore, Slovenia, Spain, Switzerland, Turkey, United Arab Emirates and the United States.
2 Siemon Wezeman cites the UN's work to address 'risks from arms transfers', including the Register of Conventional Arms (UN n.d.). These risks include:

- increased international tensions from arms build-ups
- prolonging and intensifying conflicts
- provision of means for human rights abuses
- diversion of resources from economic development
- endangering the security of allies
- diversion of legally traded weapons to the illegal circuit

3 Between 2011 and 2015 global revenues from 'defence' grew from just over $580bn to just under $680bn (Captain 2016). Large though this figure is, Paul Holden (2017) demonstrates that it is a small proportion of total economic activity, contradicting arguments for the necessity of the arms industry for prosperity.

4   The connection between trade in arms and the safety of citizens was not lost on the media when the destruction of the Malaysian Airlines flight MH17 over Ukraine led to a focus on arms sales by the UK to Russia (Milmo 2014).
5   Out of its 82,500 employees globally, BAE systems, the United Kingdom's largest arms manufacturer, employs 33,000 in the United Kingdom, or less than 50 per cent of the total, approximately the same number as it employs in the United States (BAE Systems n.d.a).
6   It is possible to find representations of damage to bodies intended for training military medics, but you have to look hard – see Figure 2.
7   'Insensitive' munitions are formulated to be less likely to explode when they are exposed to heat or shock before they are used.
8   DuPont is a chemical company that started off making explosives – the extent of its profits from the First World War stimulated the US government to enact antitrust law to stop it buying so much of the productive economy that it could control markets. Thirty per cent of Boeing's sales of $96m in 2015 were arms sales (Fleurant et al. 2016).
9   Oakley takes pains to 'civilianize' its products for the non-military customer. Other companies offer military eyewear to buy online, without any apparent concessions to this market. The American company Revision Military is one example: https://www.revisionmilitary.com/products/eyewear/view-products/# Another is Bollé who make both ski goggles and military eyewear: http://www.bolle-tactical.com

Bibliography

Abrams, Harry, N. (2014) *Disobedient Objects*, London: V&A Publishing.
BAE Systems (n.d. a) 'Where We Operate'. Available at: http://www.baesystems.com/en/our-company/about-us/where-we-operate, accessed February 2017.
BAE Systems (n.d. b) 'What We Do in the UK'. Available at: http://www.baesystems.com/en-uk/what-we-do/what-we-do-in-the-uk/uk-key-facts, accessed February 2017.
Berman, Marshall (1982) *All That Is Solid Melts into Air: The Experience of Modernity*, New York: Simon and Schuster.
Bhuta, Nehal, Beck, Susanne, Geiß, Robin, Liu, Hin-Yan and Kreß, Claus (2016) *Autonomous Weapons Systems: Law, Ethics, Policy*, Cambridge, MA: Cambridge University Press.
Blanchfield, Kate, Wezeman, Peter and Wezeman, Siemon (2017) 'Commentary: The State of Major Arms Transfers in 8 Graphics', *Stockholm International Peace Research Institute*, 22 February 2017. Available at: https://www.sipri.org/commentary/blog/2017/state-major-arms-transfers-8-graphics, accessed 7 March 2017.
Borup, M., Brown, N., Konrade, K. and Van Lente, H. (2006) 'The Sociology of Expectations in Science and Technology', *Technology Analysis & Strategic Management*, 18, 3–4: 285–298.
Bousquet, Antoine, Grove, Jairus and Shah, Nisha (2017) 'Becoming Weapon: An Opening Call to Arms', *Critical Studies on Security*, 5, 1: 1–8.
Brewster, A. (2009) 'Beachcombing: A Fossicker's Guide to Whiteness and Indigenous Sovereignty', in H. Mith, and R. T. Dean (eds), *Practice-Led Research, Research-Led Practice in the Creative Arts*, Edinburgh: Edinburgh University Press, pp. 126–149.
CAAT (2017) 'The Impact of the War in Yemen', *Campaign against Arms Trade*. Available at: https://www.caat.org.uk/campaigns/stop-arming-saudi/yemen, accessed August 2017.

Campbell, Colin (1987) *The Romantic Ethic and the Spirit of Modern Consumerism*, Oxford: Blackwell.

Captain, Tom (2016) *2016 Global Aerospace and Defense Sector Financial Performance Study*, Deloitte Touche Tohmatsu Limited. Available at: http://www2.deloitte.com/ content/dam/Deloitte/global/Documents/Manufacturing/gx-cip-aerospace-defense-financial-perform.pdf, accessed September 2016.

Chamayou, Grégoire (2015) *Drone Theory*, London: Penguin.

Chandler, Daniel (2002) *Semiotics: The Basics*, London: Routledge.

Cropley, Arthur J. (2010) 'The Dark Side of Creativity: What Is It?', in David H. Cropley, Arthur J. Cropley, James C. Kaufman and Mark A. Runco (eds), *The Dark Side of Creativity*, Cambridge, MA: Cambridge University Press, 1–14.

Cropley, David and Cropley, Arthur (2005) 'Engineering Creativity: A Systems Concept of Functional Creativity', in James C. Kaufman and John Baer (eds), *Creativity across Domains: Faces of the Muse*, London: Lawrence Erbaum Associates, pp. 169–186.

Dilnot, Clive (2014) 'Is There an Ethical Role for the History of Design? Redeeming through History the Possibility of a Humane World', Keynote address, 9th International Committee Design History and Design Studies, 8–11 July, Aveiro Portugal, Blucher Proceedings, 1, 5: 57–81. Available at: http://www.proceedings.blucher.com.br/ articlelist/icdhs2014-238/list#articles.

Dilnot, Clive (2015) 'History, Design, Futures: Contending with What We Have Made', in Tony Fry, Clive Dilnot and Susan Stewart (eds), *Design and the Question of History*, London: Bloomsbury, pp. 133–243.

Feinstein, Andrew (2011) *The Shadow World: Inside the Global Arms Trade*, London: Macmillan.

Fisher, Tom (2008) 'Objects for Peaceful Disordering: Indigenous Designs and Practices of Protest', *The Design Journal*, 11, 3: 221–238.

Fleurant, Aude, Perlo-Freeman, Sam, Wezeman, Pieter D., Wezeman, Siemon T. and Kelly, Noel (2106) *The SIPRI Top 100 Arms-Producing and Military Service Companies 2015*, SIPRI Fact-Sheet, December 2016. Available at: https://www.sipri.org/sites/default/ files/The-SIPRI-Top-100-2015.pdf, accessed February 2017.

Forty, Adrian (1986) *Objects of Desire: Design and Society since 1750*, London: Thames and Hudson.

Fuller, Charles (1934) 'Speed in Modern Warfare', in Stephen King-Hall et al., *The Book of Speed*, London: Batsford, pp. 132–138.

Gibbon, Jill and Sylvester, Christine (2017) 'Thinking Like an Artist-Researcher about War', *Millennium*, 45, 2. Available at: http://journals.sagepub.com/doi/ full/10.1177/0305829816684261

Gregory, Derek (2011) 'From a View to a Kill: Drones and Late Modern War', *Theory, Culture and Society*, 28, 7–8: 188–215.

Hand, Martin, Shove, Elizabeth and Southerton, Dale (2005) 'Explaining Showering: A Discussion of the Material, Conventional, and Temporal Dimensions of Practice', *Sociological Research Online*, 10, 2. Available at: http://www.socresonline.org.uk/10/2/hand.html

HC Deb (19 December 2016) Vol 618, Col 1215–1226. Available at: https://hansard. parliament.uk/commons/2016-12-19/debates/B8EBA03B-5FFC-44CF-8989-883F62F675D4/Yemen, accessed 7 March 2017.

Hecht, David (2010) 'Imagining the Bomb: Robert Oppenheimer, Nuclear Weapons, and the Assimilation of Technological Innovation', in David H. Cropley, Arthur J. Cropley, James C. Kaufman and Mark A. Runco (eds), *The Dark Side of Creativity*, Cambridge, MA: Cambridge University Press, pp. 72–90.

Holden, Paul (2017) *Indefensible: Seven Myths That Sustain the Global Arms Trade*, London: Zed Books.

Hunter, Matt (2014) 'What Is Design and Why It Matters', *Creative Industries Council: 'News and Views'*, accessed March 2017: http://www.thecreativeindustries.co.uk/uk-creative-overview/news-and-views/view-what-is-design-and-why-it-matters

Ihde, Don (2009) *Postphenomenology and Technoscience*, Albany, NY: SUNY Press.

Jay, Martin (1988) 'Scopic Regimes of Modernity', in Hal Foster (ed.), *Vision and Visuality*, Seattle, WA: Bay Press, pp. 3–23.

Kimbell, L. (2011) 'Re-Thinking Design Thinking, Part 1', *Design and Culture*, 3, 3: 285–306.

Kimbell, L. (2012) 'Re-Thinking Design Thinking, Part 2', *Design and Culture*, 4, 2: 129–148.

Latour, Bruno (1999) *Pandora's Hope: Essays on the Reality of Science Studies*, Cambridge, MA: Harvard University Press.

Lemonnier, Pierre (1992) 'Elements for an Anthropology of Technology', *Anthropology Papers No 88*, Ann Arbor, MI: University of Michigan

Lupton, Ellen and Abott Miller, J. (1992) *The Bathroom, the Kitchen and the Aesthetics of Waste (A Process of Elimination)*, New York: Kiosk.

Mentges, Gabriele (2000) 'Cold, Coldness, Coolness: Remarks on the Relationship of Dress, Body and Technology', *Fashion Theory: The Journal of Dress, Body and Culture*, 4, 1: 27–47.

Metz, Christian (1982) *The Imaginary Signifier: Psychoanalysis and the Signifier*, Bloomington, IN: Indiana University Press.

Milmo, Cahal (2014) 'Malaysia Airlines MH17 Crash: Massive Rise in Sale of British Arms to Russia', *The Independent*, Tuesday 22 July. Available at: http://www.independent.co.uk/news/uk/politics/malaysia-airlines-mh17-crash-exclusive-massive-rise-in-sale-of-british-arms-to-moscow-9622025.html

Mitchell, Richard, G. (2002) *Dancing at Armageddon: Survivalism and Chaos in Modern Times*, Chicago, IL: University of Chicago Press.

Montuschi, Eleonora (2010) 'Order of Man, Order of Nature: Francis Bacon's Idea of a "Dominion" over Nature', Discussion paper, *Centre for Philosophy of Natural and Social Science, London School of Economics and Political Science, London, UK*. Available at: http://eprints.lse.ac.uk/60107/

Rand, Ayn (2007 [1943]) *The Fountainhead*, London: Penguin.

Sant' Elia, Antonio and Marinetti, Filippo Tommaso (1970 [1914]), 'Manifesto of Futurist Architecture', in Ulrich Conrads (ed.), *Programs and Manifestoes on 20th-Century Architecture*, London: Lund Humphries.

Steele, G. C. (1924) 'Distant Control', *Journal of the Royal United Service Institution*, 69: 542–552.

Suchman, Lucy and Jutta Weber (2016) 'Human-Machine Autonomies', in Nehal Bhuta, Susanne Beck, Robin Geiß, Hin-Yan Liu and Claus Kreß (eds), *Autonomous Weapons Systems: Law, Ethics, Policy*, Cambridge, MA: Cambridge University Press, pp. 75–102.

Superstudio (1972) 'Microevent/Microenvironment', in W. Braham and J. A. Hale (eds), *Rethinking Technology*, London: Routledge, 2007, 196.

Tonkinwise, Cameron (2004) 'Ethics by Design; Or, the Ethos of Things', *Design Philosophy Papers*, Issue 2.

UN (n.d.) *Register of Conventional Arms*, https://www.un.org/disarmament/convarms/register/, accessed June 2017.

Verbeek, Peter-Paul (2016) 'Toward a Theory of Technological Mediation: A Program for Postphenomenological Research', in Jan K. B. O. Friis and Robert P. Crease *Technoscience and Postphenomenology: The Manhattan Papers*, Lanham, MD: Lexington Books, pp. 189–204.

Wezeman, Siemon (2010) 'The Global Arms Trade after the Cold War', in Andrew T. H. Tan (ed.). *The Global Arms Trade: A Handbook*, London: Routledge, pp. 193–207.

World Architecture News (2014) 'Aprilli Design Studio: Urban Skyfarm'. Available at: http://www.worldarchitecturenews.com/project/2014/24426/aprilli-design-studio/urban-skyfarm-in-jung-gu-seoul.html, accessed February 2017.

2

Designers and Brokers of the Mobility Regime

Mahmoud Keshavarz

Despite the promise of globalization in free movement of ideas, things, capital and bodies, globalization in practice has resulted in one of the most hardened and intensive periods of bordering and regulating of movement in the history of the world (Jones and Johnson 2014). In 2013, approximately 20,000 km of the world's borders were marked with walls or barriers and an additional 18,000 km were 'hardened' but remained unfenced (Rosière and Jones 2012). By 2015, at least seventy security barriers were initiated or expanded worldwide. This is four times more than the number of those built during the entire course of the Cold War (Vallet 2015). Looked upon through the lived experiences of refugees, asylum seekers, undocumented migrants and the travellers without the 'right' papers then, globalization's promise of freedom of movement is revealed as a myth (De Genova 2010; Khosravi 2010).

Material articulations of mobility regime

As a result of the forces of neo-liberal globalization and new economic patterns, borders have taken new forms, articulated through a set of design practices and designed things. These include artefacts, sites, spaces and practices that range in scale through passports, visa regimes, data banks, border guards and checkpoints, airports and train stations, camps and detention centres, deportation techniques and devices, etc. It is important to understand these as designed practices. They not only serve states' oppressive and purposeful policies of movement in the interest of capital and national discourses but they also actively direct, frame and articulate our *understanding* of contemporary politics in general and of mobility regimes in particular. By mobility regime I mean the ways in which under particular historical and material circumstances certain practices, including design, merge into each other, forge relations and produce realities that become given and self-evident. I understand these practices in terms of a regime (Foucault 1991) and their relations in terms of articulations (Grossberg and Hall 1996). This understanding of design's involvement in politics of movement in the form of a mobility regime thus goes beyond a dichotomy of mobility–immobility, and points to the complex ways in which the national and international circulation of goods, bodies, capital and labour requires a giant political apparatus articulated through dispersed material practices to render certain circuits possible and other circuits impossible (Salter 2013). Mobility regimes are configured through a variety of things, relations and environments, which I call material articulations (Keshavarz 2016).

In mobility regimes, specific, *directional* and contingent material articulations perform specific types of regulation and mediation. Through a set of standardized site-specific practices, models and protocols they ensure an uncontrolled, delocalized and unconditional flow of capital by regulating and blocking movements that do not follow such a flow and threaten its logic (Sassen 2010). Asylum seekers and refugees, as border transgressors, are a main target of such regulatory procedures through restrictive control, blockage and stop and check processes. Haisha Walia defines this 'border imperialism', in four parts: the free flow of capitalism and Western imperialism displaces people while securing borders against them; the criminalization of migrants, which benefits security companies; the entrenchment and embodiment of a racialized national and imperial identity in material impacts; and the denial of legal permanent residency to a growing number of migrants to ensure an exploitable and expendable pool of labour (2013: 75).

To understand and act on design's tricky nature, it is necessary to trace and intervene in the ways it co-constitutes such exclusive and discriminatory distribution and ordering of wealth and capital. This tracing is not about arguing against the co-opting of design and its epistemologies, rather it is about recognizing design's inherent violence in making a secure world for some through making it insecure for others.

This chapter identifies the passport as a material articulation of a mobility regime that contributes to and shapes much of what we perceive as legalized or illegalized acts of moving and migrating. As material articulations, passports are historically specific designed artefacts that mediate relations and actions beyond the site of both their use and their initial design. In this sense, passports are specific interfaces that produce mediating environments where certain power relations can take new shapes, beyond those anticipated by states, who seemingly are their designers. The different interests of states, security companies and individuals are performed through such a tricky, shape-shifting artefact. The mobility regime configured by artefacts and artefactual relations across and through passports does not only control, regulate or incite movement, but it also produces and articulates different modes of being and acting. Thus, passports affect how certain bodies and subjects move or do not move and how their movement is imagined, produced or articulated by design and designing, denoting what counts as human, as culture and as knowledge (Kaplan 2002).

The design and specific materialities of passports mean they can re-articulate the mobility regime. Forging a passport is a design act, rearticulating the relations the genuine artefact produces within the mobility regime. Together, designing, making and trading passports legally and forging and manipulating them illegally show how the mobility regime is designed and traded by actors with different positions and power. By rearticulating the restricted and securitized space of movement granted to privileged bodies, opening them up to bodies who are not legally entitled to move freely, forged passports show that the possibility of movement is articulated through a set of designed things and practices. Forged passports show us that the possibility of movement is both enacted and challenged through making and design.

By discussing passports, forged passports and other material practices of mobility this chapter gives an account of how the mobility regime is designed, negotiated and contested by various actors: states, smugglers or 'migration brokers', private companies and border transgressors.[1]

Passports as interfaces

Passports are designed not merely in terms of their different graphics and appearances but also to be interfaces, mediating a specific set of actions, interactions and inactions. As I have discussed elsewhere, over time and through various technologies passports have articulated themselves as a-historical products of state politics (Keshavarz 2015). However, as they are produced and circulated today, passports not only provide a service or solve a problem for national, political or economic state interests, they also shape the politics of movement in general and migration politics in particular (ibid.).

In a conventional understanding of design, users experience a passport as a material product, as information in a specific form that serves specific purposes. But the material and graphic reality users hold in their hands as passports are in practice interfaces that connect their body to specific data and software through other actors who support these connections. These actors include passport bearers, border guards, police officers, bureaucratic networks, passport reading machines and airports. So passports are not merely a designed product; they are also a set of complex interfaces. They articulate both fluid, fast and dynamic 'interactions' and a series of cautious, measured and interruptive 'inactions' between both humans and non-humans.

Moreover, passports are not only a designed interface between the databank and the bodies carrying them, they generate relations beyond their role as a product to facilitate the flow of information, as a user-friendly interface for complex interactions. The actors and technologies involved produce, regulate and mediate very specific relationships, assigning and checking the material and corporeal links between a body, its attributed nationality and its possibilities to move, reside and act across and within territories. These relations mediate and perform the nationality of a body on the move. Historical readings show that the materialization of these relationships through passports both commodifies them and represents them as given, natural and normal (Torpey 2000; Groebner 2007; McKeown 2008; Keshavarz 2015). Once the relationship of a set of other practices such as visa regimes, data banks, checkpoints, etc. is articulated through an artefact, then both the politics and history that have shaped it and the politics that it produces are concealed and easier to ignore. The existence of the artefact persuades citizens that the right to move does not look like a material articulation that is designed and traded.

Through passports individuals come to know themselves as internationally mobile, immobile or partially (im)mobile subjects and bodies (Salter 2006). They shape and co-constitute bodies on the move through categories such as nationality, class, gender, ethnicity, religion and sexual orientation depending on the economic and political context (Mongia 1999; Luibhéid 2002; Browne 2012). They are a specific technology that produces and secures the modern conception of state and nation or nationality with its origin in nineteenth-century imperial Europe (Clancy-Smith 2010). They assign this concept of state to bodies, thus fixing and regulating them geographically, spatially and temporally, producing in the process citizens, and refugees, and undocumented populations (Skran 1995; Keshavarz 2015).

However, the power to make and protect a seemingly authentic relationship between a body, its nationality and its right to move does not rest exclusively with the passport document – the relationship between a body, its nationality and its right to move can be traded legally. In 2014, the Maltese government announced that it would be selling passports to 'high value' individuals for €650,000, and this is not a new practice. Accessing first permanent residency and later citizenship through financial investment is common in many countries, particularly Western or 'desirable' ones. Foreigners who hold £10m in the UK can apply for permanent residence after two years of living in the country. US Immigrant Investor Visas are awarded to foreign nationals who invest $1m in the economy and create ten full-time jobs for US citizens within two years of arrival, granting permanent residence and, after three more years, full citizenship. Greece, Cyprus and Macedonia offer 'fast-track resident permits' to foreign investors who spend a minimum of €250,000 to €400,000 in the country. Because they are granted to high-value foreign nationals and confer extended freedom of movement, EU and US passports are high-value commodities, meaning that states, security companies and law firms are among the main traders of mobility. States design passports and the regulations around them, security companies provide techniques and technologies that sustain the mobility regime, and law firms find citizenships for 'high-value foreign nationals', together shaping an exclusionary mobility regime.

Forged passports

A history of passports is a history of how the artefact and the relations and mediating environments it produces have been appropriated for other purposes than their original designs. As long as passports are commodities with a certain value, fake versions will be traded illegally below the price set by governments. Forged passports facilitate smuggling or 'migration brokery', enabling illegalized mobility through various techniques and strategies. At the core of both is an act of negotiation, rearticulating the right to move through the material capacities of passports that forgeries enact.

Forgers' material and performative practices grant the right to move, albeit momentarily, beyond the legal establishment of citizenships and in doing so challenge the legal, that is to say immaterial, sovereignty of a nation-state. While nation-state and sovereignty are represented as 'an almost transcendental entity', as a 'nonmaterial totality that seems to exist apart from the material world of society' (Mitchell 2006: 181), forgers expose the fact that sovereign power is exercised through material articulations and can be negated by them. This is partly why forgery is considered a violent security threat, violating the law and the public good. By manipulating the passport and the relations and mediating environment produced by it, at the same time that forgers intervene locally into the artefact of the passport and its specific context of use, forgeries challenge the imagined universal transcendence of entities such as nations, territories, borders and citizenships.

Forgery can be more than forging the artefact of passports. It can extend to forging and reworking the performances and interactions in the mediating environment produced by passports. In the research behind this chapter (Keshavarz 2016) I met several travellers without the right papers who had manipulated or 'forged' their bodies to make themselves appear identical to the booklet they had obtained. They had also 'forged' certain rituals and performances to conform to established images of travellers. By being bodies frequently on the move due to easier access to the mobility regime, certain types of bodies, performances and interactions are seen more than others and thus have normalized themselves. The forgery of performances is partly about adopting and re-inhabiting these frequently seen types.

Nemat was an unaccompanied minor when boarding an aeroplane bound for Oslo from Athens with a South Korean look-alike passport. I met him in 2012 in Malmö when he was undocumented because first the Norwegian and then the Swedish authorities did not believe that he was a minor and thus rejected his asylum application. Despite not being entitled to move freely from Greece to Norway without a Schengen visa in his Afghan passport, he exercised freedom of movement with the service of a forged passport albeit temporarily, and with fear and anxiety. The migration broker told him that at Athens airport, young Korean people his age would usually be middle-class high school students there for vacation. Nemat would only pass if adopted that image, performing the scenario and role given to him by the articulation between a forged passport, his body and the knowledge given by the migration broker. He performed being Korean without speaking one single word of Korean, by dressing in certain ways, and by wearing certain shoes and gadgets to convince border guards that he was one of the many other Korean travellers.

As argued earlier, by defining people through their passports the state articulates a specific relationship to be performed at borders. A Korean crossing an international border performs a Korean subject – more than that, a Korean body with a specific class. Nemat performed his role as Korean with the help of his body, a look-alike Korean passport and a specific choice of airport and airline provided by the migration broker. Nemat rearticulated his body within the mobility regime. He affirmed that in truth, he was just like many other young men travelling. However, he had to pay for this rearticulation and had to wait in Athens for several months to find a passport in which the bearer's photo looked like him because his body from the beginning was not legalized and recognized within the mobility regime as Korean but as Afghan.

If it operates successfully, a forged passport functions in the moment and for an act of border crossing that its holder is not legally entitled to, granting a right to mobility through a forged material relation. This, however, is a temporary right. If both forged and fake passports are able to grant this, then forgeries disarticulate the political economy of the mobility regime monopolized by governments and the legalized market in citizenship. Forged passports pose a simple but important question: If freedom of movement is a right which has become commodified then why can passports, the material evidence of such rights, not be bought and sold in their imitative versions provided by the forgers and migration brokers?

Who is the 'big forger'?

Amir Heidari, a famous migration broker who was active in the 1980s and 1990s, moving refugees mostly from Iran, Iraq and Turkey to Europe and North America, puts the constructed relationship between bodies, nationalities and state revealed by forged passports forcefully:

> The world is a forged reality. Forgery is what the state does. The state is a forged entity in itself. If Sweden issues 9,000,000 passports to define a nation called Sweden, why can't I issue a hundred thousand passports to those who flee war, conflict and violence and are in urgent need of help and movement? Based on what moral position, am I a forger, a criminal and the state is not? What is forgery? Forging is an act of making something out of nothing. It is bringing to existence something unnatural and presents it as natural, like the state, like the borders made by the state. They are forged; they are made; they are unnatural things that look or make us believe that they are natural. Making borders is a form of forgery too. Now, you tell me who is the 'big forger' here? The state or me?

I met Amir in June 2015 in a European city. Now in his sixties, Amir has been working to deliver migratory services for thirty-five years. He has been arrested several times. In 1995 he had his Swedish permanent residence permit withdrawn and has served several prison sentences in Sweden and other EU countries over 14 years of his life: 2 years for falsifying documents; 4 years for 'human smuggling'; 4 years for holding 70 forged passports in Sweden alone. In 2004 he was to be deported to Iran but because he had obtained refugee status in 1980s, it was difficult to deport him. Finally, in 2010, Sweden deported him to Iran, where was arrested and sent to prison and interrogated. In 2011 he managed to escape Iran again. This migration broker who claims to have helped 200,000 refugees over thirty-five years to successfully reach different destinations in Europe and North America, with 40,000 reaching Sweden alone, now lives in a camp somewhere in Europe, having applied for asylum and been rejected due to his record in Sweden. When I met him, he was waiting for a decision on his appeal against the rejection of his asylum application.

Besides Amir, I met other individuals who became middlemen and migration brokers for various reasons (Keshavarz 2016). Their stories, like Amir's, contradict the dominant image of smugglers presented in the media of criminal traffickers operating in 'mafia'-controlled rings. In the policy discussion on migration, a consensus view has been established of the smuggler as the greedy exploiter of the vulnerable migrant, an image that fits well into discourses on security and the war on terror. However, as Ilse van Liempt's (2007) empirical study shows, the reality of smuggling is more complex and she calls for a more dynamic approach to the phenomenon. For instance, smuggling can be a way for migrants to be visible and to socialize while in transit or it can be used as a means of making money for their next trip, since they usually reside in transit countries irregularly (Papadopoulos et al. 2008; Khosravi 2010; Baird 2014). Gabriella Sanchez (2014) in her empirical study of the United States-Mexico border argues that non-state-sponsored migration brokery can also be thought as a set of services provided to facilitate clandestine border crossing. According to her, some illegal migration brokery can be understood as a collective, community and solidarity-based process rather than individual efforts towards mobility. Thus it is simplistic to consider those providing irregular migratory services, including forged passports, as mere criminals.

While states, media and the public perceive migration brokers and forgers as criminals who exploit precarious migrants, many authorized actors also engage in acts of forgery. Historically, we know of stories of diplomats and other powerful actors whose access to governmental infrastructures meant they could issue papers for Jews fleeing Nazi occupation, saving them from the Holocaust. Technically, they were 'smugglers', but they are recognized now as 'heroes'. Furthermore, states accept false passports when engaging in espionage. American diplomats were smuggled out of Iran on false Canadian passports during the hostage crisis in 1979, with Israel recently using false Canadian passports to insert agents into Jordan and Palestine (Salter 2004).

Criticalities of forged passports

Spain grants residency visas to foreigners who spend over €500,000 on Spanish property, with permanent residency following after five years, and one can buy an official Spanish passport in the streets of Athens or Istanbul for roughly €1,500. Both are originally and officially issued by the Spanish authorities, have the same materiality and theoretically function according to their use-value. However, almost all buyers of fake and forged passports use them only and exclusively for border crossing to apply for asylum. Such passports do not grant legal protection in the long run and, therefore, are less expensive – they operate outside the state mechanism to control individuals' movement.

However, both 'authentic' and forged passports affirm the materiality of citizenships and freedom of movement. The difference is that while the expensive, real, authentic, high-value and long-term passport is an affirmative material practice, the less expensive, counterfeit, forged, low-value and momentary one is a critical material practice. Nonetheless, they critique by affirming the ways the mobility regime works, a sort of 'affirmative criticality' to borrow Clive Dilnot's (2008) term. This means that the right to move facilitated by forged passports is a material critical practice, which produces its own space of functioning by refusing to engage in the dominating and hegemonic legal space. Forged passports affirm that despite states' attempts to totalize and monopolize the space and time of governance over mobility, there will always be spaces left or spaces produced that evade such governance – the 'space between bodies, law and discipline' (Asad 2004). Forged passports re-appropriate such spaces and turn them into other productive spaces of economy, politics and criticality however informal or illicit.

Forged passports make a subversive intervention, turning what is supposed to be untouchable into a threat against the source that issues it. In this sense, this specific critical and material practice enacts and releases other material forces that are suppressed by certain forms of design. A forged passport as an internal contract – the inauthenticity of which is visible only to the forger and the user – is a form of material dissent that exposes the fictive and at the same time artefactual relation between the nation and the body. Forged passports reveal such absurdities and also resist and refuse certain ways of moving or participating in the world.

The critique practised by those using forged passports is not a privileged, distant position taken by critical academic scholars. It is a question of survival. This is an important reminder that not all practices of critique are the same. Asking for forged passports, making forged passports and crossing borders using forged passports by those who are deprived of freedom of movement constitute a collective struggle that questions the violence of the mobility regime. In this sense, such critique is an act of refusal that is always in relation to something and it is through this relation that it becomes an act of refusal. It is critique as an attitude and a direction that could be understood as practice which goes beyond the concept of critique as judgement (Butler 2004; Foucault 2007). In this sense, the forging of passports can be understood as acts of refusal of what the global regime of mobility imposes on certain bodies. Forged passports then are devices through which a migrant refuses to be fixed, immobile and placed in UNHCR lines and camps.

Forged passports become the ways in which asylum seekers can enact their refusal and will to move in two parts: first, in the case of 'successful' border crossing, the possibility of momentarily enjoying freedom of movement is provided and, practically, the traveller can reach his or her desired destination and apply for asylum. Second, in the case of failure, when the passport itself or the relation between the bearer and an authentic passport is identified as 'forged', he or she becomes visible through the refusal they have made of migration policies. This however, might cause several losses for the traveller such as detention and deportation, as well as economic punishment.

As a specific critical practice of design, forged passports do not fall into the trap of making the practice of critique a statement in galleries, as is the case in practices such as critical design (Dunne and Raby 2001). While critical design is critical of mainstream product design, it never proposes or adds any meaning to the act of critique itself and is not a refusal but a passive affirmation of design. It looks 'clean', 'nice' and 'minimal' and is enacted in safe environments, such as universities and galleries. Critical design keeps the act or practice of critique within design discourse and restricts discussion to the designed artefacts rather than the mediating environments, the wider articulations that the artefact might create. In this sense, critical design dismisses relations or situations that do not necessarily discuss the future of design or technology, but negotiate the possibilities of the contingent ways that subjectivities and bodies inhabit spaces that do not historically and materially accommodate them.

Critical design is unsuccessful in its attempt to make the designed device or artefact an important part of the act of critique, instead fetishizing critique in the skin of commodity. Therefore, the artifice-based practice of critique becomes the main feature of critical design to the extent that it seems indifferent to politics as a driving force of critique and materiality. As design researchers Luiza Prado de O. Martins and Pedro Vieira de Oliveira (2015)[2] write of critical design, 'the political sphere of critical design ends where the design profession ceases its responsibility, that is, at the moment a consumer product (or a prototype thereof as "critical design") comes into being' (p. 62).

To practise critique in design, which is not separated from the political understanding of history, the status quo, and the future one should think of critique not as a category, approach, skill or methodology but as the 'very state of being of a practice' (Dilnot 2008: 177).

If design is capable of such subversion, of being critical, then forger and forgery are the designers and designerly practice in which it is able to facilitate a critical function, a use or a practical goal. They reveal the hegemony of power – in this context, the mobility regime. Also, they are not innocent, humanitarian, clean, elitist products promoting certain causes or awareness. They are not 'persuasive' or 'speculative' at all. They are real artefacts redesigned pragmatically for a particular urgent need and reproducing a business or market for irregular, less expensive citizenship, while disrupting another market for legal, expensive citizenship. At the same time, their circulation in the mobility regime exposes the vulnerability of sovereign power and hegemonic actors. A forger is a critical designer who deserves to be considered as such, as more than merely a criminal.

What violence, whose violence and towards whom?

I am sitting on a bench in downtown Athens on a hot day in 2014 listening to Rahim, an Afghan refugee in transit. He is telling me about his activities as middleman, and his time in prison in Athens. As soon as I leave Rahim and walk away from the bench, a man runs after me and asks me to stop. We shake hands and he introduces himself as Abdullah from Kurdistan: 'I was sitting next to you there and overheard your conversation. I wanted to tell you that these smugglers are like microbes. They are corrupted individuals, they are dangerous and ruin various lives including mine.' In fifteen minutes, Abdullah tells me his story of twenty-five years of statelessness, how he has been abused by states and border guards and also by migration brokers and middlemen. He has tried with four or five different brokers and has always been robbed and never received any passports or service to cross to central Europe. Completely devastated by what has happened to him, he has lost his family in these years of transit and he believes that both migration brokers and states are responsible for this loss. When I ask him what I can do for him:

> Perhaps nothing! I sleep in this park (pointing across the street where we were standing) until I find a better shelter. I have lots of contacts in different European countries, look! (he shows me a booklet with contacts of his friends) but they cannot do anything either. What you can do is tell my story so the world knows what has happened to me and how I have been betrayed by the states, borders and these individuals who benefit from such discriminations.

We exchange 'phone numbers and I promise to share his story in my writings. My conversation with Abdullah reminded me that it is dangerous as well as unethical to romanticize and generalize forgery and migration brokery as mere critical practices. Migration brokery is not entirely liberating or politically critical, as discussed in the previous section. Those who have crossed borders irregularly and had encounters with migration brokers, like Abdullah, know well that depending on their class, ethnicity, sexual orientation, gender or age they can be subject to exploitation, harassment or mistreatment. Many precarious lives are violated through such practices, which in truth are generated by the mobility regime and borders. It is important then to discuss the meaning of the different forms of violence involved in forgery and migration brokery, and how and by whom these different forms are enacted and performed upon individuals and collectives.

Walter Benjamin in his very brief but famous and much discussed 1921 essay 'Critique of Violence' distinguishes between 'divine' and 'mythic' violence. Mythic violence is equivalent to legal violence and the task of divine violence is to destroy mythic violence:

> If mythical violence is lawmaking, divine violence is law-destroying; if the former sets boundaries, the latter boundlessly destroys them; … if the former is bloody, the latter is lethal without spilling blood. (p. 297)

Among the various readings of Benjamin's essay, Simon Critchley's (2012) is one of the most interesting, framing it as an advocacy for a 'nonviolent violence' which is a form of 'subjective violence against the objective violence of law, the police, and the state' (p. 219). This means that violence sometimes is necessary to destroy the sacred image the state has even in secular times (Asad 2015). This law-destroying type of violence often comes from the 'lower' parts of society, targeting the state's sacred image and also those who enjoy and benefit from it through historical and material exploitation.

The mobility regime is violent in itself. Though its violence is invisible to those who smoothly navigate the space and time of the regime, it is partly revealed to them once the regime is confronted by other nonviolent violent practices, such as forgery and migration brokery. To understand the violence that forged passports generate, however, one needs to think of the practice of migration brokery in all its varieties, intentions and complexities, as its violence happens in different forms and towards different bodies at the same time. Migration brokery violates the sacred image of the state, as Amir Heidari told me when we were discussing his criminalization:

> The main reason they persecuted me was not my violation of the law but violation of the image of the state as the protector of people.

Migration brokery generates violence at various levels towards different bodies: the state, borders, the authenticity of citizenship and precarious asylum seekers, border transgressors and those entrapped in transit like Abdullah. The violence of migration brokerage needs a careful approach, framing it as an act of 'profanation' (Agamben 2007) of the sacredness of the state, its boundaries and its ultimate image as the only protector of people. One can think of forgery as nonviolent violence in this sense, and in doing so promote and mobilize its violence against the authenticity of citizenship and the state while restricting and stopping its probable violence against those who are the victims of the nation-state-making project.

Abdullah's experience of migration brokers is not an exception and resonates with many others who have tried to transgress borders. It points to a disagreement in the Marxist tradition of revolution. Marx and Engels would categorize migration brokers as the 'lumpenproletariat', as 'dangerous classes' (Marx and Engels 1976 [1848]) of 'vagabonds, discharged soldiers, discharged jailbirds, escaped galley slaves, swindlers, mountebanks, lazzaroni, pickpockets, tricksters, gamblers, *maquereaux* [pimps], brothel keepers, porters, literati, organ grinders, ragpickers, knife grinders, tinkers, beggars' (Marx 1979 [1852]: 149), who have no role in useful production and are unlikely to achieve class-consciousness and thus are no use to revolutionary struggle.

However, while inspired by Marxism, Frantz Fanon opposed this view of the lumpenproletariat (2004 [1963]), writing in the context of anti-colonial revolution in Algeria. Fanon believed that the potential for revolution by the colonized could not be fully understood by the traditional Marxist analysis[3] and therefore argued that such revolutionary movements cannot ignore the lumpenproletariat, as it involves both a counterrevolutionary and revolutionary potential:

> The oppressor, ... is only too willing to exploit those characteristic flaws of the lumpenproletariat, namely its lack of political consciousness and ignorance. If this readily available human reserve is not immediately organized by the insurrection, it will join the colonialist troops as mercenaries. (p. 87)

Amir Heidari suggested to me that the migration brokers of the world should organize a mass movement of refugees across borders without charging them, which aligns with Fanon's strategy in mobilizing such forces in favour of the oppressed. This is credible because migration brokers not only have the power to exploit precarious individuals, but also can easily play on the side of the states, against those in need of passports.

In October 2015 Amnesty International published a report that showed Australian officials paid six crew members who had been taking sixty-five asylum seekers to New Zealand USD 32,000 to take them to Indonesia, providing maps showing where to land in Indonesia. Amnesty implies that this was not a one-off and that the state was both involved in smuggling and, crucially, also directed it (Amnesty International 2015). This points to the potential to include forgery and migration brokery in critical practices addressing the material articulations of the mobility regime.

Design researchers can identify such seemingly criminal activities as specific critical practices of making, different from the 'critical design' found in Western academic environments, to mobilize and frame these efforts towards a collective struggle against passports and borders, by carefully attending to the power relations that these practices are embedded in.

Concluding remarks

Passports are not only artefacts or interfaces for data in the service of states but also actors that shape mediating environments that determine when and where bodies on the move are configured through dualities such as legal–illegal, productive–destructive, distinguishing between those free to move and those subject to regulation and control.

Forgery rearticulates the relations in such environments. Forgers and border transgressors use and practice forgery in both meanings of the term 'to forge': (i) to create something new, strong, and successful (simultaneously making relations that did not previously exist and were unanticipated); (ii) to produce a fake copy or imitation. Forgery is about the re-fabrication and re-articulation of given artefacts and the behaviours expected from them and their users. In this sense, forgery is an activity shared by both authorized actors, the state, and unauthorized actors, migration brokers. The state forges relations between bodies, nationalities and their positions in the mobility regime through passports for its citizens. Migration brokers re-forge the existing relations through forged passports for those who are stateless, for non-citizens who need a recognizable position in the mobility regime.

There is a danger, however, in taking forgery as a model for critical design practices because forgery is a particular act of design in a particular condition with its own operative and generative skills and utilities. To propose the same practice as an inspiration for design practices generally would risk creating a sentimental design practice and depoliticizing and de-radicalizing a practice that helps many to cross borders safely. Setting up forgery in 'safe' environments, for example academia and galleries, as a model for 'critical' or 'political' design practices would overlook the very situatedness of the politics of design.

The aim in discussing passports and forgery as designing practices is to understand how the mobility regime is organized and disrupted by various actors and how certain acts of making and designing in such a regime are presented as normal, protective and secure and others as violent and insecure. Border transgressors and forgers by their struggles against the hegemony of the current mobility regime teach us citizens that the privilege we enjoy in our right to move is not authentic or transcendental. It is historically made, designed and commodified. To change the way such privilege and right is distributed is to think its artificial, designed and material components, and thereby to reconfigure and rearticulate it.

Notes

1 I have anonymized the names of those who shared their stories with me except for Amir Heidari who wanted me to use his real name.
2 And see this volume Chapter 6.
3 This analysis is based on the concept of urban proletariat and its position in industrial production in Western societies.

Bibliography

Agamben, G. (2007) *Profanations*, New York: Zone Books.
Amnesty International (2015) *By Hook or by Crook* [online]. Available at: https://www.amnesty.org/en/documents/ASA12/2576/2015/en/, accessed 27 July 2015.

Asad, T. (2004) 'Where Are the Margins of the State?' in D. Pool and V. Das (eds), *Anthropology in the Margins of the State*, Santa Fe, NM: School of American Research Press, pp. 279–288.

Asad, T. (2015) 'Reflections on Violence, Law, and Humanitarianism', *Critical Inquiry*, 41, 2: 390–427.

Baird, T. (2014) 'The More You Look the Less You See', *Nordic Journal of Migration Research*, 4, 1: 3–10.

Benjamin, W. (1978 [1921]) 'Critique of Violence', in Peter Demetz (ed.), *Reflections: Essays, Aphorisms, Autobiographical Writing*, New York: Random House, pp. 277–300.

Browne, S. (2012) 'Everybody's Got a Little Light under the Sun: Black Luminosity and the Visual Culture of Surveillance', *Cultural Studies*, 26, 4: 542–564.

Butler, J. (2004) 'What Is Critique? An Essay on Foucault's Virtue', in S. Salih and J. Butler (eds), *The Judith Butler Reader*, Oxford: Blackwell publishing, pp. 302–322.

Clancy-Smith, J. A. (2010) *Mediterraneans: North Africa and Europe in an Age of Migration, c. 1800–1900*, Berkeley, CA: University of California Press.

Critchley, S. (2012) *The Faith of the Faithless: Experiments in Political Theology*, London: Verso Books.

De Genova, N. (2010) *The Deportation Regime: Sovereignty, Space, and the Freedom of Movement*, Durham, NC: Duke University Press.

Dilnot, C. (2008) 'The Critical in Design (Part One)', *Journal of Writing in Creative Practice*, 1, 2: 177–189.

Dunne, A. and Raby, F. (2001) *Design Noir: The Secret Life of Electronic Objects*, London: Springer.

Fanon, F. (2004 [1963]) *The Wretched of the Earth*, 4th Edition, New York: Grove.

Foucault, M. (1991) *The Foucault Effect: Studies in Governmentality*. With Two Lectures by and an Interview with Michel Foucault, Burchell, G., Gordon, C., and Miller, P.(eds). Chicago, IL: University of Chicago Press.

Foucault, M. (2007) 'What Is Critique?' in M. Foucault and S. Lotringer (eds), *The Politics of Truth*, New York: Semiotext (e), MIT Press, pp. 23–82.

Groebner, V., (2007) *Who Are You? Identification, Deception, and Surveillance in Early Modern Europe*. Brooklyn, NY: Zone Books.

Grossberg, L. and Hall, S., (1996 [1986]) 'On Postmodernism and Articulation an Interview with Stuart Hall', in K. H. Chen, and D. Morley (eds), *Stuart Hall: Critical Dialogues in Cultural Studies*, London: Routledge, pp. 131–150.

Jones, R. and Johnson, C. (eds) (2014) *Placing the Border in Everyday Life*, Farnham, Surrey: Ashgate Publishing.

Kaplan, C. (2002) 'Transporting the Subject: Technologies of Mobility and Location in an Era of Globalization', *Publications of the Modern Language Association of America*, 117, 1: 32–42.

Keshavarz, M. (2015) 'Material Practices of Power–Part I: Passports and Passporting', *Design Philosophy Papers*, 13, 2: 97–113.

Keshavarz, M. (2016) *Design–Politics: An Inquiry into Passports, Camps and Borders* [online]. PhD thesis, Malmö University. Available at: https://dspace.mah.se/handle/2043/20605, accessed 20 March 2017.

Khosravi, S. (2010) *The 'Illegal' Traveller: An Auto-Ethnography of Borders*, Basingstoke: Palgrave Macmillan.

Luibhéid, E. (2002) *Entry Denied: Controlling Sexuality at the Border*, Minneapolis, MN: University of Minnesota Press.

McKeown, A. M. (2008) *Melancholy Order: Asian Migration and the Globalization of Borders*, New York: Columbia University Press.

Marx, K. (1979 [1852]) 'The 18th Brumaire of Louis Bonaparte', in *Marx and Engels Collected Works*, Vol 11, 1851–53. London: Lawrence & Wishart, pp. 99–181.

Marx, K. and Engels, F. (1976 [1848]) 'The Communist Manifesto', in *Marx and Engels Collected Works*, Vol 6, 1845–48. London: Lawrence & Wishart, pp. 377–519.

Mitchell, T. (2006) 'Society, Economy and the State Effect', in A. Sharma and A. Gupta (eds), *The Anthropology of the State: A Reader*, Oxford: Blackwell Publishing, pp. 169–186.

Mongia, R. V. (1999) 'Race, Nationality, Mobility: A History of the Passport', *Public Culture*, 11, 3: 527–556.

Papadopoulos, D., Stephenson, N. and Tsianos, V. (2008) *Escape Routes: Control and Subversion in the Twenty-First Century*, London: Pluto Press.

Prado De O. Martins, L. and Vieira De Oliveira, P. (2015) 'Futuristic Gizmos, Conservative Ideals: On Speculative Anachronistic Design', in F. Laranjo (ed.), *Modes of Criticism 1-Critical, Uncritical, Post-critical*, Vol 1, pp. 61–66.

Rosière, S. and Jones, R. (2012) 'Teichopolitics: Re-considering Globalisation through the Role of Walls and Fences', *Geopolitics*, 17, 1: 217–234.

Salter, M. B. (2004) 'Passports, Mobility, and Security: How Smart Can the Border Be?' *International Studies Perspectives*, 5, 1: 71–91.

Salter, M. B. (2006) 'The Global Visa Regime and the Political Technologies of the International Self: Borders, Bodies, Biopolitics', *Alternatives: Global, Local, Political*, 31, 2: 167–189.

Salter, M. B. (2013) 'To Make Move and Let Stop: Mobility and the Assemblage of Circulation', *Mobilities*, 8, 1: 7–19.

Sanchez, G. (2014) *Human Smuggling and Border Crossings*, London: Routledge.

Sassen, S. (2010) 'A Savage Sorting of Winners and Losers: Contemporary Versions of Primitive Accumulation', *Globalizations*, 7, 1–2: 23–50.

Skran, C. M. (1995) *Refugees in Inter-War Europe: The Emergence of a Regime*, Oxford: Clarendon Press.

Torpey, J. C. (2000) *The Invention of the Passport: Surveillance, Citizenship and the State*, Cambridge, MA: Cambridge University Press.

Vallet, É. (2015) *Borders, Fences and Walls: State of Insecurity?* Farnham: Ashgate Publishing.

Van Liempt, Ilse. (2007) 'Human Smuggling: Types, Origins and Dynamics', in E. Berggren, B. Likić-Brborić, G. Toksöz, and N. Trimikliniotis (eds), *Irregular Migration, Informal Labour and Community: A Challenge for Europe*, Maastricht: Shaker, pp. 85–94.

Walia, H. (2013) *Undoing Border Imperialism*, Oakland, CA: AK Press.

3

Trickery in Civic Design: Co-optation, Subversion and Politics

Nidhi Srinivas and Eduardo Staszowski

Change only occurs in two ways: by accident or by prefigured intent (which is de facto design). To choose change means knowing how to identify, create and become an agent of change who is able to mobilize design to this end.

Tony Fry (2011: viii)

An effort of design, benign or malign, whether politically to the left, middle or the right, is ultimately an effort of intention, often collectively so. Yet, as an effort of intention, design can be matched, if not defeated, by the practices through which organizations and societies function. When these practices and rival intentions slip beyond the effort of the designer, it can appear a sort of trickery. This chapter is about tricks, tricksters and trickery. We argue that design for the public interest involves tricks. The designer is properly called a trickster. To discuss design in this manner is not intended to imply that designers are somehow amoral or deceitful. Rather it is to signal the manner in which design interacts with organizational and political processes, bewildering intentions.

To focus on this slippage between intentionality and practice and to foreground an image of the trickster, we proceed in three sections. First, we argue that design has a history of seeking to tether practices towards intentions in two closely related ways. Second, we argue that the contemporary trend has been to move away from a divide between intention from practice, by grounding design in forms of citizen-engagement, and participation. Third, we propose an alternative way of moving past the divide of intention and practice, by engaging directly with politics in the field of civic design. It is here that we introduce the figure of the trickster and the expertise of trickery. We consider the implications of this alternative way to approach the question of design and intentions for the public realm and reflect on the peculiar political relationship it generates between designers and their clients.

The views expressed here of the authors may not fully reflect the positions of our project partners, community groups or the official positions or policies of the City of New York or the New York City agencies discussed in this chapter. All errors and omissions are the authors' own. We are grateful to Andrew Moon for helpful suggestions in revising this chapter.

Design and intentions

A variety of applied disciplines have sought to link their practices to desired models of functioning. Management theorists, for instance, from the 1950s onward sought stable means of controlling human action within organizations, to ensure stated goals were met. They developed theories that explained how organizations adapted to their external environments, distinguished between efficiency and effectiveness, and forecast lifecycles of organizational growth. Similarly design and designers sought to identify patterns of human behaviour and establish architectural forms around them, including in terms of a science of design (Cross 2001). These disciplinary efforts ultimately sought to guide social behaviour, to enforce a set of intentions considered most beneficial for all.

In terms of urban design a famous example is the capital city of Brazil, Brasília. The city was built on a part of the vast Brazilian Central Plateau, from scratch, on an empty canvas so to speak. In broad terms, the city plan declared its modernist intentions through an artificial and abstract arrangement of geometrical shapes. These shapes became crucial in expressing the capital's grandeur, such as in its 'Monumental Axis', where state ministries and monuments were to be housed, and a grand square where Brazilian people could gather in front of their National Congress. Triangles marked the vast city's boundaries. And housing blocks, built on a separate residential axis, were constructed in the shape of quadrilaterals (Holston 1989). Literally the city was imagined into existence, architectural sketches on paper transformed into vast concrete edifices.

Brasília represents a high point in nationalist urban planning and top-down modernist design. It demonstrates the ways city planners sought to channel social energies within an artificial landscape. It exemplifies a kind of imagination that geographer David Harvey (2000: 163) describes as a historical utopian trend to define how cities should look and function. 'The roots of modern Western urban planning and design can be traced to the Renaissance and Baroque periods in Europe, when artists and intellectuals dreamed of ideal cities, and rich and powerful regimes used urban design to produce extravagant symbolizations of wealth, power and destiny' (Knox 2011: 67). Brasília's city plan sought to regulate virtually all forms of interaction; it also tried to rule out the possibility of spontaneity and disorder. It expressed a form of egalitarianism, showcasing an urban space all Brazilians could call their own. But in the process forms of expression and diversity were neglected. The city represented a mode of planned design, but severely restricted local forms of improvisation and adaptation to these designs (Scott 1998).

Design as de-sign and di-segno

Herbert Simon (1982: 129) defined design as to 'devise courses of action aimed at changing existing situations into preferred ones'. This is a blunt statement of intent. But a consideration of the etymology of design complicates such statements of intent. Early and contemporary uses of the noun form, design, mean plot, a basic structure; its verb form, designing, can mean to simulate, to draft, to sketch or even to want something from another. The word originates from the Latin *signum*, a sign. In English parlance, design was to de-sign, or to put it less pithily, construct new symbolic forms by way of de-coupling or dis-engaging a semiotic relation. Yet the Italian *di-segno*, also from the root *signum*, emphasizes 'di' (as in 'of'), meaning 'to point to'. Design as de-sign reminds us that the worlds we inhabit include symbolic worlds constructed by human beings, and are therefore amenable to being replaced, reconstructed and removed. But design as di-segno emphasizes design's creative quality, of building-upon what exists, finding an affinity between things. In both cases, we encounter design in terms of disengaging from, or engaging with, existing practices.

As a noun, *design* in its analogic mode points to something that exists in the world in a tangible and artificial form, such as a typeface, a logo, a product, an industrial process, a service, and an organization. This meaning surely impelled Simon to title his book *The Sciences of the Artificial*. But as a verb *designing*, in the sense of deconstructing a status quo (de-sign) or re-assembling a social setting (di-segno), points to the effort required to create something new, to question and reconstruct a prevailing symbolic order (Flusser 1999). Designing is a conversation to establish what could be, and what is sought. This also means that while the noun design indicates a neutrality in reference to radical change, the verb designing declares a process of partisan choice, of seeking what involved groups wish and ways to get what they want irrespective of a given state of affairs, radical novelty.

We can integrate these themes in a composite statement. Design and designing refer to a *conscious effort* to *order* (and *re-order*) the *physical and symbolic world* within which a *group* of people *function*. Each of the words that are italicized can be further explained. *Conscious*: design initiatives are thought out, often written and visualized. *Effort*: design initiatives require explanation and persuasion, and collaboration between people. *Order/re-order*: at the heart of a design initiative is a suggestion about the way in which the world we inhabit should be ordered – necessarily for life; this could be at the relatively modest level of a product design; or at a grander level such as an idealized modernist city. *Physical/symbolic worlds*: design initiatives occur in a world that has both physical features and symbolic ones. Of course, it is hard to separate these; therefore, a design initiative simultaneously involves questions of ascertaining practical answers as well as questions of ascertaining a shared meaning. *Group of people*: at the heart of the design initiative are those whose needs are to be met through this effort of ordering. Their needs may not be apparent and must be interpreted. Therefore, an important aspect of the design initiative is to be reflective on the relationship between the user citizens (who use what is designed), politicians and civil servants (who govern what is designed) and the designer (who mediates between them). *Function*: the user citizen has multiple needs often understood within a functional context of accomplishing a set of goals.

We wish to expand on this notion of design, but also directly acknowledge a slippage of intent. Simon's statement can slightly mislead us into thinking intentional efforts of change succeed. Even his assertion, which otherwise reads as a claim of rational intent, does use the word 'devise'; that is to say, Simon appears to tacitly acknowledge that whether in its verb or noun forms, design means not only an expression of intent, but ultimately a form of cunning able to adapt intents to changing circumstances.

As a set of practices embedded in a surrounding social and practical world that seek to transform and influence those who inhabit it, the intentions underlying designs will necessarily be restrained by these social forces. In fact designed objects emerge through these 'complex social relations', a fact that can be obscured by an emphasis on the intent underlying design terms (Dilnot 1984a: 18), whether in terms of de-coupling existing meanings (de-sign) or adding to these complexities (di-segno).

As these two sections have shown, civic design emerges from an urban history of linking social practices to stated intentions. Put another way, and using admittedly ideal and unrealistic extremes, designers seek constantly to make their designs speak for the ways people go about designing their lives. The social practices through which residents constitute a city were sought to be reconfigured by Le Corbusier, Lúcio Costa and Oscar Niemeyer, in the case of Chandigarh and Brasília. At a different scale, the practice of writing is 're-designed' by word processing software, which now configures what we write within this text. Design seeks to speak for these practices, negotiating possibilities, complementing, conceptually and physically, the status quo. But as we shall shortly see it also seeks to slip past the constraints in these conditions, to re-work and work-with them, to help novelty fall in line with latent expectation.

Client engagement, mapping shared intentions, participation and active cooperation

In the working contexts where design and designing occur, taking an extreme position regarding intentions would make little sense. Practical demands make it imperative to adapt initial intentions. A neutral way of stating this is in terms of a 'service relationship' where designers work with clients in adapting designs to their needs. The implication is that the designer seeks a stance of active engaged listening – a correspondence – in order to serve client needs better. Nelson and Stolterman (2012: 42) identify the importance in this process of 'empathetically drawing out (the client's) … pre-formed desires … through open communication … to discern the underlying intentions of that client's vaguely-cloaked desiderata'. By 'desiderata' the authors mean intentions that 'most often, the client does not yet recognize fully' (Nelson and Stolterman 2012: 42). So the emphasis here is on discerning what the client cannot yet state or even recognize, and presenting it back to them, in a process of mutual interpretation. This 'presenting back' is a vital part of the design process and not simply because it acts as a corrective. The designer is not trying to just ensure that they have heard the client accurately. Rather it enables a process of active cooperation, where the effort of sharing these interpretations galvanizes further involvement around a tentative but shared set of understandings. 'We can say that at the heart of design is the need to mobilize cooperation and imagination. The design process needs to be kept open to requirements that by necessity are evolving, as well as to be able to arrive at novel and sometimes unexpected solutions' (Telier 2011: 5).

Design practised in the public realm and for the public interest is often characterized by such participatory tools and methods, used to engage multiple stakeholders, in addressing often contentious social issues. 'Participatory Design' approaches are explicitly committed to generating such democratic engagement through the design process. One of the first steps in such design processes is to schedule events among a broad group of stakeholders, including citizens, corporate partners, employees and other interested parties (Dalsgaard 2012). The emphasis in these events is on identifying shared beliefs, perceptions and goals, over and above confronting divergent interests. In such design situations, citizens or non-designers are key stakeholders and can be seen as 'participants in the construction of their own futures and not only participants in the design process simply as users or consumers' (Staszowski, Brown and Winter 2013: 31).

In this perspective, the effort to stay true to the intentions of the client, the user (and the broader public), inchoate as they may be, as well as the guiding beliefs and values of the designer, enables a conversation to take place. We could use other words for this process: shared sense-making; negotiation; persuasion; manoeuvring; cajoling; guile; trickery and so on. Each of these word choices, successfully, moves us away from the relatively benign picture of two sets of actors, designers and clients, trying to work together, one actively listening, the other trying to express their needs. In fact these words gradually move us down a path of recognizing that the relationship between the client, the user, the public and the designer can also be one where initial intentions on all sides are stated, only to be defeated, by what actually emerges. As we have argued, even in the neutral terms of a 'service relationship' the effort to establish a shared understanding of the client's intentions suggests the possibility of trickery. We now turn however to a more charged setting, that of civic design, where clients, designers and citizens can have quite different goals and motivations.

Civic design and reframing intentions

In this final section we wish to suggest a way of approaching the question of design and intentions that we believe has particular relevance for civic design, and the public realm. Rather than characterizing the challenge of design as one of achieving clearer communication and understanding among actors involved, we feel it necessary to recognize that these actors can have very different goals and motivations, and ones that shift over the design process. We believe this is the case especially for a particular set of design questions involving urban planning, policymaking or issues of public interest, such as the provision of public policies and services. Such questions generate a peculiar relationship between designers, their clients and the people served. These are questions involving issues of public interest, such as public policies and services. So the clients are themselves representing other stakeholders. Public agencies with government mandates formulate policies, produce public spaces and offer services while *imputing the needs of those they serve*, namely those entitled to such services.

In this public realm, where designers work with clients who in turn represent multiple stakeholders, conflict and dissensus can be common. Such conflict however offers some opportunity for redefining goals and intentions. Consider an example. Public and Collaborative[1] is a research programme started in 2012 by the Parsons DESIS Lab[2] at the New School. The programme studies public services in New York City and how participation of citizens and civil servants can improve these services. Teams have worked with different New York City agencies on various research questions, tied together by a shared commitment to a participatory design process. The design process brought together a large number of stakeholders and generated increased agreement on the importance of such participation. Despite such consultations, however, vital decisions about design interventions still rest with city agencies.

The designers tasked with meeting the requirements of city agencies produce knowledge among public constituents on improving citizens' experiences with affordable housing services, information generated through participatory design methods. But these methods in a sense generated *excess* information, data over and above the brief offered by the client. Such excess information included citizen demands for greater empathy from public agencies, the need for more civic trust, and for transparency and accountability in the relationship between city agencies, community organizations and affordable housing advocates (Staszowski, Sypek and Junginger 2014: 2329). This excess information was not relevant to the city agency, whose interest remained strictly the initial brief offered to the designers. However, this excess information in turn offered an opportunity. Such circumstances created an opening to tackle the asymmetric relationship of city agencies and citizenry, reframing the project's original intentions. This kind of unexpected reframing, we suggest, is a form of trickery.

In these civic design settings we have observed three forms of trickery: *hiding* the designer's ultimate intentions from the client and vice versa, *adapting* to unexpected effects of intended designs and *co-owning* new intentions that emerge from these unexpected effects. For instance, the affordable housing advocates we observed were using an opportunity to improve the city agency services to generate information on areas outside the initial brief offered to the designers. In doing so it is quite possible they were hiding their initial intentions from the agency, playing along with its existing brief. Alternately it can also be argued that the excess information generated in the participatory exercise encouraged adaptation and co-ownership by the advocates and city agency.

As we use the term, tricks do not imply deceit as much as guile, not falsehood as much as social cunning. We do not argue that it is ethically acceptable for designers to fool their clients (though it is arguably the case that professional life can never approach a situation where both these sides know precisely what each thinks). Nor do we wish to argue that it is ethically desirable to fool clients, to misrepresent facts or to hoodwink. Instead the word trickery is our way of simply recognizing that unexpected and unintended effects defeat intentions. In collaborations intentions are heterogeneous, and social interactions are characterized by a great amount of negotiation and manoeuvring, where the inherent conflicts underlying these intentions are not fully stated, in the hope that their adjustment is better achieved. The peculiar relationship of designers with public clients makes conflict among these different actors inevitable, requiring indirect, 'tricky', social resolution.

Hiding the designer's ultimate intentions from the client and vice versa

Urgency and political pressures to deal with failing public services have encouraged both designers and public agencies to frame their interaction in terms of problems and possible solutions. Such an approach can lead to short-term opportunism and a kind of incrementalism that depicts 'all complex social situations either as neatly defined problems with definite, computable solutions or as transparent and self-evident processes that can be easily optimized' (Morozov 2013: 5).

But in reality it is not possible for designers to let clients know everything that they think, nor satisfactorily poll intentions and interests of the stakeholders involved. Instead what is more common is partial masking. For instance, hiding intentions can help to circumvent the public agency's risk aversion and procedures, also ensure that an idea is not discarded out of hand, even before being tested. This dissembling may go the other way too, when clients can also have good reasons as well as time pressures that reduce their ability to reveal their intentions to the designer because of time pressure or other reasons. Rather than presuming in this interaction that each side wishes to succeed and share its intentions fully or seek to hear the other side fully, it seems realistic to instead consider the possibility that neither side may always seek absolute candour.

The short-termism has a significant effect on ethical intentions in the design process. There may be simply quite different and incompatible motivations on each side. Public officials seek quick pragmatic responses to the political pressures they face. Designers, especially in a participatory design process, may have clearly held views on what is socially desirable and what is not. City officials may not oppose social justice goals, but find their actions are often curtailed by limited budgets and/ or political priorities. Even when sympathetic, their agency goals and objectives can frequently constrain what they are able to do. They have to demonstrate service reforms, as demanded by elected officials, and these reforms may have little to do with larger goals of equality and justice. At the same time the real pressures and demands of community representatives, outside the city agencies, seeking to moderate the effects of marketized government services may impel designers to seek an ethical focus. How to resolve this?

The challenge in such a setting is for designers to find ways to ensure the broader, more diverse needs of the public(s) they are being tasked to serve (indirectly) are heard by the client. For this reason design practice in the public sector can be understood not just as a 'matter of enhancing existing service structures' but in terms of 'playing a more transformative and political role' (Staszowski, Brown & Winter 2013: 31). In our experience with the Public and Collaborative research programme, the project moved away from the initial client brief due to the effort to respond to the demands of community groups. The project as a consequence generated many unexpected actions that went beyond the client's original intention of simply increasing the information available on the affordable-housing lottery application process. These actions included the growing influence[3] and expansion of a 'housing ambassador' programme designed during the project. The ambassadors are networks of community-based service providers that New Yorkers can rely upon for help in identifying and applying for affordable housing. Policies changed at the agency,[4] and even a new landlord ambassadors programme was started, to help struggling landlords more effectively resolve dangerous and unhealthy conditions in their buildings[5] (see Figure 3.1).

Figure 3.1 An example of the work done by the Public and Collaborative research programme (Author's photograph).

Adapting and co-owning new intentions

It is hard to predict what happens through the design intervention. Unexpected consequences can emerge even when strictly following the client's intentions. We have found through our research and projects that simply the experience of bringing together different groups involved in a public policy or service design initiative often generates unexpected effects. Government agencies are constrained by clearly laid out rules and regulations in terms of what they can and cannot do. These rules often lay out as well the manner in which they can consult with citizens. Just the effort to bring actors together in a manner hitherto not done can challenge existing bureaucratic norms regulating such interaction. In this way, a design intervention even when following the intentions of government clients has the potential of creating unexpected and productive consequences. Involved actors start to recognize their interdependence and become motivated to develop new stances and claims. Design becomes a set of practices that challenge the established order, a political act (Staszowski, Brown and Winter 2013: 32). In this sense, design orders a 'moment of contestation', that is, de-sign, but in doing so it is part of a process where ideas and artefacts are generated in close dialogue, building on the status quo, that is, di-segno, in an effort to change it.

As the consequences of a design intervention cascade, they generate new intentions that can be quite different from what was initially envisaged. So design proposals validated by citizen participation may end up clashing with existing policies and other conflicting government agendas. This constitutes a certain danger, being a source of uncertainty to the client. From the perspective of a public sector client the motivation for a design intervention can be to develop a suitable and favourable perceived reform to existing services. To encourage further citizen demands would be, from this perspective, to open up a Pandora's box of claims that can undermine the agency's functioning. However, from the perspective of a design activity seeking citizen engagement and better services, this heightening of political demands has a desirable effect, increasing the salience and valence of citizen claims, and placing such claims on a political agenda. It is therefore crucial to find a way to encourage co-owning of these intentions so that the client feels less threatened and indeed more validated by these changing intentions.

Conclusion: Why trickery matters

There is a distressing risk in the growing interest in social innovation from designers and public clients alike, to see it as an opportunity for technocratic reform. Government policies and services do have to be improved, and participatory design interventions are an important means to solicit user perceptions, and create the favourable climate for internal reform of government agencies. However, the ultimate goals sought by such design interventions include encouraging citizens to imagine different forms of society, to engage politically with their social world, is to make demands of their governments and state shared claims as citizens. Trickery matters ultimately because sometimes to achieve what is sought through such political action requires, paradoxically, to let go of achieving such intentions, and to be more open to what is achieved on the way. Mistakes, accidents, consequences, all offer opportunities for further political work. In this way trickery encourages design to be a politically more astute act, open to a variety of possibilities that emerge during the shared effort of designing.

Notes

1   See http://nyc.pubcollab.org
2   See http://newschool.edu/desis
3   See https://www.dnainfo.com/new-york/20161004/hudson-square/qualify-affordable-housing-lottery-rules-connect-credit-score
4   See http://www1.nyc.gov/site/hpd/about/press-releases/2017/03/03-15-17.page
5   See http://www1.nyc.gov/site/hpd/about/press-releases/2017/05/05-09-17.page

Bibliography

Cross, Nigel. (2001) 'Designerly Ways of Knowing: Design Discipline versus Design Science', *Design Issues*, 17, 3: 49–55.
Dalsgaard, Peter. (2012) 'Participatory Design in Large-Scale Public Projects: Challenges and Opportunities', *Design Issues*, 28, 3: 34–47.

Dilnot, Clive. (1984a) 'The State of Design History, Part I: Mapping the Field', *Design Issues*, 1, 1: 4–23.

Dilnot, Clive. (1984b) 'The State of Design History, Part II: Problems and Possibilities', *Design Issues*, 1, 2: 3–20.

Flusser, Vilem. (1999) 'About the Word Design', in *The Shape of Things: A Philosophy of Design*, London: Reaktion.

Fry, Tony. (2011) *Design as Politics*, Oxford: Berg.

Harvey, David. (2000) *Spaces of Hope*, Berkeley, CA: University of California Press.

Holston, James. (1989) *The Modernist City: An Anthropological Critique of Brasília*, Chicago, IL: University of Chicago Press.

Knox, Paul L. (2011) *Cities and Design*, London: Routledge.

Morozov, Evgeny. (2013) *To Save Everything, Click Here: The Folly of Technological Solutionism*, Philadelphia, PA: PublicAffairs.

Nelson, Harold G. and Stolterman, Erik. (2012) *The Design Way: Intentional Change in an Unpredictable World*, 2nd Edition. Cambridge, MA: The MIT Press.

Scott, James C. (1998) *Seeing Like a State: How Certain Schemes to Improve the Human Condition Have Failed*. New Haven, CT: Yale University.

Simon, Herbert. (1982) *The Sciences of the Artificial*, 2nd Edition. Cambridge, MA: MIT Press.

Staszowski, Eduardo, Brown, Scott and Winter, Ben. (2013) 'Reflections on Designing for Social Innovation in the Public Sector: A Case Study in New York City', in E. Manzini and E. Staszowski (eds), *Public and Collaborative: Exploring the Intersection of Design, Social Innovation and Public Policy*, DESIS Network, pp. 27–37.

Staszowski, Eduardo, Sypek, Alexis and Junginger, Sabine. (2014) 'Public and collaborative: From participatory design to design for participation'. *Proceedings of the 19th DMI Academic Conference*, London (2329–2343).

Telier, A. (Thomas Binder, Giorgio De Michelis, Pelle Ehn, Giulio Jacucci, Per Linde, and Ina Wagner) (2011) *Design Things*, Cambridge, MA: The MIT Press.

4

Guns and Morality: Mediation, Agency and Responsibility

Tim Dant

Introduction

There are three reasons why guns are interesting as a class of material objects with a distinctive moral significance. The first is the unusually limited purposes of guns as objects that can be drawn into the momentary action of a single person to have devastating consequences for other people's lives. The second is that the risks and dangers of guns have led to debate and discussion about their uses, politics and morality. The third is that guns have a moral status far beyond their actual use. These three characteristics make having anything to do with guns – as a designer, manufacturer, user or even as a creator of fiction – tricky and fraught with moral dilemmas. Those who take up a gun are able to achieve the 'trick' of personally killing large numbers of people in a very short time.

In this chapter, I want to explore this unusual relationship between guns and the life-world of contemporary societies, to argue that the moral consequence of material things is a collective issue and not one that should only be reduced to the individual subject and his or her choices. Although the individual person must be held morally and legally accountable for his or her actions, the overall responsibility for guns and the actions they make possible is one that should be taken by society as a whole. There may be good grounds for 'gun control', the regulation and restriction of the availability of guns and their uses, but more than this, I want to argue that unless the symbolic potency of guns is addressed, their moral status as real objects will not change significantly. I will begin by discussing the embodied phenomenological relationship between guns and humans as a class of objects and then mention two main uses for guns outside war: hunting and self-defence. I will then explore my central concern, the agentic status of guns in relation to human action, through the ideas of Bruno Latour and Peter Paul Verbeek about mediation and morality. Although both the Actor Network Theory (ANT) perspective of Latour and the postphenomenological approach of Verbeek have opened up understanding about the relationship between humans and material objects, they have compromised the issue of morality with their concept of a 'hybrid' form, a symmetrical combination of human and non-human.

Finally, I will draw on the ideas of Hans Jonas to argue that the morality of human relationships with the material world invokes the imperative of responsibility that includes a collective cultural responsibility for things like guns.

What guns do for people

Guns, like other weapons, are an extension of the capacity of the human body. Fists, knives, swords, clubs and so on are weapons that can deal injury and death to another person within an arm's reach. Handheld weapons extend the body's reach, but other weapons (a stone, spear, a slingshot) extend that reach by propelling a projectile beyond the 'manipulatory zone of touch' into the 'perceptual zone of vision' (Dant 2005: 115–122). The capacity to aim, direct and focus destructive energy on a point beyond reach is refined in the bow and arrow, catapult and the crossbow that store accumulated human energy and release it as an intensified propellant. Air guns further refine the gathering of human energy for propelling a small projectile down a barrel that is aimed by simply pointing it at the target. The origin of the word 'gun' seems to come from Norse words for war but the distinguishing features of its modern form are the use of a chemical explosion behind a projectile that is aimed along a metal barrel to give the weapon a high degree of power and accuracy. With a chemical propellant, the motor capacity required of the human agent is reduced to the squeezing of a trigger and his or her visual capacity is focused along the barrel to the target. The gun achieves with minimal skill or strength 'killing-at-a-distance', which dramatically changes the nature of warfare as well as violent conflict between individuals (Ehrenreich 1997).

This brief gloss on the refinement and development of weapons draws attention to the embodied phenomenological character of the gun; it channels an intention of a human being to act violently in the direction of something or someone. Perception (visual and auditory) moves up and beyond the manipulatory field to consider what is within range of the weapon's projection. At the core of phenomenology is the concept of intentionality; the direction of the contents of consciousness towards something, which orients the person to his or her life-world, ordering and organizing its materiality as well as its ideas and imaginings (Husserl 1983: 64; Verbeek 2011). What is remarkable about the gun is that in terms of intentionality it takes such a singular form; destruction or damage of a specific target. Unlike, for example, the motor car that can also wreak destruction and damage on people and things in the life-world but has a primary life-affirming purpose of enhancing mobility, the gun can do little else but issue or threaten violence. Firing a gun by squeezing the trigger is a conscious motor act that realizes the human person's intention, an act clearly directed to someone or something. The focus of conscious intentionality may be impaired by drink or the gun may be fired 'accidentally' (e.g. when 'playing' with it) but even in these circumstances simply having a gun available to be taken up and pointed involves intentionality and a prior knowledge of the risk of death and injury it can cause.

I am using the word 'gun' colloquially to refer to what is more technically a 'firearm', a personal weapon that fires a bullet using an explosive charge that includes handguns, rifles, carbines and assault weapons as well as shotguns.[1] What is important about guns as weapons is that only one person is needed to control and fire the device. In aiming it at a specific thing, animal or person the human agent shows anyone who can see – bystanders as well as the person it is aimed at – their capacity and readiness to fire at something or someone. Once triggered, the noise of the explosion 'reports' to everyone in the hearing range that a projectile has been emitted. Pulling the trigger, noise and effect are virtually at a single point in time and once fired, the bullet's trajectory cannot be cancelled and its speed means that it is too late for the victim to take evasive or defensive action. Within its range – which varies according to the type of gun – the only defence is to have a barrier or shield in place such as a wall that hides the body or a flak jacket that covers it. Ducking or running is only effective to make the firer's aim more difficult and must be a response to recognizing the preparedness to fire rather than the firing itself. A sniper's rifle with a telescopic sight that extends the zone of vision, or a gun fired from a concealed position, may mean that a victim was never aware that she or he was a target.

There are broadly two types of guns, handguns and long guns, each designed around the capacity of the human body to aim and fire. The handgun or pistol is supported by one hand, which limits the length of the barrel because a longer barrel may be more accurate but is difficult to hold steady enough to aim. A single hand grips the handle, which is at an obtuse angle to the barrel, with a trigger for firing that can be pulled towards the body by the first finger of the same hand. A second hand may support the first to steady aim and improve accuracy by sighting directly along the barrel. The handgun is lighter and easier to conceal and carry than the long gun (rifle, carbine or shotgun), which has a longer barrel designed to be supported by the second hand with improved accuracy and velocity. The handle is extended behind the trigger to a shoulder grip that transmits the recoil into the trunk of the body. The long gun can provide much better directional aim and a greater force of explosion because of the increased substance of the weapon and its greater integration within the body form of the user. As a 'standing reserve' (Heidegger 1977: 17), a gun holds contained and ready capacity to inflict mortal injury – the handgun can be holstered on the body, the long gun slung on the shoulder or kept in a vehicle or building. A gun need not be used in and need not inhibit other activities, but if loaded and nearby, little preparation is needed before it can be aimed and fired to deadly effect. Producing or revealing a gun is a form of 'unconcealment' (Heidegger 1977: 13), the enframing of a manifest technological truth, which is in itself a threatening gesture that is heightened once it is pointed or aimed, thereby indicating its preparation, direction and intention for use. The very presence of a carbine or submachine gun slung across the chest of a police officer or guard at an airport or government building shows serious intent; the gun is all too literally 'ready-to-hand' (Heidegger 1962: 100–101). Guns are associated with war, both between states and within contested states (Chivers 2010; Greene and Marsh 2012) but at the boundaries of society guns are used collectively by groups and in conjunction with other weapons and are directed at a hostile force rather than a person or animal. Within civil society guns are wielded by individuals and there are two 'uses' of the gun that are proffered as reasons for its existence: hunting and defence. It is worth briefly considering each before turning to the symbolic and cultural status of the gun.

Hunting and defence

So-called 'sporting' weapons, such as the shotgun that fires multiple pellets from a single explosion, are used for hunting game birds and small animals. The spread of the shot increases the chances of hitting even a rapidly moving object. The large cartridges need to be replaced by breaking the breach after each firing, so many shotguns have two barrels to give a second shot before re-loading. A rifle firing bullets can be much lighter and more accurate at a distance, especially with a telescopic sight, and is more likely to be used for larger game. Nicholas Govoroff (1993) describes how both types of firearm were integrated into the traditional hunting culture of rural France. Beginning with an air rifle to fire at cans, bottles, lizards and stray cats, the young hunter then learnt from his grandfather how to use a 9-millimetre rifle, shooting birds from a hunting blind outside the village. He would progress to a larger bore for hunting larger prey (hares, partridges and pigeons) on his own until at fifteen he would be allowed to use a real shotgun – *un fusil* – with greater power and range. The mature hunter uses both a 12-gauge shotgun for small game and a rifle for big game but needs a *permis de chasser* as well as the approval and encouragement of the hunting group.

What Govoroff describes is a cultural *dispositif* that includes: weapons, hunters of specific ages and gender (the pattern of use is quite different for women), local traditions, training and law enforced by game wardens and the justice system. Hillyard and Burridge have recently begun to describe in a similar way the contemporary cultural context of game shooting in the UK (2012). They explain that within the context of the Firearms Acts and the *Code of Good Shooting Practice* (BASC 2008) the etiquette of sport shooting requires the user not to remove the gun from its sleeve until she or he is in position, and not straying as the game are driven (Hillyard and Burridge 2012: 401). Although the need for provisioning through hunting has receded with industrialization, the culture of hunting with guns persists in many parts of the world as a 'sport', an entertaining and exciting activity with a collective culture of participation. Using guns for sport is an embodied practice in which consciousness and intention are focused on killing but it is also a cultural activity that involves other people and a set of social and institutional conventions, rituals and obligations. The 'pleasure' derived from the 'sport' involves killing animals but hunting firearms are also very effective as interpersonal weapons or suicide devices – their purpose of death and destruction is much the same.

Defence is the second reason for having a gun and has become a major theme in the literature on the politics of gun control, especially in the United States where there are nearly 90 guns for every 100 people (e.g. Kleck 1997; Lott and Mustard 1997; Southwick 2000; Spitzer 1998; Squires 2000; Cook and Ludwig 2002). Just showing that you have the capacity to injure or kill someone may act as a deterrent to her or him committing some violent or illegitimate act towards you – nonetheless 8 per cent of the domestic intruders in one US survey were shot at and killed or injured (Kleck 1997: 225; Kleck and Hogan 1999: 406). The academic literature uses statistics and surveys to argue that gun ownership has an impact on crime statistics – it either increases or lowers recorded crimes – but there is no conclusive evidence one way or the other, partly because of the limited accuracy of the statistics and partly because of the difficulty of using them to establish causal relationships. Whether a gun is concealed, on the person or locked away in the home alters its effect as a deterrent and 'defence' may be of others, property or 'self'. The arguments against having guns in the home or on the person for defence point to the increased numbers of 'accidents', suicides and homicides that involve a gun – again, statistics are disputed (Felson and Messner 1996; Konty and Schaefer 2012). However, the most recent work shows that higher rates of gun ownership are related to higher rates of death by firearms, homicide and victimization in gun-related crimes (Bangalori and Messerli 2013; van Kesteren 2014). The legitimate ownership of guns for sport or self-defence involves a 'gun culture' (Squires 2000; Springwood 2007) but guns also have a distinctive role in the general culture and mass media, not least in the reporting of mass shootings by rogue gunmen, especially in the United States.

Guns as mediators

Writing in 1994, Bruno Latour used the standoff between the anti- and pro-gun lobbies in the United States to explore agency and guns.[2] The anti-gun lobby believes that 'guns kill people' and that the gun 'enables of course, but also instructs, even pulls the trigger' while the pro-gun lobby – here personified by the National Rifle Association – insists that 'People kill people; not guns' using 'sociological' reasoning that 'renders the gun a neutral carrier of the will that adds nothing to the action' (Latour 1994: 30–31). Latour's argument is that the human and social should be seen as continuous and interconnected with the technical and material, a complex mode of agency in which artefacts should not be considered merely as things, because ultimately they 'are us' (Latour 1994: 64). Instead of Heidegger's understanding of technology as 'enframing' human actions, he argues that it *mediates* them: the person is transformed by the gun into a combined agent of person and thing, a hybrid, the 'citizen-gun'. The concept of 'mediation' enables Latour to abandon any subject–object dichotomy between things and people that predetermines their properties. The relations between people and things are composed of an ever-changing network although 'black-boxing' components, obscures or appears to stabilize their fluidity.

The core of Latour's argument is the notion that 'purposeful action and intentionality may not be properties of objects but they are not properties of humans either. They are the properties of institutions, *dispositifs*' (Latour 1994: 46). The term '*dispositif*', associated with the writing of Michel Foucault (1980) and often translated into English as 'apparatus', refers to the ensemble of heterogeneous elements – discursive and material, symbolic and real – that surround human actions. The sociocultural apparatus of the *dispositif* actually specifies the responsibilities of human agents in relation to objects such as a gun, clarifying what people, even different classes or people in particular legal or cultural contexts, are expected to do. The danger with Latour's merging of subject and object into the hybrid lies in obscuring the difference between the moral obligations of individual people and that of the cultural apparatus, which itself assigns quite a different level of moral agency to people and to objects such as guns. The *dispositif* does indeed have moral responsibility for the guns within its purview but that does not mean that individual users lack intentionality or responsibility for the things they use.

Moral agency

Latour makes a strong claim for 'actor-actant symmetry', which means that 'it is neither people nor guns that kill. Responsibility for action must be shared among the various actants' (Latour 1994: 34). However, Hans Jonas explains that a moral agent must have causal power over actions that have impact on the world *and* they must be able to foresee the consequences of those actions (Jonas 1984: 90). Moral agents have two types of responsibility: 'being accountable "for" one's deeds' and 'being responsible "for" particular objects that commit an agent to particular deeds' (1984: 90). The person who wields and fires a gun is responsible in Jonas's first way but it is through the *dispositif*, the media, the regulatory and legal system and the broader culture of ideas and opinions that collective moral agency is responsible in his second, responsible 'for' objects.

It is the *dispositif*, the cultural apparatus of laws, conventions and traditions that assigns individual moral agency to people and not to things such as guns. Even the users of guns accept responsibility for their use, as multiple killers Adam Lanza and Derek Bird recognized when they turned their guns on themselves (Pilkington 2013).[3] Others, like Raoul Moat and Anders Breijvik, expected to be martyred for their gun use by an armed policeman or a retributive state (Rowe 2013).[4] Even in the stress of modern warfare, a soldier is still responsible for how he uses his gun against an enemy; a UK court martial recently found a marine guilty of murdering a wounded Afghan insurgent in his custody (Morris 2013). Individual moral agency is about whether an act *should* be carried out at all – a mode of agency that an object does not have.

Peter-Paul Verbeek (2011) argues that things and technologies – such as speedbumps and seat belts (Latour 1994) – can have moral *relevance* because they become involved in moral decision-making and in shaping moral actions. He suggests that some material objects can be 'moral mediators' and 'provide "material answers" to the moral question of how to act' (Verbeek 2011: 43). But, this is to follow Latour into muddying the location of moral agency:

> When technologies are used, moral decisions are not made autonomously by human beings, nor are persons forced by technologies to make decisions. Rather, moral agency is distributed among humans and nonhumans; moral actions and decisions are the products of human-technology associations. (Verbeek 2011: 53)

He reprises Latour's discussion to claim that because the gun helps to define situations, agents and their possible actions, it is part of a 'new entity', a hybrid, the 'gunman' (Verbeek 2011: 64). The gun does indeed have material agency, moral relevance and is a moral mediator of the intentionality of whoever wields it. But, unlike the human, the gun lacks the intentionality or the consciousness to be a *moral* agent and cannot be held responsible for any action.

Material agency is a variable property of both the person and the gun; a handgun is effective at short range but useless compared to a rifle over thirty or so yards; someone who has shot someone before will find it easier to do so again.

Furthermore, the moral agency of a person can be changed by the material agency supplied by an object, such as a gun. But the moral relevance of material objects as mediators of human actions is an insufficient reason to assert that moral agency is distributed among humans and non-humans. *Moral* agency is ultimately human, however morally relevant the technology is, and the use of a gun exemplifies the personification of that agency in the intentional acts of aiming and firing. The individual person firing a gun may not be the sole and autonomous moral agent if he or she has been trained and instructed to fire the weapon by someone else or if he or she is acting on behalf of a collective moral agency (e.g. the police). It is the clear location of moral agency in the individual person that gives guns such a high symbolic value of an individual's power.

Latour's ideas have seldom come under heavy criticism beyond the sociology of science (Shaffer 1991; Bloor 1999; Tosh 2007).[5] However, the consequence of his and Verbeek's conceptual rethinking of the phenomenology of the gun is to divert attention from humans' responsibility as moral agents in technical relations. The material agency of guns does not confer any moral agency on them because they lack the consciousness and mental capacity – in phenomenological terms, the intentionality – of their human users. The moral responsibility of the gun user is not at issue in advanced contemporary societies, but the moral responsibility of the *dispositif*, the socio-technical apparatus of ideas, discourse, knowledge, institutions and attitudes that surrounds the way objects are used is in a state of flux. Once the arbitrary and unnecessary destruction of life becomes so easy, the imperative of responsibility is at a society-wide political level: 'Care for the future of mankind is the overruling duty of collective human action in the age of a technical civilization that has become "almighty", if not in its productive then at least in its destructive potential' (Jonas 1984: 136).

Responsibility and culture

Verbeek introduces the idea of 'technical intentionality' from Don Ihde (1990) to refer to the intentionality built into an object by the designer or manufacturer. But whatever intentional use is built in (such as for a shotgun to kill vermin), it may be modified by the intentions of the user (such as killing himself with the shotgun). For Hans Jonas (1984: 52), the usability of a material thing is its *purpose* which precedes its existence and emerges in its design and manufacture; an object such as a gun 'does not itself *have* its purpose at all, but only its maker and user "has" it' (1984: 53). Now a purpose can be varied by other human agents because 'purpose is set and entertained by *human subjects*' (Jonas 1984: 56 – emphasis in the original). Whereas Latour and Verbeek claim moral as well as material agency for the post-human 'hybrid', Jonas reminds us of the social-material apparatus, or *dispositif*, that gives an object such as a gun its purposes. And it is the *dispositif* that can respond to changes in the culture to re-specify the purposes of objects that already exist and to change how future objects are conceived, for example by revising the laws on self-defence or the community etiquette of hunters.

The progress of technological civilization has shifted material agency from the individual to collectively managed means. It is in the light of the changes in the technological capacities of human societies that Hans Jonas (1984) reformulated the Kantian imperative to propose an 'imperative of responsibility'.[6] Arguing that there is a 'life interest', an impulsion intrinsic and essential to all forms of life that Jonas characterizes as the 'yes' of life as opposed to the 'no' of non-being:

> In this sense, every feeling and striving being is not only an end of nature but also an end-in-itself, namely its own end. And precisely here, the self-affirmation of being becomes emphatic in the opposition of life to death. Life is the explicit confrontation of being with not being. (Jonas 1984: 81)

Is it possible to imagine the wielding of a gun as life affirming? Yes, because as an advanced hunting weapon it transforms the capacities of people to feed themselves when killing wild animals for meat. And again, when humans need to defend themselves from attacks by others, the availability of firearms can change the balance of force significantly. The use of guns, or just the threat of their use, may even bring conflict to an end more quickly. But Jonas's reformulated imperative is for a late modern world, one very different from Kant's, one in which the emergence of modern technology extends the capacity of human life to dominate and ultimately destroy all other life including all other human life. It is technological civilization, the power of human beings over nature, that changes the collective responsibility of humanity: 'Only in man is power emancipated from the whole through knowledge and arbitrary will and only in man can it become fatal to him and to itself' (Jonas 1984: 129).

As Norbert Elias (1995) has pointed out, technization – such as the introduction of the motor car – can have decivilizing effects that change human relationships and lead to unintended deaths. The tendency towards civilization however eventually brings about shifts in human practices, including emotions and the acceptance of individual responsibility, as the danger and consequences of the object are internalized by its users. These shifts are however prompted by changes in the social apparatus of discourse, regulations, institutions and technical modifications. Guns may, historically, have had a life-affirming purpose and been civilizing in their effects but their civilizing role is all but played out. In late modern societies they are *decivilizing* in terms of the deaths they threaten and the role they play in interpersonal relations (Dant 2006); they have become an anachronism.

Conclusions

Guns continue to provide a sense of personal power and security to the rampage killer, the gangland killer, the terrorist, the warlord, the insurgent, the guerrilla, the guard, the cop, the hunter and even the home defender. The power that a gun can confer gives it a symbolic power in life-worlds such as those of drug dealers, career criminals and street gangs (Stretsky and Pogrebin 2007; Hallsworth and Silverstone 2009). In these contexts, each individual user has a moral agency that gives him or her responsibility for his or her use of a gun. But the moral agency and responsibility for guns do not lie solely in the hands of those who fire them; it is for the wider society to decide on the appropriateness of guns and their use. This is not simply a matter of regulation and law because the codification of morality tends to follow the cultural recognition of moral responsibility. In the UK, the killing of sixteen children and one adult in a school at Dunblane in 1996 by a man armed with four handguns led to changes in the law that effectively made the private ownership of firearms illegal.[7] The changes were a result of inquiries, petitions and public debate in which the views of a range of interested groups were heard – this was the *dispositif* in action as moral agents negotiated the practicalities of changes that eventually became law. In 2013, Senator Dianne Feinstein introduced a bill in the US Senate to ban the manufacture and sale of semi-automatic weapons following Adam Lanza's rampage killings, but, along with other proposed changes to federal law on guns, it failed to win sufficient support in the legislature. In 2015, President Obama tried to extend background checks on prospective gun owners without a vote in congress. He, like many Americans, was aghast at the 90,000 gun deaths and 1,000 mass shootings in the three years since the massacre of twenty-six staff and children at Sandy Hook Elementary School in 2012 (Smith 2015).

The very narrow purposes of guns are always a 'no' to life and the possible life-affirming purposes of hunting and self-defence are increasingly difficult to justify in the current techno-civilization of the Western world. The risks to life of guns being present in contemporary society and culture as real, non-human actants cannot be tolerated if we are to recognize the imperative of responsibility towards life. A simple ban on the possession of guns in civil society is not practical; there is too much emotional symbolism tying the gun to ideological constructs to do with masculinity, nationalism, individual identity and the domination of nature (Ehrenreich 1997). Nor can guns be considered as simply a matter of gun crime, justice or criminal subcultures because the symbolic power of the gun extends into the broader culture through mediated images of characters using guns to exert power over others (Sheptycki 2009). As those who wanted to reduce the decivilizing effects of cars (Elias 1995) and more recently of cigarettes (Brandt 2007) have shown, challenging the cultural and symbolic status of the object is a necessary prerequisite for bringing about legal and regulatory changes in the existence of the real objects. Changing the relationship between guns and morality will come about through a stepwise modification of the symbolism of the gun as it appears in the media; in rap lyrics, movies, video games and television shows. The collective moral agency in the socio-technical apparatus, the *dispositif*, must take responsibility for the existence and tolerance of guns, both in the real world and in the symbolic world of media representations while continuing to assert the individual moral agency and responsibility of those who use them.

Notes

1   The 'Taser', a weapon that fires darts through which it delivers a disabling electrical shock, is not a gun by this definition.
2   He revisits virtually the same discussion of technical mediation in *Pandora's Hope* (1999).

3 Lanza shot dead 20 children and 6 adults at Sandy Hook, Connecticut, USA in December 2012. Bird shot 12 people dead and injured 11 others in Cumbria, UK in June 2010.

4 Moat shot dead 1 person and maimed 2 others in Northumberland, UK in 2010 before shooting himself dead. Breijvik shot dead 69 people on the island of Utøya, Norway in 2011 – police did not shoot him but he was arrested, charged, convicted and sentenced to twenty-one years in prison.

5 Pierre Lemonnier (1996) does take him to task for too rapidly dismissing the material logic of objects – their material agency often shapes the sequence of human practices in a *chaîne operatoire* that is overlooked by the 'hybrid' metaphor of socio-technology that Latour and Verbeek embrace.

6 'Responsibility' is a watchword in the arguments of the pro-gun lobby in both the United States and United Kingdom. They are keen to educate and regulate those who own and use guns to use them *responsibly* for hunting, self-defence, sport and marksmanship. But, this is individual responsibility for the guns and is not the same as the responsibility of a culture to question the *purposes* of guns.

7 Firearms (Amendment) Act 1997; Firearms (Amendment) (No. 2) Act 1997.

Bibliography

Bangalore, S. and Messerli, F. (2013) 'Gun Ownership and Firearm-Related Deaths', *American Journal of Medicine*, 126, 10: 873–876.

BASC (2008) *Code of Good Shooting Practice*. Available at: http://www.basc.org.uk/content/codeofgoodshootingpractice (accessed 13 December 2013).

Bloor, D. (1999) 'Anti-Latour', *Studies in the History and Philosophy of Science*, 30, 1: 81–112.

Brandt, A. (2007) *The Cigarette Century: The Rise, Fall and Persistence of the Deadly Product That Defined America*, New York: Basic Books.

Chivers, C. J. (2010) *The Gun: The AK-47 and the Evolution of War*, London: Penguin Books.

Cook, P. J. and Ludwig, J. (2002) *The Effects of Gun Prevalence on Burglary: Deterrence vs Inducement – Working Paper 8926*, Cambridge, MA: National Bureau of Economic Research.

Dant, T. (2005) *Materiality and Society*, Maidenhead: Open University Press.

Dant, T. (2006) 'Materiality and Civilization: Things and Society', *British Journal of Sociology*, 57, 2: 289–308.

Ehrenreich, B. (1997) *Blood Rites*, Virago: London.

Elias, N. (1995) 'Technization and Civilization', *Theory, Culture and Society*, 12, 3: 7–42.

Felson, R. B. and Messner, S. F. (1996) 'To Kill or Not to Kill? Lethal Outcomes in Injurious Attacks', *Criminology*, 34: 519–545 – reprinted in R. Hornsby and D. Hobbs (eds) (2008) *Gun Crime*. Aldershot: Ashgate.

Foucault, M. (1980) 'Confessions of the Flesh', *Power/Knowledge: Selected Interviews and Other Writings*, New York: Pantheon Books.

Govoroff, N. (1993) 'The Hunter and His Gun in Haute-Provence', in P. Lemonnier (ed.), *Technological Choices: Transformations in Material Cultures since the Neolithic*, London: Routledge.

Greene, O. and Marsh, N. (2012) *Small Arms, Crime and Conflict: Global Governance and the Threat of Armed Violence*, London: Routledge.

Hallsworth, S. and Silverstone, D. (2009) 'That's Life, Innit': A British Perspective on Guns, Crime and Social Order', *Criminology and Criminal Justice*, 9, 3: 359–377.

Heidegger, M. (1962) *Being and Time*, Oxford: Blackwell.

Heidegger, M. (1977) *The Question concerning Technology and Other Essays*, New York: Harper Torchbooks.

Hillyard, S. and Burridge, J. (2012) 'Shotguns and Firearms in the UK: A Call for a Distinctively Sociological Contribution to the Debate', *Sociology*, 46, 3: 395–410.

Husserl, E. (1983) *Ideas Pertaining to a Pure Phenomenology and to a Phenomenological Philosophy: First Book*, Dordrecht: Kluwer.

Ihde, D. (1990) *Technology and the Lifeworld: From Garden to Earth*, Bloomington, IN: Indiana University Press.

Jonas, H. (1984) *The Imperative of Responsibility: In Search of an Ethics for the Technological Age*, Chicago, IL: University of Chicago Press.

Kleck, G. (1997) 'Guns and Self Defence', in D. B. Kates Jr and G. Kleck (eds), *The Great American Gun Debate*, San Francisco, CA: Pacific Research Institute for Public Policy.

Kleck, G. and Hogan, M. (1999) 'National Case-Control Study of Homicide Offending and Gun Ownership', *Social Problems*, 46: 275–293 – reprinted in R. Hornsby and D. Hobbs (eds) (2008) *Gun Crime*. Aldershot: Ashgate.

Konty, M. and Schaefer, B. (2012) 'Small Arms Mortality: Access to Firearms and Lethal Violence', *Sociological Spectrum: Mid-South Sociological Association*, 32, 6: 475–490.

Latour, B. (1994) 'On Technical Mediation – Philosophy, Sociology, Genealogy', *Common Knowledge*, 3, 2: 29–64.

Latour, B. (1999) *Pandora's Hope: Essays on the Reality of Science Studies*, Cambridge, MA: Harvard University Press.

Lemonnier, P. (1996) 'Et pourtant ça vole! L'ethnologie des techniques et les objets industrials', *Ethnologie Française*, 26, 1: 17–31.

Lott, J. R. and Mustard, D. B. (1997) 'Crime Deterrence and Right-to-Carry Concealed Guns', *Journal of Legal Studies*, 26, 1: 1–68.

Morris, S. (2013) 'Royal Marine Found Guilty of 'Executing' Afghan Insurgent', *The Guardian*, 8 November. Available at: http://www.theguardian.com/uk-news/2013/nov/08/royal-marine-guilty-executing-afghan (accessed 13 December 2013).

Pilkington, E. (2013) 'Firearms Lobby Stands Firm Despite Wave of Revulsion', *Guardian Weekly*, 10 May 2013.

Rowe, M. (2013) 'Just Like a TV Show: Public Criminology and the Media Coverage of 'Hunt for Britain's Most Wanted Man', *Crime Media Culture*, 9, 23–28.

Schaffer, S. (1991) 'The Eighteenth Brumaire of Bruno Latour', *Studies in the History and Philosophy of Science*, 22, 1: 174–192.

Sheptycki, J. (2009) 'Guns, Crime and Social Order', *Criminology and Criminal Justice*, 9, 3: 307–336.

Smith, D. (2015) 'Obama Looks to Expand Background Checks for Guns with Executive Action', *The Guardian*, 10 December.

Southwick, L. (2000) 'Self-Defense with Guns: The Consequences', *Journal of Criminal Justice*, 28, 351–370.

Spitzer, R. J. (1998) *The Politics of Gun Control*, 2nd Edition, New York: Chatham House.

Springwood, C. F. (2007) *Open Fire: Understanding Global Gun Cultures*, Oxford: Berg.

Squires, P. (2000) *Gun Culture or Gun Control?*, London: Routledge.

Stretesky, P. B. and Pogrebin, M. R. (2007) 'Gang-Related Gun Violence: Socialization, Identity and Self', *Journal of Contemporary Ethnography*, 36, 1: 85–114.

Tosh, N. (2007) 'Science, Truth and History, Part II. Metaphysical Bolt-Holes for the
    Sociology of Scientific Knowledge?' *Studies in the History and Philosophy of Science*, 38,
    1: 185–209.
Van Kesteren, J. N. (2014) 'Revisiting the Gun Ownership and Violence Link: A Multilevel
    Analysis of Victimisation Survey Data', *British Journal of Criminology*, 54, 53–72.
Verbeek, P.-P. (2011) *Moralizing Technology: Understanding and Designing the Morality of
    Things*, Chicago, IL: University of Chicago Press.

5

The Magic That Is Design

Cameron Tonkinwise

For (said he) any of us being resolved to undertake any thing of importance, we first of all search out a God to prosper our designed Undertaking; and going out of doors with this Design, take the first creative that presents itself to our Eyes, whether Dog, Cat, or the most contemptible Animal in the World, for our God; or perhaps instead of that any Inanimate that falls in our way, whether a Stone, a piece of Wood, or anything else of the same Nature.

William Pietz (1958: 8)

The most mysterious and wonderful thing about technology is that reality, Being, should allow itself to be manipulated by one of its evolutes, human beings. The truth is that the clay that shaped into us after billions of years, allows itself to be manipulated by us to form all manner of artifacts and things.

Ignacio Götz (2001: 39)

Why must the Moderns resort to complicated forms in order to believe in others' naïve beliefs, or in knowledge without belief among themselves? … Why not just admit that there is no such thing as fetishism – and no anti-fetishism either – and recognize the strange efficacy of these 'action displacers' with which our lives are intimately bound up?

Bruno Latour (2010: 11)

Dwelling with spirits

Every now and then, I pause to think, 'How strange, I live with an animal.' This brown furry dog follows me from room to room, making liberal use of the furniture for his excessive sleep habits. On these occasions, when I am noticing that a completely alien species inhabits my human dwelling, I can sometimes glimpse that this is not just the case for this quite sociable mammal. My house contains a plethora of creatures. I do not mean the unwanted insects and perhaps rodents, let alone mites, fungi and bacteria, but all the other things. There are the devices that crowd together in the kitchen or occupy my desk and shelves. There is a whole badly curated set of equipment in the bathroom and a few more dignified products in the living areas. Each device has its own personality (Janlert and Stolterman 1997), in terms of not just appearance, but also expectations and demands. The expensive blender on the kitchen work area looks at me in its ugly way, judging how little use it gets. The stereo in the lounge seems to conceal its disdain for the laptop that does most of my music-ing these days. But there are also less noisy things. There are chairs and cabinets and doors and rugs, each reliably performing important tasks in my house in much more direct ways than devices, though each with no less character. I made none of these things; I have no idea who did make them; for many I cannot even remember where they came from. But on these occasions, prompted by an eerily human sigh emanating from my dog, I suddenly feel surrounded in my most private spaces by all these alien things, hanging around me, more or less calling attention to the few actions that give them their only occasionally well-executed reason to exist.

To some extent, to be Western is nothing more than playing this convoluted trick on ourselves that is only noticeable as a result of something like an estranging dog-effect. We global consumers live charmed lives surrounded by these spirits that do things for us. Yet we insist that all these products and environments are just neutrally material, denying the spells each weaves to keep our lives comfortable and convenient. Why deny these animisms? Why take pleasure in what they deliver without acknowledging how they do so?

Magic happens

People who believe they are advancing humanity through their design innovations are fond of Arthur C. Clarke's third law: 'Any sufficiently advanced technology is indistinguishable from magic' (1973: 38).

This statement is a deceptive trick. It seems to insist that products of design are in fact distinguishable from magic, but that, if of a sufficiently advanced design, they will look and feel magical. The 'user experience' of these devices will be that they perform 'services' in ways that cannot be readily explained, and so they will delight their users with their apparently magical animistic operation.

But the products of design do not *seem* magical; they *are*. If something well designed is indistinguishable from magic, that is because it *does* have magical powers. And the magic that such designs accomplish is not reserved for that fetishized subset of products we worship as 'technology'. Forks and kettles, chairs and wardrobes, bicycles and kites, doors and windows, books and street signs, as well as laptops and jumbo-jets – all are magical, by design. Or so I believe, and so I want you to believe by the end of this chapter. (And belief is actually what is at issue here.)

It is probably part of the deception that Clarke claims to have come up with his third law, which is certainly his most famous, just so that he could have three.[1] The previous two concern the line between what is possible and impossible. The first claims that predictions, by scientists, are probably right if they are about what is possible but probably wrong about the impossible. In other words, there is more that is possible than scientists know and are prepared to believe – because predictions are by definition beliefs (or hopes) not knowledge. The second law explains why you can only discover what is impossible by believing it is possible and so trying to build it – in other words, the limits of the possible are stretchable, by technologists. In this context, the third law appears to qualify the first two by indicating that the technologist only seems to accomplish the impossible but in fact does so by shifting our sense of what is possible.

Clarke is of course a science fiction writer, formulating these laws when essaying about 'Hazards of Prophecy: The Failure of Imagination'. The source of these 'laws' is therefore a strange in-mixing of fact and fiction, science and imagination, prediction and technological advances. It is part of the trick of their argument therefore to hide the possibility that seemingly impossible things like magic might actually happen. The affect of magic is appropriated by these laws but precisely in order to reinstate the fictional privilege of technoscience.

Contrary to this privileging, I will insist instead that magic is possible, and real, that it does happen, by design.

Decolonizing the magic of design

I will argue this seemingly dangerous idea, that design is magic, for three related reasons. The first is merely pragmatic: I will run this argument to demonstrate how much of the way we talk about design, about designs and designing, proceeds by way of magic or at least magical thinking.

If the first reason is descriptive, the second reason is more prescriptive. Clarke's talk of laws concerning what is and is not possible clashes with Herbert Simon's arguments in *Sciences of the Artificial* (1996). As Clive Dilnot notes, to live in the historical epoch of the Anthropocenic artificial, where built environments are ubiquitous and 'nature' is reduced to managed pockets, means to be where, or when 'there is no absolute "what-is", which means that there is no law … Consider a half-dozen chairs … in their configuration they obey no law. Plato was thus wrong in this instance. No ideal chair exists. In artifice there are only chairs. This reflects the general truth that the artificial does not know law but only instances and possibility' (Dilnot 2014: 191–192).

Dilnot argues that this condition is precisely one that makes ethics central to what design is:

[the artificial] gives content, demand, to Simons' 'preferred situations' … [it] delineates the radical responsibilities that the inescapably anthropomorphic subject must take on board as the price paid for centrality. The onset of the artificial as world is the condition where this responsibility can no longer be so easily sloughed off. (Dilnot 2014: 196)

Precisely because the era of design is one of seeming limitlessness, in which everything and so anything can be designed, designers must ethically self-impose constraints. Bruno Latour (2008) calls this the condition of a 'cautious Prometheus' who must 'love their monsters'. In other words, if design is actually magical, with

Promethean powers to demiurgically transform the entire planet into piles of the artificial, there are no laws to fall back on to excuse our decisions. Magicians must temper their own powers. Bruce Mau's challenge – 'now that we can do anything, what will we do?' (Mau 2004) – acquires full ethical force only when we fully acknowledge that design can magically do anything.

The final reason to make this argument, on design's magical nature, is political. Magic is pejorative because, we moderns are supposed to think, it is impossible. Magic is a phenomenon only in primitive world views. Magic was the enslaved error that we, in the developed West, matured out of via the Enlightenment; it is the mistake that unenlightened, underdeveloped peoples around the world continue to make. Magic is the very definition of being unscientific, or more accurately, pre-scientific; to believe in the possibility of magic is, according to science, to suffer the psychological pathology of 'magical thinking'. By freeing themselves from false beliefs in things like magic, Europeans differentiate themselves from all those Others who have not yet designed their way to civilization.

This is, of course, offensively and oppressively colonialist. Usefully, Clarke (and Simon, Dilnot, Latour, etc.), by relating the discourses of design to those of Promethean sorcery, have made clear how central design (technology, the artificial) is to this colonialism. To decolonize design involves not only opening the practice and discourse of design up to others outside the North Atlantic, but also deconstructing the existing hegemonic account of design. If magic can be found to be taking place in and as design, then design can no longer be a factor differentiating colonizers and the colonized. Or to put it more starkly, if design is magical, then what was derided in Others as instances of magic are actually more like forms of design.

Magic tricks

The following definitions will make it clear what is at stake in this argument. First, I want to clearly distinguish between *magic* and *trickery*. In the part and period of the world that thinks of itself as post-magic, the word 'magic' usually refers to an entertaining deception: a 'magic act' is a performance, a pretence, not actually an act of magic. To preserve the latter, I think that the former should be called a 'trick'. An audience is 'tricked', that is, manipulated, usually through distraction, by a magician's 'trick' or technical skill.

A theatrical magician is like a comic who announces that they are about to tell you a joke: listen to me carefully, says the joker, see if you can follow this story or answer this question or remember this everyday action; no matter how hard you concentrate, I bet I can still manage to surprise you with some unexpected conclusion. Laughter seems to be the spasm our body has when we realize that we were indeed again tricked by the comic. Stage magicians of this same 'now watch me carefully' kind can spark wonder, precisely in the form of the question 'how did you (really) do that?' There is always the presumption that a positivist explanation, based on material causality, is possible for what seemingly a magical act has taken place; all that has happened is that the 'magician', who is in fact just a 'trickster', has mastered some complex mechanics so skilfully that they almost disappear beneath what is accomplished. One way that such a trickster might 'cheat', for instance, is by having some sort of device that performs some of the mechanics – string or elastic, a hidden chamber, a duplicate object, etc. Without knowing that those mechanisms are there or understanding how they operate, the audience cannot explain what just occurred. This is the kind of trick Clarke was probably talking about: miniaturization, digitalization and now 'algorithmicization' allow mechanisms to be buried inside products, accomplishing things we find miraculous only because they are, as experienced, inexplicable.

Certainly design is a highly skilled profession in arts that are not widely taught: letter-form, three-colour, website-coding, video-editing, joinery and fastening, moulding and folding, etc. And certainly design makes use of a wide range of other, black-boxed technologies that generate complex final effects – photography, vacuum-forming, lighting and HVAC, CSS and PHP, etc. Designers also make liberal use of practices like distraction – perceptual gestalts, intuitive behavioural nudges, etc. All these suggest that designers can fake magical effects because they have mastered a wide range of technical tricks to dazzling effect.

John Kolko uses precisely this argument to motivate his *Exposing the Magic of Design* (2011). Kolko's focus is not the material side of design crafting, but rather the conceptual side of design that makes creative leaps between contextual research and proposition:

> Despite the acknowledged importance of this phase of the design process, synthesis appears magical when encountered in professional practice. This sense of magic is both good and bad. The idea of designers as magicians is an intriguing metaphor, because their work is mysterious and the output can be phenomenal and tremendously emotional ... Because the act of synthesis – the revelation of clarity – is frequently performed privately ('in the head' or 'on scratch paper'), the outcome is all that is observed, and only after the designer has explicitly begun the form-making process. Unlike other aspects of the design process (such as drawing, which even a naïve or detached audience can observe and generally grasp), synthesis is often a more insular activity, one that is harder to understand or even impossible to see. (Kolko 2011: xi)

The bad side of seeing synthesis from research to design as magical, according to Kolko, is that designers do not perform it rigorously, and clients come to doubt the validity of what is proposed because they cannot see where and how the abduction has happened. Kolko's book therefore seeks to demystify synthesis, laying out the techniques and tools that designers are using to accomplish the trick of synthesis. However, as the following will suggest, I am not sure that Kolko's talk of models, patterns and abduction does not just bury the magic of design under a set of tricky concepts and distracting systems maps and diagrams.

I am therefore pushing beyond this account of design as trickery. This means defining magic as a real power, a capacity to make actual changes to things rather than just changes to how they are perceived, an ability to draw on mysterious forces in order to craft outcomes that exceed 'the sum of the parts'. Design, I will argue, involves this 'more than the tricking version' of magic. This means that design has an efficacy that defies technical explanation, no matter how complex or mechanically assisted. It has a power to cause change beyond direct mechanistic contact; it assembles materials into forms that can act at a distance on groups of people in lasting ways that those people find difficult to resist and that consequently become predictive of their future habits.

This definition of magic should at this point seem insufficient. The argument of this chapter requires the development of a thicker description of just what magic means in the context of design. If I manage to get you to believe that design is a form of magic, it will be because you have richer understanding of the meaning of that word in the context of design.

This is not to say that trickery is not part of design's magic. In fact, to understand the magic of design, we must first understand that the most blatant trick that designers perform is to conceal the true magic of designing – in a way that parallels the logic of Clarke's third law.

Magically disappearing

Design conceals itself. Designed things are everywhere but are rarely acknowledged as having been designed, and when they are, almost nobody can give an account of what their origin entails. Perhaps this is like the orientalist cliché of the best doctor being the one no one has heard of because of pervasive health. Real magic does not announce itself like a comic telling a joke; it simply accomplishes quietly.

Let me try to underscore this from another perspective. We often hear that nature 'works' because it is the result of millennia of evolutionary experimentation and testing. By contrast, when humans make things, especially when they make new things, things with new forms and functions that have never previously existed, there is no such long timeframe system to ensure reliability. 'Naturally', many designed artefacts fail: they do not do what they claim to be able to, or they are difficult to use, or they break. Nevertheless, if you compared the failure rate of products to the planet-devastating number of products in use each and every day, the fact that so few disrupt the practice of everyday life seems quite magical. How does design materialize things that never previously existed that can so quickly be taken for granted as doing repeatedly what they were designed to do?

When a process is everywhere, to some extent being conducted unknowingly, or unartfully, by millions of people – such as the crafting of this or that object, this or that service – we are at risk of thinking that it is nothing or at least nothing special. When the designing behind something does manifest – either because something breaks down or because it works with delightful noticeability – that designing often appears obvious: of course you would make it fit the hand, and not be too heavy, with a button right there so that you can press it while using the device, etc.

Much of what passes for 'design thinking' seems to expose designers as unclothed emperors. The blackbox of designing apparently involves little more than superficial observation, empathetic play, randomized creativity and some hasty categorization. However, given the scale and power of design's accomplishments, designing is clearly more than, if not quite distinct from, 'design thinking' – perhaps so much so that the latter is the 'sleight of hand' obscuring what is actually being done by design proper.

Conversely, design is very conspicuous when it results in profit. Its outcomes not only have high cultural capital, but can be revered as iconic classics or history-making breakthrough innovations. In these explicitly visible manifestations of design, it has a transcendent power, to transform matter into value, and is indeed recognized as magical, in the quite literal sense of creating fetish objects. However, these 'iconic' consumerist fetishizations seem to be excessively salient distractions from design's real powers, which manifest more mundanely, and more in terms of usefulness than symbolic value. To explain, I need to explain something about the history of fetishes.

Fetishizing fetishism

As with magic, the history of the notion of the fetish is the history of colonialist differentiation. Over a series of essays (1985, 1987, 1988), Pietz has analysed many of the original encounters between European traders and a variety of African communities out of which the concept of the fetish emerged. Along with others who have commented on the origin of this term (Graeber 2005; Latour 2010), Pietz notes two important historical factors that contextualized these encounters, at least from the European side. These could be characterized as the two different sides of materialism. On the Enlightenment side, there were efforts to narrate the West as developing from myth and magic through religion to rationality. On the capitalist side, there were efforts to disembed systems of exchange from messy social relations.

To the Europeans, certain practices of African peoples were at first bewildering, then challenging and so finally belittled. The communities that traders encountered valued things in ways that were initially incomprehensible. The resources the traders wanted were often not valued by the locals, or if they were, they were valued for the wrong reasons – i.e. not for their use but rather for their symbolic power, or vice versa, valuations that consequently seemed to the Europeans to be capriciously applied. A trader could, as the fable goes, secure gold in exchange for beads, which was good from an emerging capitalist point of view. However, to do so traders were often required to participate in some kind of ritual that sacralised the beads, which was awkward from an Enlightenment point of view:

> To effect economic transactions, merchants had to accept the preliminary swearing of oaths upon Fetissos – a perversion of the natural process of economic negotiation and legal contact. Desiring a clean economic interaction, seventeenth century merchants unhappily found themselves entering into social relations and quasi-religious ceremonies that should have been irrelevant to the conduct of trade were it not for the perverse superstitions of their trade partners. The general theory of fetishism that emerged in the eighteenth century was determined by the problematic specific to this novel historical situation. (Pietz 1987: 45)

The original Portuguese term, *feitiço*, means made, both in the sense of physically constructed, and so artificial, and socially made-up, so fictitious and even fraudulent (Pietz 1987: 25). The traders also chose the term to differentiate fetishes from idols, since the former in most cases made no pretence of being a likeness of some deity (Pietz

1985: 7–8). The label therefore claimed that African peoples seemed to be able to find religious significance in things that they themselves had made or perhaps even found. On the one hand, this seemed wilful, as if belief was something you could choose to do rather than something you suffered or felt externally compelled to do. On the other hand, this seemed nonsensical, because if you chose the fetish, or worse, if you made it, how could you then insist that that thing was filled with some god's power over you?

What was unnerving about fetish-based peoples for the Europeans is that it exposed the Europeans' own combination of materiality (why wear and carry these sorts of things?) and religiosity (which are appropriately church-sanctioned non-idolatrous artefacts of and for worship?) as possible social constructions: 'We see one group of people covered with amulets scoffing at another group of people covered with amulets. We do not have iconophiles on one side and iconoclasts on the other, but iconodules on both sides (one side being of selective iconoclasts)' (Latour 2010: 5). The ambivalence of this situation is what seems to motivate an almost violent attempt to differentiate the Other's beliefs from those of Europeans, as Latour paraphrases:

> How can you so sanctimoniously admit that you have to make, fabricate, seat, situate, construct these divinities that grip you and yet remain out of reach? Are you so unaware of the difference between making what comes from yourselves and receiving what comes from elsewhere? … If you admit that you fabricate your own fetishes yourselves, you must then acknowledge that you pull their strings as a puppeteer would. The whole thing is engineered to impress others through disguising itself … Or else, if you let your own marionettes take you by surprise and you start believing in the airs they (or rather you) put on, this proves such a degree of naiveté that you are condemned to join the eternally credulous and hoodwinked masses who make up – again according to lucid observers – the gullible rabble of the history of religions. (Latour 2010: 6)

The force behind this reaction to what potentially undermined emerging modern life perhaps explains why a term used to account for Euro-African relations in the seventeenth century goes on to become a central term in ideology critique. The two most famous versions are Karl Marx's and Sigmund Freud's. For Marx, fetishism is a phenomenon that follows alienation. A labourer works to create a product that is removed from her or him by the capitalist who owns the means of production and sold on the market as a commodity with no reference to its human origin. After being alienated from their producers, those products then act like fetishes, taking on a life of their own, commanding prices, networks of distribution, systems of use, etc. – and, if then valuable, even seeming to have compelled the worker to produce them in the first place.

The process is similar for Freud: during psychological development, someone finds (i.e. appears to choose) sexual pleasure in something apart from heteronormative acts of reproduction. Later, that thing can begin to command the behaviour of that individual. A combination of Marx and Freud's use of the term refers to consumers deriving perverse pleasure from certain products, even to the point of suffering compunctions to buy products of which they have no need.

In either modern case, the notion of fetish is used pejoratively just as when traders and the European philosophers used the term to deride non-Europeans: the worker is being duped and needs to re-learn that he or she is the true source of value creation; the pervert is fixated and so needs therapy to return to normal modes of pleasure. The term fetish is therefore these days a metonym for being suspicious of people's everyday beliefs. It is almost as if we these days fetishize the word fetish, believing its utterance to have a critical power beyond the analytic work it was coined to do.

This is the trick that fetishism performs, concealing beneath its conspicuous critique a real magic that it itself is still subject to. Latour makes this point insistently: because fetishism was a defensive European reaction to the realization that the Europeans themselves were as fetishistic as the non-Europeans with whom they were establishing trade relations, the critique itself draws on and reproduces the fetishism that it sought to divide itself from: 'since according to the anti-fetishists the effect of the fetish is efficacious only if its creator is unaware of its origin, it must be capable of dissimulating its own manufacturer' because otherwise the fetishist is at once a 'cynical manipulator' deliberately making fetishes and at the same time 'an ingenuous dupe' (Latour 2010: 9). The critique of fetishism is a double accusation: that the fetishist is just making stuff up, inventing, for example, the power of things to compel people to act and that the fetishist is subjecting himself or herself to the power of things, feeling compelled by things that he or she should be able to choose to resist. For the accusation of fetishism to hold in both cases, it must be that in certain circumstances, things can, despite having been designed by humans, in turn design those humans in ways more compelling than their artifice suggests.

The critique of fetishism seems to assume the existence of the very magic transformations that it aims to be distinct from; it not only assumes the existence of this magic but appears to be deploying this magic itself. The critique believes that it is enough to announce the existence of a fetishism to break the spell. It is as if fetishism is itself the magic word that once and for all rids the world of magic, just as when a hypnotist says, 'when I count to three, you will awaken (I suggest) and then be free from suggestion'. If the critique works, it is only because its pronouncement has the very power it wishes to dispel. But as we know, from the persistence of consumerist capitalism and/or scientistic positivism alongside various religious beliefs, the critique has not worked (Latour 2004); fetishized products continued to circulate with magical value around our globalized world.

Making up things

Latour explores this magical confusion around fetishism with respect to how we come to know things. Science conducts rigorously controlled experiments in which things are made to happen. At the conclusion of an experiment, the scientists draw conclusions about what happens in the world outside of the experiment. In this translation, the scientists insist that what they made happen was in fact just what ordinarily happens anyway, that the things being experimented on were in fact doing things (to) themselves as they would outside of the laboratory. We can rest assured that what the scientists have observed are facts of the world and not artefacts that they made up. Designers, despite the rise of design research as both a phase of designing and an academic discipline, are less interested in making something be known than in knowing how to make something come to be. Even so, the process of designing bears a remarkable similarity to the scientific process, though in reverse – which means that it involves translations that are just as magical.

Consider a conventional version of problem-solving product design. First, designers feel other people's problems. This in itself should not seem magical. However, in this era of bigoted politics and sociopathic corporate leadership, design thinking does manage to sell itself as having tricks for being empathetic, as if that were not an inherent aspect of sociality. What is magical about designers is that they do not just feel other people's pain, but feel it in ways that compel them, or at least inspire them, to do something about it. Further, what they are motivated to do is not offer some direct response – comforting the person who is suffering then and there – but instead invest in innovating some other way of dealing with the situation. They feel for the other, and so seek to help, but do not do so directly.

It is worth pausing to think on how strange this is: when designing, there is an emotional relation strong enough to cause action, but that action goes the long way round as it were, through a process of design ideation and manufacture. This detour, which Latour calls technological mediation (1994), is where the magic happens.

I have written often (following Clive Dilnot's (1993) lead) about Elaine Scarry's poetic account of artefact creation (Tonkinwise 2006, 2017). Scarry's rich descriptions describe the way in which design is not only initiated by empathy, but is empathetic throughout. The very mechanics of detailing the form of the proposed product-based response to someone's 'pain point' are best characterized as forms of 'applied empathy'. Scarry describes, for instance, how someone feeling another's weight-bearing pain performs a kind of dance as they empathize, perhaps cradling the one suffering, and thereby gesturing in a way that begins to describe the form of chair that could be materialized to permanently offer weight relief (Scarry 1985: 290). The designer's magic involves being able to translate empathy into material form, to convert feelings into things – which means being able to magically speak with things.

Designing involves being able to empathize not only with people and the problems they are suffering, but also with materials, components and products. Designers project themselves into the 'mind' of what they are designing. They imagine the forces involved in someone holding and interacting with some thing; they think through how those mute materials might signal themselves to their users, instructing them as to the best ways to interact. Donald Schön (1992) calls this a 'conversation with materials', such as when Louis Kahn asks 'what does the brick want?'. The outcome, Scarry insists, is that designed artefacts come alive to the needs and habits of humans. Designers put 'smarts' into things so that they are attentive to their users, prompting users as to how they can best be used. The chair magically knows my anatomy but also my need for not just comfort but also support. The phone knows (or should, if well designed) that I am driving, and so puts a 'spell of concealment' on my notifications so as to ensure my safety and that of others around me. My house now seems haunted by more or less friendly pet-devices, each promising help whenever I might need it.

All of this sounds somewhat plausible but mostly ridiculous. It provides access to distinctive aspects of designing, but probably still seems like an exaggeration or at best an inadequate account that should be easily replaceable with 'this is actually how I do it'. This is exactly the reaction we moderns are supposed to have when we hear something that seems magical – we want to take these almost shamanistic acts and codify them into design methods structured by legible design tools. But I want to try to show how converting empathy into interactive things responsive to people's problems is indeed magical. It is not inexplicable; it is just that explanations will always still contain some conversionary power, some magical translation that brings inanimate things to life.

Apprentice to a studio mage

How do designers learn the magical power of animating things to interact well with people and their needs? A traditional Bauhaus foundation has design students experimenting extensively with key materials. The materials, and later products, are experimented on, or rather, since the process is more improvisatory than controlled, the materials and products are performed, in order to reveal their possibilities and impossibilities, to recall Clarke's framework. The process is not a materials science study of qualities, but rather a process of learning to let the materials speak.

This is why the education involves shared crit (though for a critical account of studio critique conventions in art education, see Elkins 2001). These art experiments with materials are collectively interrogated by studio leaders and fellow students by way of a strange array of terms that try to capture what material assemblages are trying to say about themselves: that design feels 'blocky' or 'blobby', 'lop-sided' or 'resolved', 'dynamic' or 'in tension', etc. In the process of the education, designers develop a shared vocabulary for coaxing materials into new forms (Fleming 1998). These are magical terms, in that they are shorthand for how to make materials do what they may not at first seem capable of doing.

Another aspect to this education in the magic of material design involves something like Philippe Lacoue-Labarthe's account of mimesis (1998). Lacoue-Labarthe is a Derridean philosopher who noted that there are two kinds of imitation. I can imitate something by developing a likeness of it. But I can also imitate something not by imitating it directly, but instead by 'reverse engineering' what it appears to be imitating, what it is modelled on, and then producing another variation of that model. I imitate what that thing appears to be imitating. This can be a generative activity, freed from (representational) imitation, or the figurative. But that generativity risks being open ended: anything could be said to be a variant of this or that model that appears to lie behind whatever is being imitated. How to contain these variations, how to limit what is and is not an appropriate imitation? Lacoue-Labarthe, following Derrida (1981), calls this effort to control the generative side to mimesis, mimetology: a magical version of differences that remain contained within some kind of model sameness.

This appears to be precisely the magical knowledge that designers learn through their studio education and constant exposure to precedents throughout their professional career. As design students play with how materials perform, they are not merely learning what a material can do, but what else it can be made to do without losing its identity. Enigmatic statements are made in the studio about whether some material innovation remains within the modernist edict to be 'true to materials', even when those materials are magical artifices without inherent form, such as concrete or plastic. This mimetology extends beyond crafting materials to problem-solving in general, and the pursuit of parsimonious or elegant solutions, interactions that flow, services that delight, etc. In each case, an aesthetics of coherence becomes the magical aspect that design adds to what are otherwise an infinite set of logistical options.

All of design education involves this kind of magical mimetology. As Schön noted when first encountering design education (1985), designers mysteriously learn to design by designing. Design is mostly taught not as a set of self-conscious principles extracted from practice, but instead by undertaking studio projects in the presence of expert studio leaders. That practitioner never explicates a model of what the designer is to do, but rather provides examples that students must reverse engineer in order to get at what those examples are examples of. Schön, in his studies of the design process (1992), once distilled these mimetologies into an odd experiment in which students were asked to develop a rule set in their head and then create three manifestations of that rule set out of lego. Another student would then try to determine the rule behind the three design cases and so build a fourth iteration. The originator of the first three would then try to judge whether that fourth was a successful implementation of the rule they were implicitly using. The experiment was mostly unsuccessful, but it points to Schön discerning what he considered to be a key aspect to how designers learned to perform precedent-informed pattern recognition. Or rather, the experiment was unsuccessful because it tried to rationalize what is in fact a fairly magical process of case-based reasoning by expert designers.

Delimiting use

Design then is quite literally a constructivism, magically causing valuable things to come to be. It assembles materials and components into things. Part of the designer's job is to make an array of discrete parts look like they all comprise one coherent thing. Some of this magic is engineering: bonding or fastening this and that material together, and then making components causally interact such that when one part does one thing a subsequent part does something else. But in addition to this systematization of components, the designer's job is to give them all an aesthetic sense of belonging together.

This assembling magic is apparent in its absence, when you open a package and wonder where a loose part is supposed to go, or when a product's casing is clearly a distinctive wrapping around other components with very different qualities. When the magic works, things appear as finished, complete, with a reliable object permanence. When after a while, a designed artefact stops working, when a part halts the chain of causality within the product, or literally becomes disconnected, there is a sense that the magic holding the thing together has become undone.

Designers do not just generate any old thing where previously there was nothing: they design valuable things, that is to say, useful new artefacts. Use troubles philosophers (see for instance Houkes and Vermaas 2010) because on the one hand it appears to be a quality merely imposed on things. Humans are adept at making use of any old thing lying nearby when a need arises – i.e. they can spontaneously make things useful for a task even if those things had not been designed for that purpose. Uta Brandes and colleagues collected instances of these tricks under the title 'non-intentional design' (Brandes and Erlhoff 2006, but see also Brandes et al. 2009). On the other hand, usefulness for a task does also lie in particular facets of certain things; having a particular form lends those things, as opposed to others, to being more useful for that particular job. It is of course the job of designers to enhance this way in which things can afford usefulness for specific purposes. Designers craft the form of things so that they are not only able to be used to perform actions, but so that they invite, persuade and even cajole people into performing those actions. Designers make things that make people use them in particular ways.

All of this should sound very familiar. The logic – that any thing at hand can be made to be useful for accomplishing a task, but that certain classes of people are skilled at making things more useful, so much so that things begin to have their own agency with respect to those tasks – is precisely that which required European religious traders to coin the term fetishism. This isomorphism, between usefulness and fetish is precisely because design, the design of things to make them useful, is magical. Because pretty much any more or less appropriate thing can be made to perform a needed function, just what is it that makes one thing seem more useful than another? What is the trick designers perform that makes designed artefacts seem more valuable to specific use contexts than other un-designed artefacts? How do they delimit usefulness given the generative creativity behind humans making use of things?

User-centred design makes clear that the constructivism by which things come to appear useful is necessarily a *social* constructivism. Usability can only be identified experimentally rather than in principle. Designers play the role of users as they test prototypes. Then 'outsiders' are brought in, delegates who must represent the wider population. They are encouraged to play with the designed artefacts to test their usability, just as designers play with materials to discover their inclinations and resistances. As Steve Woolgar (1990) has articulated, what actually are being tested in these 'user trials' are not just the artefacts but also people: Will they comply with the guidance they are being given by the animated design artefact? Will they accede to the power of the thing, playing along with how it is saying it wants to be used? Will people fall under the spell of the design and transform themselves into 'users'? This mutual configuring of both the artefact and the people using the artefact happens as the magical moment in which belief in a design is realized.

Distributed (non-)beliefs

While design is a material craft, its magic then is that it is, in fact, a social practice. It is learned in the sociality of the studio via the development of shared languages for speaking with materials. It is a series of experiments through which social learning can take place that allow things to be animated by usefulness. The social constructivism of design is the magic of establishing a convention, a sociomaterial convention that comes to accept that this form of a product can accomplish a needed activity. Components are convened into objects that magically become conveniences, spirited devices that live with each of us in our houses offering, and sometimes even imposing, their help.

In this sense, magic happens when a set of people come to accept that it is happening. Magic, or specifically the magic that is designing, is coming to take for granted that a certain assemblage works. Designs become magical when we accede to relying on their doing what they declare they are designed to do.

There are some nuances here that are important to capture. Anthropologists of cultures that accept what Westerners would characterize as magic often argue that magic should not be framed as a belief. Magical occurrences are things that happen for those involved, not beliefs about how things happen. They are in the nature of how the world is experienced rather than value systems framing an account of the world. In the practice turn within religious studies (Vasquez 2011; Meyer et al. 2014), this phenomenon is described as lived religion, to distinguish it from the world view version of religion. What is at issue here is again very precisely issues to do with coloniality. The secularized West tolerates religion only as a set of beliefs about how to behave in the world, not as something ontological. As a result, Western scholars want to conceive of magic as a framework that people are choosing to believe, precisely so that it can be displaced by non-magical versions of scientific knowledge. As Latour (2010) and in a different context Michael Polanyi (2015 [1958]) point out, scientific ways of knowing are nevertheless themselves modes of belief, ones that choose to deny the magic performed by scientific instruments, experiments and discourse.

A more symmetrical account allows acknowledgement of the Western magic of design. Let me quote at length Ariel Glucklich's introduction to his study *The End of Magic* (1997):

> Magic is rarely a simple matter of belief. Belief implies a set of intellectual assumptions and conclusions that is bridged by uncertain means. This process plays no key role in healing, cursing or other forms of magic I have observed. Few magicians and clients in Banaras ever ask themselves why their magic works or what it means. It works as a matter of nature. A man who inserts a key in the ignition of his Honda and turns it does not believe that the engine will start as a result of some causal chain. The act of turning the key and the firing of the engine are one event. Belief rarely figures in this type of action. But this is just a metaphor, and it should not convey the message that magic is based on ignorance of mechanics, or on taking mechanics for granted. The point is different. Claude Levi-Strauss once noted that magic has a kind of necessity that resembles natural forces. Magical acts are performed because they are connected to certain natural phenomena, and this connection is sensual and intuitive rather than intellectual. The magical act and the natural fact 'register' in the awareness of the practitioner by means of the senses. Act and result are perceived as parts of one pattern …
>
> Magical actions are no longer interpreted as symbols. They constitute a direct, ritual way of restoring the experience of relatedness in cases where that experience has been broken … Magic does not seek to 'fix' an objective world; it addresses an

awareness of a bond that is neither subjective nor objective. It straddles the line between the perceiver and the world because the two are part of a unified system, a mental ecology. I call this bond 'empathy.' (Glucklich 1997: 11–12)

To convey the outcome of his study of magic, Glucklich characterizes it as identical to the experience of interacting with a car. And his explanation of this leads him directly to what designers would recognize, having appropriated the notion from James Gibson's ecological perception theory, as affordances. An affordance is not a symbol, nor even a belief in unknown causal mechanisms; it is an aesthetic surety of efficacy – 'press here and hear that action-at-distance will result'.

Limiting power

What is the (magical?) result if I have successfully convinced you that design should be understood as magical? At the least it should mean that design education embraces or better enhances its process of socializing students into the arts of making materials speak and animating products to the needs of users. Rather than methodologizing design, design educators should advance their distinctive languages for discerning case-based patterns of human–thing interactions. This is partly the argument that design researchers working with human–computer interaction have tried to make in relation to *Research through Practice* (Koskinen et al. 2011); the 'black arts' of design (Wolf et al. 2006) should be allowed to be ludic and speculative (Gaver 2012).

More significantly, the design profession should acknowledge its constructivist powers. While prominent designers tend towards arrogance, design as a profession casts itself as subservient to the inertia of markets, with respect to both industry sponsors and consumer adoption. Seeing design as magic should restore the power of design to constitute any kind of future. Given the right conditions – I will come back to this – design is a sovereign act of creating, one that can magically make the seemingly impossible not just possible but materialized as what people will take for granted. This is not a technoutopianism. Precisely because design's magic lies in everyday sociomaterial practices, it concerns the creation of new ways of living, not current ways of living merely amplified by exponentialized versions of current technologies. To put it more politically, the magical powers of design mean that there is no one-way linearity to efficiency and convenience. Design's magic means that it is possible for design to restore ways of doing things that feel burdensome given today's economic expectations. Usability is not just about existing tools and techniques becoming easier and easier; it is rather the profoundly reconstructable nature of what we consider to be usable. Design as magic promises us that we could design lifestyles that centre on what appears at the moment to require effortful sacrifice – more sustainable ways of living for instance, more diverse forms of societal governance, more equitable systems of resourcing.

This is why asserting that design is magical is decolonial. Ways of life that the West colonized with its anti-magical scientism should now be seen not as capriciously mired in false beliefs, but as in fact having designed their own ways of being in the world. As a result, those ways of organizing society are not inefficient, but rather constituted around their own versions of the useful and usable. This is why, should the West decide for ethical reasons, to try to recover some of those ways of living, it would not be a de-ratcheting of Western senses of comfort and convenience, but just their redesign. Magically, slower, more local and inclusive ways of living would, by design, manifest as habitual if not enjoyable.

This way of understanding design's magical powers already points to the fact that those powers are not limitless. They cannot be conscripted into the hubristic ambitions of proactionary technosolutionists. There are mimetological constraints, what Marxists call parametric determinisms: 'Humans are history makers, just never in conditions of their own choosing.' In the terms of this chapter, the limits on design's constructivism are social. Design is always co-design, or more accurately, the transition management of sociotechnical co-evolution (Irwin et al. 2015).

What design professionals should learn from design-as-magic is that magic is social. Just as design education is social, so too the construction of futures involves the hard work of enlisting allies into extensive spells. Useful and usable things are collective enterprises. I will conclude by trying to underline this in reference to the politics of personas.

Socializing magic

One of the most powerful interventions in the last couple of decades into the modern expert practice of designing, specifically interaction designing, has been the promotion of the use of personas (Cooper 2004). This technique was developed in order to improve the use value of digital devices.

I should pause to underline that digital devices are particularly magical because their mechanisms are electronic, that is, not readily discernible. One of the major problems for early digital devices was that there were no existing patterns of use, no 'natural' affordances. Designers (or at that point, software engineers) were in a realm in which anything was possible; that is to say, there was no model to imitate.

Alan Cooper lighted upon a very mimetologically magical process for helping determine how to digital devices could be made useful and usable. This magic was fundamentally social: research people, observe and talk with those who may be made into users of these things. Such research however tended to be a never-ending task exposing ever-increasing differences. Cooper proposed synthesizing that research into one or two characters. To be done well, the process should involve determining something like a model that might lie behind a diverse segment of the people researched, and then fictioning a singular persona based on that model.

Importantly, there is another mimetological aspect to personas. What is captured in that individual character is a range of their likes; a persona is described in terms of their taste regime (Bourdieu 1984 [1979]) – food, films, leisure and life goals. The magic of persona is the capacity of a designer to translate between their cultural practices and their technical behaviours. Just as designers translate materials into forms, empathy into products, so too they translate tastes into practices (Tonkinwise 2011). Designing always involves a series of these conversions between the social and the material; personas merely focus that conversion very explicitly.

I am calling attention to personas because they succinctly foreground the opportunities and dangers inherent to the magical powers of design. Designers can make futures only ever socially, in which case their power is completely dependent on who is delegated into that sociality. When designers make futures, they do so with reference to only a particular mimetological model of a certain social group. Personas are always caricatures (Turner and Turner 2011). They are effective because caricatures are powerful ways in which our societies constrain what is a permissible variant of that model. The magic of design can therefore make a population uniform, norming particular ways of being human by materializing futures that cater to only certain kinds of people. In Latour's (1990) insightful phrase, the magic of design involves making society durable – which means determining which class of people will be serviced by things. Designers must be always highly aware of this selective power to their magic, and so always work concertedly at designing with and towards diversity.

Do not let design trick you about its magical powers

Design has successfully tricked the modernized global consumer class into believing that it is not magical, despite being the demiurge behind every manifestation of those modernized built environments. We must now acknowledge that design is a form of magic, so that the worlds that designed artefacts colonize might not be eradicated by mere variants of the same capitalist modes of society. We must see that design could magically undo consumerist uniformity, and make more diverse ways of living more valuable. Do not be tricked into thinking that current modes of designed existence are irrevocably efficient and that technical devices are the only form of effectivity. Designers have magically transformed what we experience as comfortable and convenient, and could do so again. They can reanimate ways of living and working other than those under the hegemonic spell of neo-liberalism.

Note

1   Clarke added a footnote in his revised edition of *Profiles of the Future* to the sentence 'But the only way of discovering the limits of the possible is to venture a little past them into the impossible,' which reads: 'The French Edition of this book rather surprised me by calling this Clarke's Second Law. I accept the label, and have formulated a Third... As three laws were good enough for Newton, I have modestly decided to stop there' (Clarke 1973: 38). Clarke had eponymously titled what then is considered the First Law: 'When a distinguished but elderly scientist states that something is possible, he is almost certainly right. When he states that something is impossible, he is very probably wrong' (31).

Bibliography

Bourdieu, Pierre (1984 [1979]) *Distinction: A Social Critique of the Judgement of Taste*, Cambridge, MA: Harvard University Press.

Brandes, Uta and Erlhoff, Michael (2006) *Non Intentional Design*, Cologne: Daab.

Brandes, Uta, Stich, Sonja, and Wender, Miriam (2009) *Design by Use: The Everyday Metamorphosis of Things*, Basel: Birkhauser.

Clarke, Arthur C. (1973) *Profiles of the Future: An Inquiry into the Limits of the Possible*, New York: Harper & Row.

Cooper, Alan (2004) *The Inmates Are Running the Asylum: Why High-Tech Products Drive Us Crazy and How to Restore the Sanity*, Indianapolis, IN: Sams.

Derrida, Jacques (1981) 'Economimesis', *Diacritics*, 11, 2: 3–25.

Dilnot, Clive (1993) 'The Gift', *Design Issues*, 9, 2: 51–65.

Dilnot, Clive (2014) '"Reasons to Be Cheerful, 1, 2, 3 … " (or Why the Artificial May yet Save Us)', in Susan Yelavich and Barbara Adams (eds), *Design as Future-Making*, London: Bloomsbury.

Elkins, James (2001) *Why Art Cannot Be Taught: A Handbook for Art Students*, Chicago, IL: University of Illinois Press.

Fleming, David (1998) 'Design Talk: Constructing the Object in Studio Conversations', *Design Issues*, 14, 2: 41–62.

Gaver, William (2012) 'What Should We Expect from Research through Design?', *Proceedings of the SIGCHI Conference on Human Factors in Computing Systems* 937–946.

Glucklich, Ariel (1997) *The End of Magic*, Oxford: Oxford University Press.

Götz, Ignacio (2001) *Technology and the Spirit*, Westport, CT: Greenwood Publishing.

Graeber, David (2005) 'Fetishism as Social Creativity: Or, Fetishes Are Gods in the Process of Construction', *Anthropological Theory*, 5, 4: 407–438.

Houkes, Wybo and Vermaas, Pieter E. (2010) *Technical Functions: On the Use and Design of Artefacts*, Dordrecht: Springer.

Irwin, Terry and Kossoff, Gideon (2015) 'Transition Design Provocation', *Design Philosophy Papers*, 13, 1: 3–11.

Janlert, Lars-Erik and Stolterman, Erik (1997) 'The Character of Things', *Design Studies*, 2, 2: 297–314.

Kolko, Jon (2011) *Exposing the Magic of Design: A Practitioner's Guide to the Methods and Theory of Synthesis*, Oxford: Oxford University Press.

Koskinen, Ilpo, Zimmerman, John, Binder, Thomas, Redstrom, Johan, and Wensveen, Stephan (2011) *Design Research through Practice: From the Lab, Field, and Showroom*, Amsterdam: Elsevier.

Lacoue-Labarthe, Philippe (1998) *Typography: Mimesis, Philosophy, Politics*, Stanford, CA: Stanford University Press.

Latour, Bruno (1990) 'Technology Is Society Made Durable', *The Sociological Review*, 38, 1: 103–131.

Latour, Bruno (1994) 'On Technical Mediation', *Common Knowledge*, 3, 2: 29–64.

Latour, Bruno (2004) 'Why Has Critique Run out of Steam? From Matters of Fact to Matters of Concern', *Critical Inquiry*, 30, 2: 225–248.

Latour, Bruno (2008) 'A Cautious Prometheus? A Few Steps toward a Philosophy of Design (with Special Attention to Peter Sloterdijk)'. *Proceedings of the 2008 International Conference of the Design History Society*.

Latour, Bruno (2010) *On the Modern Cult of the Factish Gods*, Durham, NC: Duke University Press.

Mau, Bruce and The Institute without Borders (2004) *Massive Change*, London: Phaidon.

Meyer, Birgit, Morgan, David, Paine, Crispin, and Brent Plate, S. (2014) 'Material Religion's First Decade', *Material Religion*, 10, 1: 105–110.

Pietz, William (1985) 'The Problem of the Fetish, I', *Anthropology & Aesthetics*, 9, 1: 5–17.

Pietz, William (1987) 'The Problem of the Fetish, II: The Origin of the Fetish', *Anthropology & Aesthetics*, 13, 1: 23–45.

Pietz, William (1988) 'The Problem of the Fetish, IIIa: Bosman's Guinea and the Enlightenment Theory of Fetishism', *Anthropology & Aesthetics*, 16, 1: 105–124.

Polanyi, Michael (2015 [1958]) *Personal Knowledge: Towards a Post-Critical Philosophy*, Chicago, IL: University of Chicago Press.

Scarry, Elaine (1985) *The Body in Pain: The Making and Unmaking of the World*, Oxford: Oxford University Press.

Schön, Donald (1985) *The Design Studio*, London: RIBA Publication Ltd.

Schön, Donald (1992) 'Designing as Reflective Conversation with the Materials of a Design Situation', *Knowledge-Based Systems*, 5, 1: 3–14.

Simon, Herbert (1996) *The Sciences of the Artificial*, Cambridge, MA: MIT Press.

Tonkinwise, Cameron (2006) 'Thingly Cosmopolitanism: Caring for the Other by Design', *The Radical Designist*, 1, 1.

Tonkinwise, Cameron (2011) 'A Taste for Practices: Unrepressing Style in Design Thinking', *Design Studies*, 32, 6: 533–545.

Tonkinwise, Cameron (2017) 'The Practically Living Weight of Convenient Things', in Leslie Atzmon and Prasad Boradkar (eds), *Encountering Things: Design and Theories of Things*, London: Bloomsbury.

Turner, Phil and Turner, Susan (2011) 'Is Stereotyping Inevitable When Designing with Personas?', *Design Studies*, 32, 1: 30–44.

Vásquez, Manuel (2011) *More than Belief: A Materialist Theory of Religion*, Oxford: Oxford University Press.

Wolf, Tracee Vetting, Rode, Jennifer A., Sussman, Jeremy, and Kellogg, Wendy A. (2006) 'Dispelling Design as the Black Art of CHI'. *Proceedings of the SIGCHI Conference on Human Factors in Computing Systems*, 521–530.

Woolgar, Steve (1990) 'Configuring the User: The Case of Usability Trials', *The Sociological Review*, 38, 1: 58–99.

Part Two

Tricky Processes, Tricky Principles

6

Designer/Shapeshifter: A Decolonizing Redirection for Speculative and Critical Design

Pedro J. S. Vieira de Oliveira and Luiza Prado de O. Martins

> Pero es difícil *differentiating between* lo heredado, lo adquirido, lo impuesto ... *She reinterprets history and, using new symbols, she shapes new myths ... She strengthens her tolerance (and intolerance) for ambiguity ... She becomes a* nahual, *able to transform herself into a tree, a coyote, into another person* ... Se hace moldeadora de su alma. Según la concepción que tiene de sí misma, así será.
>
> Gloria Anzaldúa, *Borderlands/La Frontera*, (2007 [1987]: 104–105)

Shapeshifters and tricksters are figures present in Latin American mythologies, from the *Nahual* and the *Coyote* in Mesoamerican culture, to the *Anhangá* in Brazilian folklore. These creatures are often known to possess more than one soul, and to transit among different universes: humans, animals, nature, the living and the dead. The knowledges possessed by the shapeshifter are often understood beyond folkloric magic; rather, they are perceived more as a *faculty,* which extends one's own awareness and allows for a more comprehensive, if not complete, perception of the world as whole. Acknowledging the existence of such extended perceptions challenges conventional ontologies simply because they do not fit within the narrative and rationale of a dichotomous existence. They require a predisposition to think in terms of metaphors, contradictions and borderlessness.

Feminist writer Gloria Anzaldúa has dealt extensively with these capacities, which she calls *facultad* or *conocimientos* (2007 [1987], 2015). For instance, she recalls being forewarned by her mother not to go out late at night, otherwise the axolotl, a mythical creature, could make her pregnant; the axolotl, she contends, was in fact men who could assault and rape her, should she go out late at night by herself (2015: 26). Allowing both types of knowledge – about otherworldly creatures and about men – to coexist is a way of extending the mind beyond given notions of what constitutes reality; it is a way of understanding that knowledge expresses itself in multiple ways. Whether it takes the shape of real men or a mythical creature, danger is very much real in that cautionary tale. Anzaldúa wrote extensively on the necessity for the non-conforming subject – in her case a Latina and lesbian of colour living in Texas – to acquire abilities akin to those of the Nahual, of the shapeshifter to 'stretch the psyche horizontally and vertically, ... to juggle cultures [... to operate] in a pluralistic mode' (1989: 101) by embracing diverse forms of knowledge. The colonized body, she contends, has a shapeshifting nature, living and speaking from the borders of different languages, identities and knowledges.

As researchers from the Global South, living and working in the Global North, we, too, dwell on such a border – albeit voluntarily. Nevertheless, living in this in-betweenness often requires us to act as shapeshifters ourselves. Throughout our research and practice we have often encountered epistemologies that diverge significantly from our own local histories. Our position – academic and geopolitical – thus requires us to critically assess hegemonic and Eurocentric systems of knowledge. In doing so, we strive to find ways of evidencing their contradictory nature, while at the same time negotiating their coexistence with other ontologies. In this chapter, we discuss how we address these issues in our own research and practice within and around the discipline of speculative and critical design (SCD), taking into account our 'tricky' position as designers and as border subjects. First, we introduce what we see as a core foundation of the systems of knowledge that design is part of – what decolonial authors call the colonial matrix of power, or coloniality for short (Quijano 2000; Mignolo 2007). Examining through the lenses of coloniality how designerly knowledge is validated, and how methods are constructed and endorsed requires us to challenge the very constitution of such expertise. We then discuss how the logic of coloniality manifests itself in SCD by analysing two projects: 'The Republic of Salivation' by Burton-Nitta (2011) and 'The Non-Earth State' by Elliott P. Montgomery and Chloe Brillatz (2013). The choice of these specific examples is not intended as a personal critique of their authors, but rather to demonstrate how the colonial matrix of power is not only perpetuated by a lack of deeply and critically informed research but also fostered, supported and financed by Western institutions. Lastly, we propose 'yarn sessions' as an articulation of the decolonial concepts of yarning and siting; they are used as our method for dialoguing with the hegemonic systems of knowledge in SCD in a divergent manner, thus exercising a form of shapeshifting to redirect and redistribute power in narratives about the future.

Without futures, without pasts: Universality and representation

Coloniality is an ongoing project. While the invasion of land, exploitation of resources, and the genocide and enslavement of Amerindian and African peoples in past centuries might be its most obvious facets, the consequences of the colonial project extend to the very way human beings relate to the contemporary world, ontologically and epistemologically. The project of violent dominance undertaken by Western Europe in the fourteenth and fifteenth centuries worked to eliminate difference and homogenize systems of hierarchies, knowledge and culture, originating a set of interrelated practices that Peruvian sociologist Aníbal Quijano (2000) describes as the 'colonial matrix of power'. These practices situate the Western European (male) body as the sole narrator of history; all others are relegated to a state of 'uncivilization', which validates their serfdom, assimilation and obliteration. The colonized subject is forced into the sovereign culture, reproducing it in its own designs, activities and subjectivities. To become 'civilized' is to be fully assimilated into the dominant (European) culture, to seek 'progress' and 'development' through technology and industrialization, and to achieve 'salvation' through Christianity (Quijano 2000).

Among the unfoldings of the colonial matrix of power lies the idea that human knowledges are homogeneous, globally transferable and, most importantly, universal truths; that all that can be known is known from the same point of view (Quijano 2000; Connell 2007; Mignolo 2007, 2011). Design, as a discipline with historical ties to colonial institutions, often reproduces the same discourse. In most Latin American colonies, for instance, design education was promoted first and foremost as a way to teach both technical and artistic skills to a creole society that had previously relied on slave labour, and needed to overcome a 'lack of labour force' to move towards modernization and development (Cardoso 1999: 76, translated by the authors). Until then, they were deemed to remain 'behind in time, far in space' (Mignolo 2007: 472). Hegemonic design discourses thus enforce coloniality by understanding the material practices of the colonized to be primitive, and therefore undeveloped. Moreover, by assigning these practices to a space outside design, these narratives define design's own 'legitimate heirs of a tradition' (Cardoso 1999: 14).[1]

The assumption of design as a set of practices coming from a supposedly universal (i.e. Eurocentric) perspective reproduces and assimilates the ethos of coloniality. This process, however, should not be understood as a mere matter of correlation/causation. Rather, it is necessary to develop a profound reflection on the agency of design within a much more complex web of relationships, among them the erasure of other ontologies and epistemologies that challenge dominant preconceptions about the world. In designing things into an already established context, the ability of design to shift or reorganize a previously existing order is limited, though not negligible. Thus, knowing these constraints, a radical epistemological shift in the terms, forms and contents of the conversation becomes imperative (Mignolo 2011). Design needs to be critically scrutinized in its role of securing hegemonic futures: which worlds are fostered, and, more importantly, which worlds are negated by design. Or, put simply, we need to challenge what design designs (Fry cited in Willis 2006). We believe it is through this process of acknowledging possibilities, of analysing adjacent territories, of listening for echoes – of shapeshifting – that design ontologies might be stripped of its colonial foundations to embrace other forms of making sense of the world.

When it comes to design's role in world creation/negation, the discipline of SCD that appeared in the UK in the early 2000s seems a significant contribution to a supposedly counter-hegemonic design vocabulary. This type of designerly practice concerns itself, at least in theory, with visualizing and making tangible 'probable, plausible, possible, or preferable futures' (Dunne and Raby 2014: 2), through fiction and storytelling. However, SCD relies instead on the superficial spectacle of uncomfortable, mysterious technologies designed to disgust and shock audiences (DiSalvo 2012; Tonkinwise 2014; Prado de O. Martins and Vieira de Oliveira 2015). In so doing, we argue, SCD acts as the mildly dystopian wing of the status quo, an asset of and for coloniality; instead of questioning hegemonic discourses, it depicts futures in which the systems of the colonial matrix of power are still intact, only glazed with a thin layer of middle-class dystopia (Vieira de Oliveira 2016). Modernity, capitalism, patriarchy and whiteness are not only assumed to be 'universal' or 'neutral' modes of existence in the world, but also to continue to be the pillars upon which the future must be built.

The format with which SCD works is partly responsible for these shortcomings. By relying on representation as its driving force, SCD projects are consumer goods displayed in a 'market place of ideas' (Kiem 2014). The exhibition is the language of the absolute majority of these projects, and galleries, museums and universities its strongest funders and supporters. However, despite what Dunne and Raby (2013: 140) claim, these are not spaces that allow for diversity; instead, they are strongly segregated by social and economic markers such as literacy, class or economic power. These 'invisible markers' not only limit the scope of SCD's audiences, but also assign clear roles: the visitor, the object and the author[ity]. In enforcing a disconnection between bodies and worlds, through the device of imagetic representations, political complexities and accountabilities are flattened into a picture of an estranged world, of somewhere else, disengaging the observer from the reality observed (Mitchell cited in Kiem 2014).

An example of this is 'The Republic of Salivation' (2011). Developed by London-based design studio Burton-Nitta, with support from Dutch arts centre STROOM, this project depicts a dystopian food scarcity scenario, focusing on the life of an industrial worker who lives on a high-energy, starchy diet rationed and provided by the government. His daily routine is described through objects, photographs and an installation exhibited at STROOM in 2012; in 2014 the project was integrated into MoMA New York's 'Design & Violence' collection. The authors write that the project[2] 'starts with the food shortages and famine we will face in the future [...,] where inhabitants of the city are allocated a quota of food according to their employment' (Burton-Nitta 2011).

Despite what the project seems to suggest, famine is far from a dystopian future nightmare. The United Nations World Food Programme (WFP) updates yearly its 'World Hunger Map', which depicts nations in danger of, or already struggling with famine and malnutrition. In 2016 famine continued to be an endemic problem in many countries of the Global South (World Hunger Map 2015). Brazil, for instance, has only in 2014 and for the first time in its history left the WFP's threshold of famine (2015). This is partly due to a stark increase in the scope of distribution of the 'cesta básica', a food basket containing thirteen types of basic nutrition items, including among them several in the high-energy, starchy category; still, hunger is far from a ghost left in the country's past. Such a harsh reality was obviously overlooked by the London duo in their speculations. While this could be easily attributed to a lack of profound research, or oversimplification for shock value (as the project's images strongly suggest), we argue that such a narrow world view begs the question of who exactly are the 'we' they refer to in their description.

The answer becomes clearer as we delve further into the project. 'The Republic of Salivation' is part of 'The Feast after Agri', 'an investigation into future evolutions to our food systems' (Burton-Nitta 2011). Speculating on what kinds of food cultures and ethnic identities might exist in the year 3000, the designers depict Africa and Oceania as populated by 'Subterranean Troglodytes' [sic], describe inland Asia, Iraq and Japan as 'No Man's Land' and group all of the American continent together (save Canada) as a 'Symbiotic Bacterial Nation', while Western Europe is named 'Bovineopolis' (2011). These choices resonate profoundly problematic world views: populations in Africa and Oceania are – not even subtly – suggested to be backwards and animalistic; Asia remains a mysterious, exoticized land; North America and Europe, however, retain traces of 'civilization'. The assignment of non-Western/southern populations to a state of 'barbaric uncivilization' is anything but speculative; rather, it is an ontological narrative responsible for the justification of colonial violence upon 'peoples without history', who were thought to live 'in a state of nature' (Mignolo 2007: 471). Moreover, such geopolitical speculations echo much of Walter Mignolo's thoughts on the inherently fictional aspect of modern cartography, which for him was a 'powerful [tool] with which western civilization built its own image by creating, transforming and managing the image of the world' (2014).

Confining SCD to representations such as these exempts designers from debate. It undermines contestation and critique because it sets clear boundaries, limited to the gaze. The visitor – the observer – is only able to project herself onto uncanny futures and try to fit into the scenario that is already there, to watch as the story unfolds before her – 'a form of window shopping', as explained by Dunne and Raby (2013: 140). There is no space for questioning where that scenario came from, what sequence of events preceded it; history is already written, the future already secured 'in a specialist shop selling state-of-the art material culture' (Dunne 2005: 86). There is only space for one narrative – the one devised by the designer; no rough edges, no place for those who cannot afford to have their stories up for display. A future secured is, after all, a future that does not need to be deeply debated.

Coloniality in SCD is perpetuated not only by prefiguring futures, but also by rewriting pasts. Elliott P. Montgomery and Chloe Brillatz's 'The Non-Earth State' (2013) consists of a 'performative reenactment of research conducted by geologists August Haquet and Alex Milfort, who in 1996, proposed the notion that portions of Earth are not native to our planet'. This project locates its 'portion of Earth' in Brazil and presents evidences that the geologists, basing themselves on the 'profundity of their discovery' (2013), wanted to expropriate a piece of Brazilian land. The work bases its central point in a specific part of the world that is not only physically distant from the designers' own reality, but also perceived as exotic enough to have its history re-written by a 'discovery' of 'interstellar matter'. In this process of distancing and othering, the violent act of expropriating land is rendered as performance. While one could argue that their work embraces this colonial move as an act of irony or sarcasm, there is a sensible historical and ontological problem when European designers re-enact the appropriation of native land. This act of 'overidentification' as mimicry, as Mexican artist Pedro Lasch (2012: 27–29) argues, cannot be a critical endeavour when the colonizer does not do anything but act exactly like himself.

In these terms, the 'Non-Earth' in Montgomery and Brillatz's Brazil is not metaphorical but rather literal alien matter. A 'no-one's-land', waiting to be claimed as soon as European researchers – geologists or designers – 'discover' something that supposedly justifies expropriation. Historically, Europeans have used similar rhetoric to invade 'portions of Earth' – Brazil among them – and annihilate entire populations;

however, this historical fact did not seem relevant to the project's narrative. According to the story, the geologists' 'legal claim' for the ownership of this piece of land was not further pursued because of its conceptual absurdity (even for a piece of fiction), or due to any thorough response from the Brazilian Congress, but rather to 'Haquet's diminishing health' (Montgomery and Brillatz 2013). The Brazilian side of the story – i.e. the perspective of those facing the threat of re-colonization – is not part of the narrative devised by the authors; such a decision not only silences any attempt at refusal or resistance, but also depicts the Brazilian government as a peaceful savage – a regular trope in (colonial) fiction – mesmerized by the colonizer's alleged superior intellect and scientific apparatus. In other words, the project's description leaves enough room for speculation that the geologists' endeavour might have been successful otherwise. Quijano (2000: 555) argues that 'from the Eurocentric perspective, certain races are condemned as inferior for not being rational subjects. They are objects of study, consequently bodies closer to nature …, dominable and exploitable'. In the project's view, Brazilian land remains, as of 1996, 'closer to nature' than Europe, as alien as when the Portuguese first invaded and found enough goods to pillage. This time, however, such an act becomes a performance endorsed by the colonizer's institutions – Imperial College in London – without any further consideration of the profound historical and geopolitical implications this narrative may have. Coloniality is, in their speculation, validated through a re-enactment of and direct homage to colonialism.

Brazilian playwright Augusto Boal (2008 [1979]: 120) maintains that finished performances are stories made by and for the bourgeoisie, depicting their reality; only those whose futures are secured are able to display them as completed. Based on the above analyses and following Boal's thoughts, we believe SCD could benefit from the rehearsal instead of the spectacle (2008 [1979]); that multiple, often contradictory realities, knowledges, pasts and futures can coexist on their own. Appropriating contemporary tragedies of the Global South and transposing them to the context of whiteness and privilege, or re-enacting past tragedies in order to pay them homage in a displaced reality is, unfortunately, not exclusive to SCD projects – but are phenomena much present in its methods nevertheless. If SCD practitioners actively worked not to erase pasts and futures, but rather to assess the tricky nature of design decisions and how they impact past and future in both directions, we believe the practice could become a platform for the dispute and enactment of change.

Such an assessment yields a more profound reflection on the designer's own position in the world, and in turn evidences the complexities of political/colonial issues SCD tends to ignore. Negotiating these complexities and making them research assets requires designers to act as trickster figures: debating, listening and crafting possible, speculative world views as we design them. It is an exercise in the type of shapeshifting Anzaldúa has written about; one that 'creates a split in awareness' (2015: 28) to allow a 'divergent thinking' (1989: 101): the ability to navigate between hegemonic and non-hegemonic world views, designing 'an in-between space, *el lugar entre medio*' (2005: 28). To do so, we articulate two concepts from decolonial and feminist thinking: yarning – storytelling as a method for transmission of knowledges – and siting – an informed awareness of a 'locus of enunciation' (Mignolo 2011: 280) as the source of one's own knowledge.

Yarning: Rehearsing speculation

Feminist philosopher Donna Haraway once compared complex systems to balls of yarn: tangled, chaotic masses that could 'be loosened [and] pulled out, [leading] to whole worlds, to universes without stopping points, without ends' (2004: 338). It is the process of untangling these balls of yarn that allows one to understand their underlying structures, analyse their implications and assess their impact in the world. The loose threads revealed by this process may lead us to multiple paths: unclear futures, worlds-to-be ripe for inquiry.

SCD offers its audiences the ball of yarn: ready-made stories, things to be observed, perhaps even reflected upon for a brief moment, but with no loose ends. The disconnection between designer and audience is thus cemented: the designer, as the enlightened subject, speaks and exhibits; the silent spectators in the audience merely listen and observe. There is no call for the yarn to be untangled, no possibility for reply. A fixed narrative emerges: points in time that are impossible to change. Audiences become the passive subjects of a future already speculated and pre-packaged for them, representing but a single angle – that of the author – from which to analyse that specific subject; a single thread, a single voice.

We argue that speculation needs to be enacted in transient spaces in which any perspective could become a loose thread for exploring the future or an amalgamation of untold pasts and uncertain presents – in Boal's (2008 [1979]: 120) words the rehearsal, not the spectacle. This requires, of course, a substantial change in the strategies used in SCD. First, it becomes clear that the exhibition format cannot attend to those needs; thus, the act of speculating must shift from static, self-contained narratives to dynamic, open-ended participatory projects. Second, the authors need to be present, to become a part of the story, to acknowledge the fragility of their versions of the future and to make themselves accountable for the debates that may emerge. They need to become shapeshifters, moving between roles, negotiating the repercussions that their actions and ideas have in the worlds of others, and understanding that these worlds may entail knowledges that directly confront those of the authors or other participants. These sessions are not workshops, nor theatre pieces; they cannot be understood as seminars or courses either. They are, in fact, the projects themselves, in which the process of speculation unfolds collectively, simultaneously, and may or may not reach a common point.

In these sessions, participants cease to be passive recipients of knowledge to become agents for its emergence. They are thus encouraged to become actors in the stories being told, with the power to suggest and enact changes. According to the *Oxford Online Dictionary* (n.d.), 'to yarn' means to 'tell a long or implausible story'. It is also a 'way oral-based cultures use stories and conversation as a process of making meaning, communicating, and passing on history and knowledge' (Terszack 2015: 90). Yarning is a method of generating knowledge about complex matters through 'living engagement' and 'relational patterning' (Sheehan 2004: 38). In other words, it is an understanding that individuals can only possess a fraction of knowledge that directly relates to their personal engagement with said knowledge; by negotiating the relations among every individual's portion of knowledge, a group is able to extend their perspective to a collective one, while respecting the fact that a collective world view implies diversity and allows for contradictions (2004: 40).

In a session, yarning may occur through a variety of outlets: oral storytelling, drawings, sounds, performances, prototypes, whatever allows each actor to tell their own versions of what might happen, what is happening now or what has happened in the past in the context of the presented scenario. Traditional speculative proposals – props, fragments of stories, semi-fictional accounts, photos, sound – are only starting points offered by the authors: participants are confronted with fragments of one version of a story to be explored. From the moment these proposals are introduced in the session, participants are free to untangle and weave them into any direction they see fit. In order to accommodate these processes, the authors need to shift their role, acting more like what Boal described as the 'Joker': a 'contemporary and neighbour of the spectator' (2008 [1979]: 152), someone who 'ensure[s] that those who know a little more get the chance to explain it, and that those who dare a little, dare a little more and show what they are capable of' (2002: 245). This provides that a session is a safe space in which all knowledges are welcome, and they are welcome in any format as long as they keep stories going and creating new paths. These new stories, assuming an improvisational character, are naturally incomplete, mismatched and often end up leading to other places and paths. What is important here is that by sharing knowledges through yarning, we are able, as a group, to extend our conscience on the subject matter of each session.

Siting: Observing diffractive patterns

In a yarn session, ambiguity and incompleteness are not consciously applied assets of speculative proposals (Gaver et al. 2003), but rather their intrinsic nature. These proposals are only able to tell the story with the biases and intentions of the designer, and thus are open to challenge and questioning. Therefore, their ambiguous nature requires the acknowledgement of one's position as an observer and actor in the world, or, in other words, where one's knowledge is situated. In her dissection of the myth of scientific objectivity, Haraway (1988) postulated the notion of situated knowledges, questioning the idea of the researcher as an observer capable of extracting objective truths about the world. She maintains that inherent to research is its partiality – as opposed to universality or objectivity; researchers are only able to read the world through the position they occupy in it, be it in terms of gender, race, class, ethnicity or education. Hence any version of the future, described by the objects and actors that inhabit it, sets a clear boundary, delimited by the author's own bodily knowledge of the world (Haraway 1988: 591–596).

As participants engage in yarning, creating their own stories out of the initial fragments and expressing their own perspectives on the subjects at hand, they tend to naturally – often unknowingly – situate their outlook in the world. It is of utmost importance, then, to elicit reflections within the group that foster this engagement with one's situated knowledge, making clear that this is a positive process that only adds to the untangling of the story. Each group of participants, when confronted with the designers' initial narrative, may imagine completely different worlds, completely different timelines. Notions of time and space – what one's present looks like – are intimately linked to social, cultural, economic and political contexts, and so-called 'objective' depictions of the future work as an endorsement of privileges. Situating speculation creates a specific marker in time – be it in the past, present or future – that is particular to the moment, the location and the group.

Siting is, then, a core process within yarn sessions, a strategy for making sense of the raw material offered by the act of yarning. It happens within each session, through a number of designerly languages; in turn, the designer acts as a nurturer of ideas, allowing reflections to unfold, embracing anachronism and difference. Dissenting accounts are embraced as part of the process; the more different knowledges the project is able to yield, the richer the results will be. Instead of delimiting a boundary through speculative proposals, each session provides multiple, intersecting, and more often than not fluid, situated knowledges. Siting ultimately works as a tool to investigate the value of anachronism as an expression of different ontological values in speculative futures.

A further form of siting may be carried out by applying diffractive lenses to the relational patterns of a particular instalment or multiple sessions of the same project. Haraway (2004: 70) argues for diffraction in place of reflection as a strategy with which to analyse worldly phenomena, for 'diffraction does not produce "the same" displaced ... Diffraction is a mapping of interference, not of replication, reflection, or reproduction. A diffraction pattern does not map where differences appear, but rather maps where the effects of difference appear'. Adding to Haraway's reflections, physicist and philosopher Karen Barad (2007: 90) clarifies that 'a diffractive methodology is a critical practice for making a difference in the world. It is a commitment to understanding which differences matter, how they matter, and for whom'. By observing how patterns of repetition and patterns of difference emerge in or throughout sessions, and analysing how they are articulated by the participants, the designers may gain a layered perspective on the social and cultural impact of speculation through design. Repetitions often indicate assumptions informed by colonial impositions of economic, political, epistemological and cultural systems; they tend to expose what is perceived as 'neutral', 'global' or 'universal' about the world. Conversely, difference tends to emphasize the non-obvious, that which goes unnoticed; they describe how a problem might be articulated within a given group of participants. Patterns of difference provide an ontological portrait of what it means for a specific group to be part of that moment in space and time.

The identification and analysis of diffractive patterns in speculations do not seek to level contradictions and eliminate dissent. Rather, they aim at acquiring a deeper understanding of how and why each situated knowledge entails different needs with different modes of addressing said needs. This form of 'relational patterning' understands knowledge to be composed by a multitude of lived experiences, ontologies and epistemologies between systems (Sheehan 2004: 41). Thus, if each future described by each actor is equally important/real in the collective scenario, it is imperative to ask why some futures focus on certain aspects, while others ignore them altogether. Inevitably, considerations about these emerging patterns will be subject to the designers' own knowledge, partial understandings informed by their own siting in the world as well. It is, thus, fundamental that researchers interested in decolonizing design processes be not only merely aware of their own underlying biases or take them for granted; rather, these must be acknowledged, clearly stated and discussed as an integral aspect of any SCD project.

Conclusion: A decolonial redirection

Shapeshifters are beings living at the intersection of multiple worlds, shuffling between different realities. To be able to stand 'on both shores at once', Anzaldúa remarks, is a faculty for taking action rather than resorting to mere reaction; it is what allows the border subject to remain in a state of 'perpetual transition' as a strategy for survival (1989: 100–101). Even when we actively cross the border, we cannot escape this type of confrontation; there is only so much one is able to adapt to, before losing their ability to retain their identity and ontologies.

Border subjects who are designers – or designers who become border subjects – have to develop novel *conocimientos* recognizing the emergence of patterns and points of contact between different ontologies and differentiating the acquired from the imposed, the 'imported magic' from our own devices (Medina et al, 2014). The decolonization of design processes requires negotiating the existence of multiple perspectives within the same project while avoiding hierarchies, listening to one's surroundings and adapting communication accordingly and discussing how one's social and cultural position informs how one engages with the material world. Moreover, the designer/shapeshifter has the task of communicating and accommodating these novel understandings to his or her peers and audiences. This happens through actions that acknowledge and demonstrate how bias is a 'pathological condition' in some research contexts, and in turn may directly inform a group's perception of reality (Sheehan 2011: 79); or by de-centring ontologies to critically inquire what constitutes knowledge or what validates certain knowledges above others.

Good design practice should be not only speculative, but also encourage its audience to be critical and speculative in return (Tonkinwise 2015). In this chapter, we have demonstrated how SCD reproduces and perpetuates coloniality by subscribing to modes of representation founded in colonial understandings about the world. In proposing 'yarn sessions' as a possible decolonial redirection of SCD, we aim to start a discussion about problems that are not only particular to this discipline, but also endemic in the general field of design. Due to its history in the Western[ized] world, design has long subscribed to narrow, Eurocentric ideas about what constitutes knowledge. While other fields have, in the past, greatly benefited from discussions initiated by decolonial and feminist thinking, Design has yet to sufficiently address them. We maintain that design praxis should not silence and marginalize non-hegemonic and de-centralizing forms of knowing; strategies such as yarning and siting have the potential to yield richer worlds and to contribute to the creation of futures where power is better distributed, and multiple world views are able to respectfully coexist. Research becomes the vessel for accessing the future and the processes that frame its inherently unequal character; design – that through which research is done – is in turn one language to speak about the shaping of these futures, and to perform the politics within these articulations. Designers must nurture this language by transmitting and translating it to others; in doing so, new doors for accessing the (right to have a) future are created.

Notes

1   For instance, Gui Bonsiepe writes that he is 'wary of unearthing design in pre-colonial peripheral countries', claiming that these notions often rely on 'bucolic ideas of rural communities preferring simplistic technologies stemming from old traditions' (1997: 107–108, translated by the authors). The dismissal of traditional knowledges as 'simplistic' is a clear example of the notion of 'development' within colonial understandings of design and technology.
2   http://designandviolence.moma.org/republic-of-salivation-michael-burton-and-michiko-nitta/ (accessed January 20 2016).

Bibliography

Anzaldúa, G. (2007 [1987]) Borderlands/ La Frontera: The New Mestiza, 3rd Edition, San Francisco, Aunt Lute Book Company.
Anzaldúa, G. (2015) *Light in the Dark/Luz En Lo Oscuro: Rewriting Identity, Spirituality, Reality*, Durham, NC: Duke University Press.
Barad, K. (2007) *Meeting the Universe Halfway: Quantum Physics and the Entanglement of Matter and Meaning*, Durham, NC: Duke University Press.
Boal, A. (2002) *Games for Actors and Non-Actors*, London and New York: Routledge.
Boal, A. (2008) *Theatre of the Oppressed*, New Edition, *Get Political*, London: Pluto Press.
Bonsiepe, G. (1997) *Design: Do Material ao Digital*, Florianópolis: FIESC/IEL.
Burton, M. and Nitta, M. (2011) The Republic of Salivation [WWW Document]. Burton-Nitta. Available at: http://www.burtonnitta.co.uk/republicofsalivation.html (accessed 20 January 2016).
Cardoso, R. (1999) Uma introdução à história do design. Ed. Blucher, São Paulo.
Connell, R. W. (2007) *Southern Theory: Social Science and the Global Dynamics of Knowledge*, 1st Edition, Cambridge and Malden, MA: Polity Press.
Definition of 'yarn' (n.d.) Oxford Online Dictionary.
DiSalvo, C. (2012) 'Spectacles and Tropes: Speculative Design and Contemporary Food Cultures', *The Fibreculture Journal*.
Dunne, A. (2005) *Hertzian Tales: Electronic Products, Aesthetic Experience, and Critical Design*, Cambridge, MA: MIT Press.
Dunne, A. and Raby, F. (2014) *Speculative Everything: Design, Fiction, and Social Dreaming*, Cambridge, MA; London: The MIT Press.
Gaver, W. W., Beaver, J. and Benford, S. (2003) 'Ambiguity as a Resource for Design'. *Proceedings of the SIGCHI Conference on Human Factors in Computing Systems, CHI '03*, New York: ACM, pp. 233–240. doi:10.1145/642611.642653.

Haraway, D. (1988) 'Situated Knowledges: The Science Question in Feminism and the Privilege of Partial Perspective', *Feminist Studies*, 14, 575–599.

Haraway, D. (2004) *The Haraway Reader*, London: Routledge.

Kiem, M. (2014) Is a Decolonial SCD possible? [WWW Document]. Medium. Available at: https://medium.com/@mattkiem/is-a-decolonial-scd-possible-30db8675b82a (accessed 17 August 2015).

Lasch, P. (2012) Grand Gestures and (Im)modest Proposals: A Project for Documenta 13 AND AND AND. XCO/Documenta 13 AND AND AND, Kassel, Germany.

Medina, E., Da Costa Marques, I. and Holmes, C. (2014) 'Introduction: Beyond Imported Magic', in E. Medina, I. Da Costa Marques and C. Holmes (eds), *Beyond Imported Magic*, Cambridge, MA: MIT University Press Group Ltd, pp. 1–23.

Mignolo, W. D. (2007) Delinking, *Cultural Studies* 21, 449–514. doi:10.1080/09502380601162647.

Mignolo, W. D. (2011) *The Darker Side of Western Modernity: Global Futures, Decolonial Options*, Durham, NC: Duke University Press.

Mignolo, W. D. (2014) The North of the South and the West of the East: A Provocation to the Question. Ibraaz.

Montgomery, E. P. and Brillatz, C. (2013) The Non-Earth State [WWW Document]. Blyth Gallery. Available at: https://www.union.ic.ac.uk/arts/artifact/wp-content/uploads/2013/02/Artifact-Catalogue.pdf (accessed 20 January 2016).

Prado De O. Martins, L., and Vieira De Oliveira, P. J. S., (2015). 'Futuristic Gizmos, Conservative Ideals: On Anachronistic Design', in: Laranjo, F. (Eed.), Modes of Criticism, Modes of Criticism 1 – Critical, Uncritical, Post-critical available at: http://modesofcriticism.org/futuristic-gizmos-conservative-ideals/.

Quijano, A. (2000) Coloniality of Power, Eurocentrism, and Latin America, *Nepantla: Views from South*, 1, 533–580.

Sheehan, N. (2004) 'Indigenous Knowledge and Higher Education: Instigating Relational Education in a Neocolonial Context.' University of Queensland, Brisbane.

Sheehan, N. W. (2011) 'Indigenous Knowledge and Respectful Design: An Evidence-Based Approach', *Design Issues*, 27, 68–80. doi:10.1162/DESI_a_00106.

Terszak, M. (2015) *Orphaned by the Colour of My Skin: A Stolen Generation Story*, London: Routledge.

Tonkinwise, C. (2014) 'How We Intend to Future: Review of Anthony Dunne and Fiona Raby, Speculative Everything: Design, Fiction, and Social Dreaming', *Design Philosophy Papers*, 12: 169–187. doi:10.2752/144871314X14159818597676.

Tonkinwise, C. (2015) Just Design: Being Dogmatic about Defining Speculative Critical Design Future Fiction [WWW Document]. Medium. Available at: https://medium.com/@camerontw/just-design-b1f97cb3996f#.i9jowd6lz (accessed 20 January 2016).

Vieira De Oliveira, P. J. S. (2016) 'Design at the Earview: Decolonizing Speculative Design through Sonic Fiction', *Design Issues*, 32: 43–52.

Willis, Anne-Marie (2006) 'Ontological Designing', *Design Philosophy Papers*, 4, 2: 69–92. https://doi.org/10.2752/144871306X13966268131514.

World Hunger Map, (2015) World Food Programme, United Nations.

7

Making 'Safety', Making Freedom: Problem-Setting, Collaborative Design and Contested Futures

Shana Agid

The point of departure of the movement lies in the people themselves .... Accordingly, the point of departure must always be with [people] in the 'here and now', which constitutes the situation within which they are submerged, from which they emerge, and in which they intervene. Only by starting from this situation – which determines their perception of it – can they begin to move. To do this authentically they must perceive their state as not fated and unalterable, but merely as limiting – and therefore challenging.

Paolo Freire (1970: 85)

While it is important to seek to better understand why people do the things they do and to reduce harm, we need to reject 'crime' as a lens of analysis and excavate and separate from 'crime' the topics buried within it that matter to us, while drawing attention to power-infused processes of criminalization and punishment.

Melissa Burch (2014)

In May 2013, one year before the police killings of Michael Brown in Ferguson, Missouri and Eric Garner In Staten Island, New York set off massive public protests and the racist violence of policing reached the main stage of US media and political discourse, I met six members of the Critical Resistance (CR) *Oakland No Cops* working group to begin planning their new campaign. We were in an office with a soft couch, colourful posters, sunlight and just enough space. A group member, Susan,[1] and I had planned the agenda together, with feedback from everyone. I facilitated so she could be a full participant. I brought snacks and sticky notes purchased with funds from a small grant. We grabbed markers and big paper from the CR office and got to work.

CR is a US-based organization seeking to abolish the prison industrial complex (PIC), which they define as 'the overlapping interests of government and industry that designate surveillance, policing and imprisonment as solutions to economic, social and political problems' (2004: 59). The No Cops group focuses on fighting the impacts of policing in Oakland, California, including the targeting of people of colour, former prisoners, immigrants, queer people and others. Their organizing *against* police incursions is supported by organizing *for* other ideas and resources to foster community well-being and self-determination.

We started the workshop by making a timeline of significant ideas, events, policies and memories from members' research into the recent history of policing in Oakland on the only available vertical space – a wall of windows. Backlit, the timeline showed five years of strategies, elections and a rotating cast of characters in charge. It showed a body count, people of colour of all ages killed by police. It showed changing neighbourhoods, and blocks missing neighbours to prisons around the state. It showed some organized resistance, as well, limited only by our having forgotten to include what CR members called 'fight back' as a research focus of its own. As timelines do, it told stories.

No Cops members talked through what they saw, adding memories and analysis as connective tissue. While they talked, I listened and wrote, making a list on big paper of their key concerns and arguments: *funding for a range of social issues, like poverty, domestic violence and drug use, is filtered by city and federal governments through police agencies; city residents are told that more police will create more safety; people don't feel they have options other than calling the police; there is a story being told by media, police and even city government that Oakland is terrible; the city keeps picking cops over alternative resources.* From the organizers' perspectives, these were areas of meaning making with which the campaign would have to contend.

I began to see how the stories they found in the timeline had historically, and contemporaneously, shaped the problem of policing and harm the No Cops group set out to challenge. What I saw, while specific to Oakland, and therefore new to me in its details, also reflected what I believed from my own years of work with CR. I turned the page on the easel pad and began to draw the problem as I heard it. On the left of the fresh sheet of paper, I made a big box representing the story the Oakland Police Department told about policing and itself. To its right, linked by a not-equal symbol, I drew another box representing stories Oaklanders told about policing. Below them I made a third box representing what we imagined would be the stories from the new campaign. I connected this to the Oaklanders' stories box with arrows moving between the two (Figure 7.1).

What struck me as I drew was that this was a representation not only of what No Cops members' knew, but of an idea of policing that contradicted 'common sense', accepted notions of where the *problem* rests in matters of 'crime', 'violence' or 'safety'. Additional notes and shapes accumulated to annotate my drawing as the group began to speak back to it and we talked through the context and aims of the campaign. Policing fails Oakland, they argued, and this campaign would build and amplify people's stories, resources and power, because people don't have to rely on police.

This chapter explores the critical nature of naming, and framing, the focus of designing in what Bannon and Ehn (2012) call the 'socio-material assemblies' in which collaborative design work takes place. I draw on long-term embedded design research with CR to propose that 'problem-setting' (Schön 1983) is a deeply political component of design processes and the contexts in which designers and participants work. No Cops members and I designed capacities, materials and a collective practice

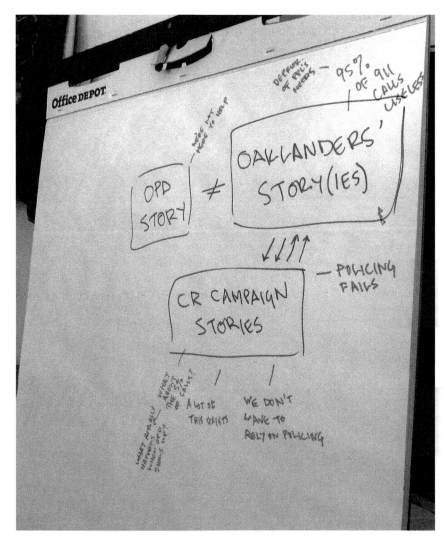

Figure 7.1 Author's in-the-moment drawing, reflecting the group's conversation about shifting common sense understandings of harm and responses to it (Author's photograph).

for moving forward with their short- and long-term (political) goals in mind. With my work grounded in theirs, what we determined needed to be designed both shaped, and was shaped by, those goals and the problems, and the possible actions they suggested.

Here, I argue for a rethinking of 'problem-setting', often imagined as an *act of designers*, through the lens of Paolo Freire's (2010) concept of 'problem-posing' as *a collective and dialectical process*. This chapter suggests that as designers work with people, especially towards social and political change, we participate in the tricky work of setting the terms by which designing takes place. This calls for designers to have a deep awareness of the complex, contested and messy conditions that form design's contexts, and how those are experienced and defined by people most affected by them.

'Problem-setting': Parameters of and contexts for designing

Donald Schön's (1983, 1987, 1988) theory of reflective practice articulates how ways of thinking and reflecting shape how practitioners know what they know, generalize this knowledge and make decisions about what comes next. As I argue elsewhere (2011, 2012), Donna Haraway's (1991) and Lucy Suchman's (2002) theorizations of situated knowledge help to expand Schön's theory of reflective practice, suggesting other frameworks for seeing what designers and others are 'reflecting through' as we bring our experiences and beliefs into design practices. In other words, *how* we understand what we bring to design meant to create social or political change matters.

Reflective practices of designing have at their core what Schön considered the concomitant practices of 'problem-setting' and intervention on that problem space. Schön (1983: 40) explains:

> When we set the problem, we select what we will treat as the 'things' of the situation, we set the boundaries of our attention to it, and we impose upon it a coherence which allows us to say what is wrong and in what directions the situation needs to be changed. Problem setting is a process in which, interactively, we *name* the things to which we will attend, and *frame* the context in which we will attend to them. (emphasis in original)

Problem-setting is setting the terms of what comes next, as designers bring what we already know, from experience or investigation, together with the questions raised by the specific situation. Through this process designers begin to make sense of the nature (and parameters) of the problem with which a design will need to contend. While Schön's framing of the nature of 'the problem' remains important to understanding design processes, a more critical investigation can shed necessary light on the systems and structures in, around or against which we design with people by asking: Who defines the problem? Who sets the parameters? And how? With what results?

Schön warns that the routine of practice can foster 'selective inattention' through which designers eliminate what 'doesn't fit' bypassing messy data, people or other characteristics of a situation that differ from expectations. He warns, too, of 'overlearning', only practising what is already known. However, he does not address the systemic factors present in designing with people, which influence what a designer does or does not see to begin with. When the contingencies of naming the problem are left behind, the mostly unspoken *political* contexts of design practices that fall under the loose (and sometimes contested) umbrella of design for social change are also lost. Design meant to alleviate *conditions* of structural inequality often ends up 'sustain[ing] the unsustainable' (Fry and and Dilnot 2003: n.p.), as different understandings of 'ideal' worlds, and how they might be produced are often under-theorized or un-discussed (Agid 2011).[2]

Designing with people, and in the contexts of community organizing, means working with problem framing practices and ideas that are *already in place,* in collaborators' organizational mission and vision statements, individual or collective experiences and their histories. A decade before Schön published his work, Scandinavian practitioners developed participatory design (PD) as a part of the workplace democracy movement, creating an approach to design practice rooted in ethical questions: *Who* used designed things and how should what they know and articulate as needs for their work guide designing? As they involved people in the (re)design of systems with which they would be working, PD practitioners centred people's right to a voice in the design of things that would impact their lives (Ehn 2008; Robertson and Simonsen 2012). Contemporary PD continues to expand on this principle, in emergent political and social contexts (Karasti et al. 2010; Bannon and Ehn 2012; Clement et al. 2012; Light and Akama 2012), providing one model of how designers might engage in the politics inherent in design as a practice of making things and systems (Fry 2010).[3]

In my research with CR, the work we did was shaped by CR members' understanding of the 'PIC' and of its impacts on Oaklanders. This included how members framed the PIC as a problem, named the parameters of acceptable and legitimate action to take in relation to it, including what they hoped would come from that action and who would lead it.[4] As new situations arose in practice, we imagined, tested and honed strategies and tactics in relation to new questions. We came to do what Paolo Freire (2010) has called 'problem-posing', a situated, collective process for naming the things of the situation and placing 'the problem' and what might be done about it in socio-historical and relational context. This emerged as a combination of what CR members had 'represented the problem to be' (Bacchi 2009) over time, what emerged as specific needs and ideas as we created a new campaign, and what we all individually brought to the table through previous organizing (and design) experiences.

Framing contexts and meanings: 'Crime', 'safety' and 'freedom'

The United States incarcerates more people per capita than any other country (Schmitt et al. 2010). In 2014, while overall numbers of people locked up decreased slightly from prior years, rates of incarceration for women continued to rise, and people of colour were incarcerated at rates two to five times higher than white people (Carson 2015). Geographer Ruth Wilson Gilmore (2007) has argued that the expansion of the prison system in the United States since the late 1970s grows out of that era's crises of capital and labour, deindustrialization and the continued racialization of punishment as social control. Rapidly expanding rates of incarceration, especially for poor people and people of colour, in the decades since, she explains, are linked to *systemic* conditions, to structures of race, class and capital in the post-Civil Rights Era, post-industrial United States (12–13), rather than to the fact of 'crime'. This analysis demonstrates the importance of systemic thinking for designing in relationship both to these structures themselves and to organized opposition to them. Additionally, media and political discourses in this era emphasized 'tough on crime' rhetoric and policies (Hall et al. 2013), shifted government spending towards personnel working in 'enforcement' jobs and away from 'service' roles (Bohrman and Murakawa 2005), and subjected poor and working-class people to dwindling access to economic assistance and other 'safety nets' (Kandaswamy 2008).[5]

This landscape has deeply affected many Oakland residents, especially people of colour, and poor and working-class people (Rios 2011). The 'Riders Case', in which a police unit was charged with routine abuse, planting evidence and making false arrests in the mostly African American West Oakland neighbourhood, led in 2003 to federal court oversight of the Oakland Police Department (Monmaney 2000; Moughty 2011). This oversight was still in place during my research, and police violence, including the killing of Oscar Grant in 2009 and the severe injury in 2011 of an Occupy Oakland participant by 'non-lethal' projectiles, led to protests and continued scrutiny. In the workshop which opened this chapter, group members discussed the multiple and conflicting stories about policing and communities' needs and desires operating in the city at any given time. At the nexus of these sometimes conflicting, sometimes overlapping, reports, members proposed making policing irrelevant as a strategy for producing both safety and freedom.

As concerns about rising incarceration rates in the United States and internationally have become mainstream, designers working from a range of perspectives have also taken notice.[6] The UK Design Council-funded project at The University of the Arts London, Design Against Crime (see Chapter 11), proposes that social design methods can reduce 'crime'. Lizzie Coles-Kemp (2013), of the Possible Futures Lab, asks how people define and determine ideas of security in multiple settings, including with families of prisoners.[7] The Public Policy Lab (PPL) in New York, whose mission is to 'help Americans build better lives by improving the design and delivery of public services', highlights 'Courts and Criminal Justice' projects as one of many sites of intervention on its blog. Here, the PPL focuses on work in various design fields to 'improve' people's experiences of, or in, systems of policing, courts and prisons. Alternatively, the US-based Architects/ Designers/ Planners for Social Responsibility (ADPSR) has led efforts to organize designers to refuse to design execution chambers and solitary confinement units, and has worked through public charrettes to reimagine and repurpose prison sites in California.[8]

Although these examples are not exhaustive, they highlight how different approaches consider different routes to, and frameworks for, design responses to 'crime', policing and imprisonment. While the PPL blog example of a 'better designed' police and prison complex presumes that such a space can be designed to work well for people caught in it (Routson 2013), the ADPSR's campaign questions the very possibility of designing 'humane' cages, especially for solitary confinement and asks designers to consider the lives and experiences of the people in those cages (Sperry 2014). Gui Bonsiepe (2006) argues that participation is a process through which 'dominated citizens transform themselves into subjects opening a space for self-determination' to create projects of their own. In this light, participation in the context of incarceration, policing and feelings of security raise questions about who defines the impetus and aims for design in relationship to harm and safety.

The generally accepted notion that the aim of policing is to 'create safety' by 'reducing crime' offers a simple cause and effect relationship that could seem to be an appropriate point of intersection for designers interested in addressing 'crime'. But if 'crime' itself can be called into question as a stable term or category (Burch 2014; Gilmore 2007; Hall et al. 2013; Muhammad 2010), and definitions of 'safety' are understood as contingent, the sense of the problem shifts. Melissa Burch (2014) maps the social and political factors that have helped to create today's 'common sense' understandings of 'crime'. Burch notes that criminal laws and enforcement mechanisms were shaped by eugenics in the late eighteenth and early nineteenth centuries, by reform movements in the 1910s and 1920s focused on the rehabilitation of white ethnic immigrants to the United States, and by the pathologizing of African American families in the 1960s, especially in the 1965 Moynihan Report (see also, Muhammad 2010). Resistance in the 1960s and 1970s to these characterizations and policies and the resulting backlash from the political right (and centre) in the 1980s and 1990s shifted the discussion from social and political conditions of inequality back to personal responsibility and to 'crime' as individualized and not systemic (Davis 2003; Gilmore 2007; Hall et al. 2013; Burch 2014).

Despite the complex social and political construction of 'crime', and the ways in which laws are made and changed in different political moments and places (Gilmore 2007), the idea persists that 'crime' is a constant and clear category. In their study of the mugging panic in Britain in the early 1970s, Hall and colleagues (2013: 72) argue that in representations of 'mugging' by media, police and courts 'dominant definitions' emerged to reify a specific 'problem with crime', setting the terms of debate, narrowing possible understandings of the conditions at hand and limiting alternative interpretations. Burch (2014: n.p.) reminds us that 'when people say "crime," they rarely mean "unlawful act," much less, "action which happens to have been labeled unlawful in this particular place at this particular time, according to the prevailing social, political and economic order"'. This historically grounded unsettling of the notion of 'crime' necessarily affects both the work of, and the potential for, designing in this arena. It raises other critical questions: Whose safety is at issue, how is it defined, and how is it compromised?

If crime is understood as not only *not constant*, but as a designation of social, political and economic relationships, then how might designing with other needs in mind change approaches taken by designers? My work with the No Cops group opened up a different way to think about policing in relationship to the 'problem' presented by both discourses of 'crime' and the actual harm taking place in Oakland. Our designing began by reframing policing's function as what Rachel Herzing (2015: n.p.) calls the 'armed protection of state interests', which 'increases clarity about what policing is meant to protect and whom it serves'. This argument shifts the problem field from 'crime' as the problem, and 'police' as the solution or as those in charge of defining possible solutions. What might it mean to design *for* 'freedom' or 'well-being' instead of *against* crime?

Many design projects in the 'social' realm presume a naturalized idea of 'crime', or a necessarily beneficial 'justice system'. However, CR frames the problem in a specific historical and political context, and poses it differently. From this point of view, systems of policing and imprisonment are not 'broken', rather they are doing what they are meant to do: mobilizing logics of incarceration, surveillance and policing to lock up ever larger numbers of people of colour, poor people, immigrants and others. The aim of abolitionist organizing is not to *improve* the system so it affects fewer people or is less damaging to those caught in it, but to fight the PIC as a system of harm, and build alternatives to it. Shifting the understanding of the problem shifts ideas of who might be best positioned to address or rethink it, and shapes possibilities for imagined futures.

A 'yes' campaign: Problem-posing and designing political 'tasks'

While group members articulated this long-term goal in relation to the problem(s) identified through our design processes, this ability to name the 'things of the situation' (Schön 1983) on a large scale did not always generate understanding of how to either organize or to design together. To design a campaign that reflected and furthered the group's mission and bring it to Oaklanders, the problem had to be posed on multiple scales together, considering both a vision for the future and a plan for the immediate present. In meetings leading up to the group's decision to take up a campaign, CR members discussed both this context and the kind of campaign they wanted to begin. These conversations shaped our understandings and articulations of the 'problem' and possible interventions into it. One member, Jeanne, raised interlocking concerns:

> I … think that Oaklanders are ready to build something together and not just battle the cops. While I'm definitely down to keep fighting the cops and I think it's essential, I also wonder what it would be like to try to build something that could move in the direction of 'making the cops obsolete' rather than reacting against and resisting what they do. (personal communication)

This is one example of how the group named the problem they chose to engage. They knew campaigns *against* policing were made more difficult by the way police positioned themselves through public relations efforts, which had been one focus of this conversation, and at the same time, people in Oakland seemed 'ready to build something together'. This recognition suggested possibilities for designing a new way of working, what some in the group called a 'yes' campaign. Their problem-posing began from a political understanding of the PIC that shaped strategies to chip away at its base. This, in turn, determined how we would design together, to what ends and shaped what we would (need to) make.

Freire's argument for 'problem-posing', as a collective and dialogical process of identifying what Schön would call 'the things of the situation', introduced above, offers an expanded, and socio-historically grounded, approach to both theorizing and doing the work of problem-setting, evident in CR's work. Problem-posing, Freire writes (2010: 83), engages people in 'develop[ing] their power to perceive critically *the way they exist* in the world *with which* and *in which* they find themselves; they come to see the world not as a static reality, but a reality in process, in transformation' (emphasis in original). He argues that this takes place through reflection and action, or praxis, creating capacities for doing and changing things by first *seeing* or *perceiving* them.

While Schön (1987) suggests that acts of designing over time hone a designer's experiences and knowing through 'beliefs ... rooted in worlds of our own making that we come to *accept* as reality' (36, emphasis in original), Freire focuses on the critical act of the *perceiving* one's own position. He suggests 'problem-posing' as a way to reveal socially constructed realities with material effects. Both emphasize a constructivist understanding of 'reality', but Freire's focus rests on the actions through which people first see through a theoretically 'static' reality, and imagine and transform the dynamic conditions and boundaries through which it is made and maintained, what he calls 'limit-situations'. These, he argues (2010: 102), 'imply the existence of persons who are directly or indirectly served by these situations, and of those who are negated or curbed by them'. People's critical reflection on their own conditions, and their contexts, Freire (2010: 101) explains, reveals themes – 'ideas, values, concepts, and hopes, as well as the obstacles which impede people's full humanization'. This knowing helps to determine 'tasks', or 'limit-acts', active engagements with limit-situations as what Alvaro Vieira Pinto (as cited in Freire 2010: 99 n. 15) calls the 'real boundaries where all possibilities begin'. These same conditions of knowing, engagement and possibility determine how a problem is imagined in any given design scenario.

As CR members considered taking on a 'yes' campaign shaped by what they wanted to argue for and work towards creating, they did so through an analysis of the limit-situation and by identifying ways to push against its boundaries. Members' conversations about the nature of the problem of policing and about the time- and context-specific problem of how to combat it opened up possibilities for new approaches that could address the 'problems' identified on these multiple scales. The campaign they envisioned grappled with and sought to engage in what Freire (Freire 2010: 102) calls the 'untested feasibility', in this case, alternatives to police in the service of the abolition of policing.

We did this through designing and using systems for internal communication and reflection as well as for outreach and engagement. In the new campaign, the Oakland Power Projects, group members determined 'tasks' through interviews with Oaklanders about their needs for well-being and how to meet those needs without police (Figure 7.2). This allowed us to move through short-term goals with long-term goals in mind (Agid 2016). Our working process raised up differences in how we imagined what would be useful to make, and pushed forward concerns and ideas about how to shape the campaign itself. In this way, problem-posing became a means for imagining both *ways of* building collaborations and *approaches to* grounding design with people focused on social or political change. Rethinking 'problem-setting' through Freire's 'problem-posing' re-casts this intrinsic component of design processes as a collective dynamic engagement with the multiple experiences of participants identifying and revealing 'limit-situations' in dynamic relation to the analysis of larger socio-historical contexts.

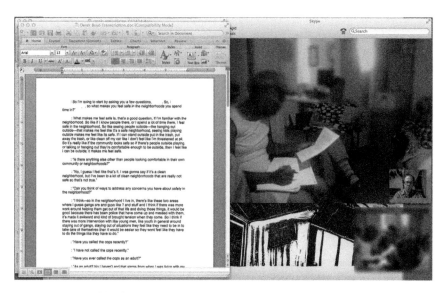

Figure 7.2 CR Oakland No Cops members conducted listening sessions of interviews with Oakland residents to test a tool for gleaning ideas and information (Author's photograph).

Problem-setting is/as political

Schön's efforts to imagine and address the idea of the 'problem' in design has a precursor in Rittel and Webber's 1973 articulation of 'wicked problems', brought into contemporary design by Buchanan (1992). He describes such problems as unwieldy, constantly changing and accessible only in parts. Similarly, Alain Findeli (2001) argued a decade later that designers needed a new epistemological understanding of their practices to account for the prevalence of systems that are contingent, situated and systemic, rather than fixed. He proposed reimagining design as moving a system from 'State A' to 'State B', while recognizing that both designers and stakeholders are a part of, and acting within, it. Findeli acknowledged that 'State B' might reflect designers and stakeholders values, but like Schön, stopped short of critically analysing how those values are determined or what their implications are for different kinds of systems.

Kees Dorst (2015) has recently revisited the issue of values through his articulation of 'framing' as a means for naming, and reimagining, a given 'problem' with people through first conceiving, and then re-framing it to arrive at new (design) ideas. In this way, 'framing' begins to address some of the tricky ethical questions about problem-setting by proposing a role for people central to a site to name its issues and concerns. This process creates space for contesting definitions and ideas intrinsic to the design process through working with multiple, possibly conflicting frames. However, Dorst also insists that design outcomes proposed through framing must be limited to what is possible for and desirable to the 'stakeholders' in the process (2015: 79). This presumes that the people or institutions with power to implement the design must be able to both imagine it and agree to it. Indeed, an implementable system, service or structure is perhaps what a *design* process is unique in being able to accomplish. This is rarely straightforward when designing with people in opposition to state or normalized sociopolitical systems, especially where short-term 'solutions' engender roadblocks to long-term goals. (The prison itself, as Foucault (1995) demonstrated, was imagined as an humanitarian reform to public and corporal punishment.) How, instead, might designers practice problem-posing that strategically *engage with* the limits, conditions and possibilities of imagining 'change'?

In the growing areas of design that seek to create social or political change, or to collaborate with people who are impacted by the systems that designers (and others) seek to change, Schon's (1983: 40) emphasis on 'select[ing] the "things" of the situation … the boundaries of our attention to it … and say[ing] what is wrong and in what directions the situation needs to be changed' is critically important. To meaningfully engage in problem-*posing* means acknowledging that *all* design processes, and the problems set through them, are ideological, not only those based on ideas that run counter to prevailing logics. Designers' and others' beliefs about structures that act on or for people shape our perceptions of limit-situations, and our capacities for and interests in problem-posing (Hall 2009). Sometimes what we perceive differently is shaped by what we have known: what is threatening versus safe; what is familiar versus unusual; what is routine versus exceptional. Designing with people and for social change, in other words, is always already taking place in the spotlight (or shadow) of 'common-sense' notions about anything from 'order' to 'safety', to what a desirable neighbourhood looks (and feels) like.

Reflecting on the shifting nature of the problem of the PIC, another member of the group, Evans, noted:

> Something that we've been talking about as a chapter has been how to identify what are the … windows of opportunity to organize against the PIC. And then how do we move ourselves – our labor, our skills, our resources – into a … formation that takes best advantage of that? … Because we're thinking … of long term resistance in Oakland, or to the logic of policing … there is not this small window of opportunity [that means] we need to figure out how to gather around this particular thing … We're having to do a formation that … seems newer to the organization, and this [design research] project is helping us do that. (personal communication)

Problem-posing emerged as ongoing and cyclical, taking place at multiple scales and in different contexts. The shared political goals of the group that shaped our collaboration did not mean that there weren't also disagreements along the way. Conversation and debate were a means to move towards deeper understandings of policing in Oakland, and of how to use the organizing experiences and tools on hand, as well as new strategies emerging from the work. Members and I uncovered new 'problems', or did 'problem-posing' as a constant part of our long-term practice, which, in turn, shaped the way forward.

Design meant to impact issues related to prisons, policing and surveillance happens in the very particular and contested contexts that produce and maintain the systems designers seek to intervene on, whether to 'improve', 'change' or 'abolish' them. As designers and participants in design processes, we must ask how problem-posing in a design context is informed by it, and how it shapes design processes with people. This opens up possibilities for the 'controversies' (Bjögvinsson et al. 2012) that emerge through discourse and the negotiation of meanings and goals that are often central to participatory design. Following Lucy Suchman's (2002: 96) call to 'become answerable for what we learn how to build', I propose that rethinking the positions from which we design, and those through which problems are imagined, is critical. If we engage the contexts of our work and the different relationships we, and those with whom we work or seek to work, have to the 'limit-situations' with which such designing contends, we gain the capacity to be clear and honest about both the present we imagine and the futures for which we are working.

Notes

1 CR members are identified by pseudonyms, and quotes are used with permission.
2 Thorpe (2008, 2010) writes about the value of using design to address 'social' concerns, but presumes a shared sense of what those concerns are and how they can be framed or addressed. Writing on designers' interest in manifesting British prime minister David Cameron's 'Big Society', Montgomery (2010) ignores what it means to design for the elimination of government services. Routson (2012) writes on the role of design in re making a centrally located all inclusive police station/court/jail/social welfare hub but does not reflect on how this might not work the same for everyone. Manzini and Rizzo (2011) assert that Design for Social Innovation can develop shared ideas of sustainability, but do not specify those ideas, or how they may be influenced by different perceptions or experiences.
3 Participatory design, human-centred design, HCI, along with service design and social innovation, foreground people's experiences in setting the problems they contend with. These practices have changed over time, shaped by debates about how and why to involve people in design processes (Parker and Heapy 2006; Morelli 2007; Jégou and Manzini 2008; Sanders and Stappers 2008; Oosterlaken 2009; Sangiori and Meroni 2011; Hargraves and JafariNaimi 2012). A discussion of ongoing debates falls outside the scope of this chapter, but they demonstrate the range of historical and emergent practices in which designing with people is a focus (see Bannon and Ehn 2012; Bjögvinsson et al. 2012; DiSalvo et al. 2012; Lee 2008; Light 2010; Light and Akama 2014; Manzini and Rizzo 2011; and Suchman 2002 for some key arguments).
4 Members evaluate campaigns and projects through CR's mission statement to be sure they do not run counter to it. It is published at: http://criticalresistance.org/about/
5 This rhetoric is being reinvigorated in contemporary political strategies in the United States and internationally.
6 See, for example, the popular news media coverage of what gets called 'mass incarceration', exemplified in this *New York Times* editorial from May 2014: 'End Mass-Incarceration Now', 24 May 2014, http://www.nytimes.com/2014/05/25/opinion/sunday/end-mass-incarceration-now.html?_r=0

7   See also the Possible Futures Lab website: http://pflab.rhul.ac.uk/
8   See ADPSR, Prison Design Boycott and Prison Alternatives Initiative, http://www.
     adpsr.org/home/prison_alternatives_initiative1

Bibliography

Agid, S. (2011) 'How Can We Design Something to Transition People from a System
    That Doesn't Want to Let Them Go?': Social Design and Its Political Contexts, *Design
    Philosophy Papers*, 3, 1–11.
Agid, S. (2012) 'World-Making: Theory/Practice Practices in Design', *Design and Culture*,
    4, 1: 27–54.
Agid, S. (2016) It's your project, but it's not necessarily your work…: Infrastructuring,
    situatedness, and designing relational practice. *Proceedings of the 14th Participatory
    Design Conference, Aarhus, Denmark*, 1, pp. 81–90.
Bacchi, C. L. (2009) *Analysing Policy: What's the Problem Represented to Be*, Frenchs
    Forest, N.S.W: Pearson Higher Education AU.
Bannon, L. J. and Ehn, P. (2012) 'Design: Design Matters in Participatory Design',
    in J. Simonsen and T. Robertson (eds), *Routledge Handbook of Participatory Design*,
    New York: Routledge, pp. 37–63.
Bjögvinsson, E., Ehn, P. and Hillgren, P.-A. (2012) 'Agonistic Participatory Design:
    Working with Marginalized Social Movements', *CoDesign*, 8, 2–3: 127–144.
Bohrman, R. and Murakawa, N. (2005) 'Remaking Big Government: Immigration and
    Crime Control in the United States', in J. Sudbury (ed.), *Global Lockdown: Race,
    Gender, and the Prison Industrial Complex*, New York: Routledge, pp. 109–126.
Bonsieppe, G. (2006) 'Design and Democracy', *Design Issues*, 22, 2: 27–34.
Buchanan, R. (1992) 'Wicked Problems in Design Thinking', *Design Issues*, 8, 2: 5–21.
Burch, M. (2014) *Keywords in critical prison studies II: We used to think…but now we
    know: 'Crime'*, Paper presented at the American Studies Association, 6–9 November,
    Los Angeles, CA [unpublished].
Carson, E. A. (2015) *Prisoners in 2014* [online]. U.S. Bureau of Justice Statistics. Available
    at: http://www.bjs.gov/index.cfm?ty=pbdetail&iid=5387 (accessed 15 June 2016).
Clement, A., McPhail, B., Smith, M. L. and Ferenbok, J. (2012) Probing, mocking, and
    prototyping: Participatory approaches to identity infrastructuring. *Proceedings of the
    12th Participatory Design Conference: Research Papers*, pp. 21–30.
Coles-Kemp, L. (2013) *Families disconnected by prison: A scoping study in barriers
    to engagement* [online]. London: Proboscis. Available at: http://bookleteer.com/
    publication.html?id=2784 (accessed 1 March 2016).
Critical Resistance Abolition Toolkit Workgroup (2004) *The CR abolition organizing
    toolkit* [online]. Available at: http://criticalresistance.org/resources/the-abolitionist-
    toolkit/ (accessed 1 March 2016).
Davis, Angela Y. (2003) *Are Prisons Obsolete?* New York: Seven Stories Press.
DiSalvo, C., Clement, A. and Pipek, V. (2012) 'Communities: Participatory Design
    for, with and by Communities', in J. Simonsen and T. Robertson (eds), *Routledge
    International Handbook of Participatory Design*, Routledge: New York, 2012,
    pp. 182–209.
Dorst, K. (2015) *Frame Innovation: Creating New Thinking by Design* [eBook], Palo Alto,
    CA: The MIT Press. Available at: ProQuest ebrary.

Ehn, P. (2008) Participation in design things. *Proceedings of the Tenth Anniversary Conference on Participatory Design Research Papers, Indiana University*, pp. 92–101.

The failure of enforcement tactic and the need for effective public safety strategies [online]. Justice Policy Institute. Available at: http://www.justicepolicy.org/uploads/justicepolicy/documents/07-07_rep_gangwars_gc-ps-ac-jj.pdf (accessed 15 June 2016).

Findeli, A. (2001) 'Rethinking Design Education for the 21st Century: Theoretical, Methodological, and Ethical Discussion', *Design Issues*, 17, 1: 5–17.

Foucault, M. (1977) *Discipline and Punish: The Birth of the Prison*. Translated by A. Sheridan, 1995. New York: Vintage.

Freire, P. (1970) *Pedagogy of the Oppressed*. Translated by M. Bergman Ramos, 2010. New York: Continuum.

Fry, T. (2010) *Design and Politics*, New York: Bloomsbury Publishing.

Fry, T. and Dilnot, C. (2003) 'Manifesto for Re-directive Design', *Design Philosophy Papers*, 2: n.p.

Gilmore, R. W. (2007) *Golden Gulag: Prisons, Surplus, Crisis and Opposition in Globalizing California*, Berkeley, CA: University of California Press.

Hall, S. (1997 [2009]) 'The Work of Representation', in S. Hall (ed.), *Representation: Cultural Representations and Signifying Practices*, London: Sage Publications and Open University, pp. 36–51.

Hall, S., Critcher, C., Jefferson, T., Clarke, J. and Roberts, B. (1978 [2013]) *Policing the Crisis: Mugging, the State and Law and Order*, 2nd Edition, New York: Palgrave Macmillan. References refer to the 2013 edition.

Haraway, D. J. (1991) *Simians, Cyborgs, and Women: The Reinvention of Nature*, New York: Routledge.

Hargraves, I. and JafariNaimi, N. (2012) Questioning the Centre of Human-Centred Design. *Zoontechnica: The Journal of Redirective Design* [online], 2. Available at: http://zoontechnica.com/occ_web/issue_02/issue_02.default.html#pg_issue_02.default.html (accessed 1 March 2016).

Herzing, R. (2015) Big dreams and bold steps toward a police-free future. *Truthout* [online], 16 September. Available at: http://www.truth-out.org/opinion/item/32813-big-dreams-and-bold-steps-toward-a-police-free-future (accessed 15 June 2016).

Jégou, F. and Manzini, E. (eds) (2008) *Collaborative Services: Social Innovation and Design for Sustainability*, Milan: Edizioni Polidesign.

Kandaswamy, P. (2008) 'State Austerity and the Racial Politics of Same-Sex Marriage in the US', *Sexualities*, 11, 6: 706–725.

Karasti, H., Baker, K. S. and Millerand, F. (2010) 'Infrastructure Time: Long-Term Matters in Collaborative Development', *Computer Supported Cooperative Work*, 19 (3–4): 377–415.

Lee, Y. (2008) 'Design Participation Tactics: The Challenges and New Roles of Designers in the Co-Design Process', *CoDesign*, 4, 1: 31–50.

Light, A. (2010) HCI as heterodoxy: The queering of interaction design. *Proceedings of CHI*, pp. 1–8.

Light, A. and Akama, Y. (2012) The human touch: From method to participatory practice in facilitating design with communities. *Proceedings of the 12th Participatory Design Conference: Research Papers*, 1, pp. 61–70.

Light, A. and Akama, Y. (2014) Structuring future social relations: The politics of care in participatory practice. *Proceedings of the 13th Participatory Design Conference: Research Papers*, 1, pp. 151–160.

Manzini, E. (2014) 'Making Things Happen: Social Innovation in Design', *Design Issues*, 30, 1: 57–66.

Manzini, E. and Rizzo, F. (2011) 'Small Project/Large Changes: Participatory Design as an Open Participated Process', *CoDesign*, 7, 3–4: 199–215.

Monmaney, T. (2000) Rampart-like scandal rocks Oakland justice system, politics, *Los Angeles Times* [online], 11 December. Available at: http://articles.latimes.com/print/2000/dec/11/news/mn-64091 (accessed 15 April 2016).

Montgomery, A. (2010) 'Designers Want to Be Part of David Cameron's "Big Society"', *Design Week*, 25, 30: 7–7.

Morelli, N. (2007) 'Social Innovation and New Industrial Contexts: Can Designers "Industrialize" Socially Responsible Solutions?', *Design Issues*, 23, 4: 3–21.

Moughty, S. (2011) The Oakland police department's troubled history, *PBS: Frontline* [online], 27 October. Available at: http://www.pbs.org/wgbh/frontline/article/the-oakland-police-departments-troubled-history/ (accessed 15 April 2016).

Muhammad, K. (2010) *Condemnation of Blackness: Race, Crime, and the Making of Modern Urban America*, Cambridge, MA: Harvard University Press.

Oosterlaken, I. (2009) 'Design for Development: A Capability Approach', *Design Issues*, 25, 4: 91–102.

Parker, S. and Heapy, J. (2006) *The Journey to the Interface. How Public Service Design Can Connect Users to Reform*, London: Demos.

Rios, V. M. (2011) *Punished: Policing the Lives of Black and Latino Boys*, New York: New York University Press.

Robertson, T. and Simonsen, J. (2012) 'Participatory Design: An Introduction', in J. Simonsen and T. Robertson (eds), *Routledge Handbook of Participatory Design*. New York: Routledge, pp. 1–18.

Routson, E. (2012) Designing a new justice system. *Policy x Design Blog, Public Policy Lab* [online blog], 10 April. Available at: http://publicpolicylab.org/2012/04/designing-a-new-justice-system/ (accessed 1 March 2016).

Sanders, E. and Stappers, P. J. (2008) 'Co-Creation and the New Landscapes of Design', *CoDesign*, 4, 1: 5–18.

Sangiori, D. and Meroni, A. (2011) *Design for Services*, Burlington: Ashgate Publishing.

Schmitt, John, Warner, Kris, and Gupta, Sarika. (2010) *The High Budgetary Cost of Incarceration*, Washington, DC: Center for Economic and Policy Research.

Schön, D. A. (1983) *The Reflective Practitioner: How Professionals Think in Action*, New York: Basic Books.

Schön, D. A. (1987) *Educating the Reflective Practitioner: Toward a New Design for Teaching and Learning in the Professions*, San Francisco, CA: Jossey-Bass.

Schön, D. A. (1988) 'Designing: Rules, Types and Worlds', *Design Studies*, 9, 3: 181–190.

Sperry, R. (2014) 'Discipline and Punish', *Architectural Review*, 235, 1406: 22–23.

Suchman, L. (2002) 'Located Accountabilities in Technology Production', *Scandinavian Journal of Information Systems*, 14, 2: 91–105.

Thorpe, A. (2008) SES! (Social Equity and Sustainability), *Innovation*, 27, 1: 20–23.

Thorpe, A. (2010) 'Design for social impact – Is it activism?' *Design Activism Blog* [online blog], 15 September. Available at: www.designactivism.net/archives/262 (accessed 1 December 2015).

8

The Nature of 'Obligation' in Doing Design with Communities: Participation, Politics and Care

Ann Light and Yoko Akama

This chapter examines the commitments that designers and design researchers make – or perhaps ignore or neglect – when they embark on work in the unbounded field of designing with and for communities. This work is growing in prominence, fuelled by a desire to contribute meaningfully to the world and our collective futures. We set about here revealing the trickiness of designing with communities when a designer comes into an environment to make change – and ask what responsibility we should take in responding to complex social systems.

Design comes historically out of industrial contexts, such as the workplace and corporate lab (into which sample participants are invited), which are clearly bounded by role, scope and intention. By contrast, in designing with nebulous and dynamic clusters of people, classical distinctions, such as those between 'designers' and 'users', may collapse, and, instead, many people can become collaborators in pursuit of a common, often evolving, objective. If we are looking for trickiness, we have found it here.

With this trickiness as a starting point, ethics cannot be viewed as a static condition, but, instead, something created and manifested in the relations of dynamic ecologies of actions and roles. We consider how we can understand *obligation* and *care* as two contrasting, sometimes complementary, lenses with which to trouble our relations as designers in emergent and unpredictable engagements. By obligation, we refer to ways we attend to explicit duties and rights in a structural politics that pre-exists our encounters. In care, we offer a concept that speaks to an ecological view of relations made in the moment. We might see this unstable entanglement of perspectives embodied in the figure of the Trickster; a figure that unsettles and provokes, rather than providing solutions.

The *Everyday Disruptions* project (EIA 2014) invoked the Trickster as part of co-design project exploring how social action is inspired, designed and maintained, characterizing the figure in these ways:

> Trickster is not a comfortable figure to rally around, not bright and hopeful like the Hero, not good or bad. Trickster guards against pomposity, superiority and hubris.

One minute funny, the next sinister, Trickster is the perfect image of this time, where by our very existence – the way we consume, eat, work, move around – many of us are implicated in violence and destruction, sometimes under our very noses, often outsourced to somewhere else.

Trickster does not lead us, but disrupts us, keeps us on our toes. One can try to be a follower of Trickster, but Trickster is no guru or icon. Sometimes Trickster saves the day, other times we may find ourselves betrayed and left to rot. Trickster is a mirror, constantly reminding us of our real and imagined imperfections while equally showing us the power of our humour, creativity, adaptability and resilience. Of our power in the face of power'.

Becoming irreverent generates agency, through a critical standpoint and by shifting energies; speaking from decentred discourse with a serious (not solemn) voice; resisting solutions and not being nice, clean, shiny or pure; welcoming the trickster and understanding that role – especially at times of crisis in opposition EIA 2014, n.p.

Doing responsible design

All designers have to consider the effect of the designs they produce, but there are particular aspects relevant to working with communities and these are what we address in this chapter. We need only think about the design of weapons (see Chapter 1 of this volume) or of public spaces (see Chapter 11 of this volume) to see that shaping materials has consequences. In working directly with other people, not only do the outcomes matter, but there are short- and long-term impacts that come from the collaborations of the group, beyond the use of the final product or system. These are a meeting of the immediate engagements of the process and the wider context of the social and political realm in which they take place.

Something particular happens when we undertake a participatory approach, sharing decisions and evaluations. Perhaps the designers are not the only moral custodians shaping the process and outcome. Whose version of ethics pertains? Our idea of design facilitation is well documented (in Light et al. 2011; Light and Akama 2012, 2014). In these contexts all the participants can be considered as 'design researchers', engaged in 'mutual learning' (Robertson et al. 2014) and exploring the best way to achieve their ends together. There is no gatekeeper to relationships, either during or after the design process. Instead, we are in the unmade world of emergent issues, unexpected tensions and unpredictable outcomes. Things can reverse fast and progress does not follow simple lines.

In this spirit, Meskell and Pels (2005) argue that ethics cannot be abstracted from the way in which research is practised. If guidelines for conduct are needed, they should not take the shape of rules assuming expertise beforehand, out of context, but facilitate the negotiation of expertise. Particular interventions are thus 'performances' in a particular setting, open to reformulation and public negotiation. Enshrined in this approach to ethics is a broader issue of relevance for anyone intervening in a complex situation and seeking to make change in the materials or social structures to be found there. Collaborative research on the spot is often the only way to find out how to be ethical in that situation. In this rejection of the traditional way ethics is framed, we embrace other moralities of knowing, such as trust and social learning. And we have to consider afresh how these happen in every situation and at every moment. This has implications for how we understand a designer's role, as we go on to discuss. For instance, it turns any design project into a research project.

First, we look at what kinds of issues will inform these on-the-ground insights and lead to an ethical position. For that we need to consider, more generally, whom we are talking about. Who are these people? And how are they arranged?

Then, we consider how the two approaches of obligation and care can interrelate in our understanding of an embedded and embodied ethics.

Messing about in communities

We talk about 'communities' to define something almost indefinable. The groups we mean in this context are not linked by workplace or any other single umbrella structure. If we look too closely, community can melt into hundreds of separate people all with their own priorities.

For instance, consider a village in a remote part of internal Ghana, such as the one in which the first author has worked. We might think we would be talking about one community, a group of people from the Ashanti region with some commonality of culture, history and experience. Certainly, the village has a specific and observable geography, marked by fields belonging to the villagers and cut off from the main road by a long dirt track. Things that happen there affect everyone. There is, for instance, one water source and everyone collects their water there, even if there is a hierarchy in who carries it. Yet, one member of the village is from the very north of Ghana, a Fulani: in other words, of a group which, while still semi-nomadic, has become distributed and settled in many parts of West Africa. And the teacher, as is policy, is from outside the area, posted there as part of getting a teaching job. Coming to the village and working there is approved by the Elders of the village in concert with a Chief, so there is a clear entry point and an etiquette to learn and follow, but that is not the whole story. There are currents of difference that make the identity of the village more complicated. As Merritt and Stolterman (2012) point out, cultural hybridity is a norm in a postcolonial world.

And if we are doing research in partnership with Indigenous nations in Australia, as the other author is, there are contrasting cultural dynamics. Nations, such as the Ngarrindjeri or Gunditjmara, have a particular identity, culture, language, country, kinship network and eldership system of passing down knowledge systems. They politicize their identity as *nations* – self-defined collectives that have authority over issues that matter to *that* group – rejecting the label and perception of a pan-Aboriginal *community* to signify that there are multiple self-determining and self-governing nations in pursuit of nation-determined social, economic, cultural and political goals. Yet, determining borders is hard and, once determined, these may not remain static. For some Indigenous nations, this is an acute issue of governance and decision-making because colonialism and government policies led to the break-up of families and kinship ties, often forcing different nations to settle together in a single reserve, mission or land. Some are responding to this state of affairs by trying to reunite fragmented members and build a nation, and others are learning how to work together under a single governing system.

Stepping into such contexts demands a heightened consciousness of structures, customs, relations and boundaries.

In the multicultural areas where we usually work (in the UK and Australia), urban sprawl and the 'melting-pot' that has resulted from many waves of immigration make the picture even more complicated. Sen (2006) talks of the 'disparate pulls – of history, culture, language, politics, profession, family, comradeship, and so on [… which] cannot all be drowned in a single-minded celebration only of community' (p. 38). Life is multi-threaded, down to the level of individuals who identify as 'multi-local' (Selasi 2014). Furthermore:

> Designers and participants can freely move among their cultural identities, taking up whatever cultural blend is situationally appropriate – within boundaries of pre-determined cultural positions. Of course, each person possesses several concurrent cultural identities, going beyond those of nationality and ethnicity. Designers should reflexively observe changes in cultural positions and correlating situational influences and similarly seek to discover the cultural hybridities of design participants. (Merritt and Stolterman 2012)

Responding to this hybridity, theorists have shifted the emphasis from geographic boundaries and lived experience of neighbourhood to *community as imagined*, a symbolic structure made significant by shared cultural concerns and 'meaning' (Anderson 1983; Cohen 1985). The slippage between community as an actual group and as a felt or *imagined* category has prompted anthropologists like Pink (2008) to forgo the term, instead examining experiences of social relations situated in a physical environment. Similarly, Light, Miskelly and Thompson (2008) explain why they do not use the word in their analysis of habitat, but prefer *locale* or *neighbourhood* to refer to an area of people. Working to make the term useful, Akama and Ivanka (2010) describe ways in which their participatory methods facilitate awareness and reveal tacit knowledge about who and what *community* is for local residents, to 'avoid "imagined" notions of a community that can hide social heterogeneity' (p. 11). Likewise, writing about the growing interest in participatory design work in communities, DiSalvo and colleagues (2013) suggest the importance of negotiating the plurality that exists within them. They offer a useful framing of participatory design as 'work that foregrounds the social constructs and relations of groups in settings that include, but go well beyond, formal organization structures' (2013: 183).

In other words, *community*, the term, is tricky, just as working with community is tricky on the ground. Yet, this elusiveness is not often unpacked in design literature. The detail of encounters is often ignored, and there is a lack of analysis and a tendency towards uncritical do-goodism (Bødker 2015). Thus, on the ground, *community* is an opaque notion. Accounts do little to specify the awkward features, such as the power dynamics.

There are reasons for this. In social settings without formal institutional shape, nothing is standardized and practices are heavily and non-systematically interwoven. Beginnings of engagement are less clear-cut and so are endings. There are projects that continue long after their official end. For example, Light occasionally works with the participants in a project that notionally ended in 2008, but is still running (see Clarke et al. 2016).[1] Informal arrangements can allow for flexibility and creativity, but can also create problems – such as mismatched expectations – without offering easy ways to resolve these. Where there are no representatives and intermediaries, keeping everyone briefed and maintaining a dialogue can be a major part of the work.

All these factors mean design work cannot be neatly delineated: it has become unbounded. Design often comes with a large degree of serendipity and some unexpected circumstances (Storni 2012). Some of these circumstances are independent of the design context. Some are introduced by it. Unboundedness, then, belies any simple ethical approach, giving cause for a framing that prioritizes rights and responsibilities and also the mutual concern of a different politics. In the next section, we introduce the idea of using obligation and care as frames to consider our engagements.

Choosing our ethical path

It is apparent from the discussion above that to work together is an ethically complex business – it is tricky in terms of what to do and also why. We have looked at the nature of making change and begun to consider the particular ethical issues raised by the social structures we might work among. Here we compare approaches to ethics, looking at the politics of both rights and mutuality.

The dominant ethical position in participatory design (PD) can be summed up by PD scholar Joan Greenbaum, who, more than twenty years ago, argued that 'as system designers, we have the *obligation* to provide people with the opportunity to influence their own lives' (1993: 47, author's emphasis). Here, we have an understanding of obligation defined by rights and principles that are acknowledged among a group of people, in this case, participatory design researchers.

We most often meet rights-based ethical concerns in dealing with people's personal information. We know, for example, that confidential information should not be rendered public through our actions. This is legislated for in various ways across the world, so we know this is a rights-based consideration.

We contrast this obligation with the feminist notion of care. For Puig de la Bellacasa (2012), 'care' is a pre-condition of interdependency; for 'not only do relations involve care, care is itself relational' (p. 198). Interdependency is inevitable, not something forced upon us by moral order, but a condition of living, and 'for life to be livable, it needs to be fostered' (Puig de la Bellacasa 2012). We are obliged to each other, but it is not a personal ethical relation; it is a fact of sharing a world.

Based on this interpretation, we have understood care as existing in the practices of creating space for people to come together to re-examine relationships, re-make their environments, re-imagine familiar places and to reflect, learn and debate about making futures (Light and Akama 2014). It follows that *designing with care* is to structure ways to support sustainable and flourishing relations in ecologies of beings and materials.

This is a different understanding of ethical relations to the rights-based notion of obligation. If we are already intimately connected to everything and this primordial interrelatedness precedes our actions, there is an ethics, but not one of rights. Instead, we have the call of pre-existing mutuality, from the symbiosis of our bodies to the collectivism of our preferences. How does acknowledging this mutuality affect the ethics of designing?

Obligation and care

We can look at the interplay between the approaches of obligation and care to produce an embedded and embodied ethics.

Participants United (Light et al. 2011) was a research project to explore how community participants themselves recommended they should be treated in design research. It took the ethics of informed consent particularly seriously, working for half a day with each of four community groups brought in from former participatory projects to prepare for a two-day meeting at which issues of inclusion, representation and credit could be discussed. The outcomes involved a policy on 'voice' and appropriate uses of anonymity, suggesting that participants' contributions should not be obscured, but credit for ideas and opinions (and intellectual property) given where due.

In the identification of areas to consider such as voice and credit (Light et al. 2011), we hear similar concerns to those expressed by Robertson and Wagner (2013: 65) that people have 'rights to represent their own activities to others, rather than having others do this for them'. The work is framed in discussion of hierarchies, power relations and institutional frameworks that marginalize the voices and interests of participants. Those marginalized by organizational politics can also include designers and researchers, who might be seen to wield power in terms of choosing how to represent others in their work, but who may have no impact where they seek it, in changing policy at the organizational or national level.

While this valuably demonstrates principles of equity, transparency and respect, this could be viewed as a rights-based way of enacting obligation that shapes the way informed consent is sought and given, credit and recognition are shared, and research disseminated.

However, if we look closely at many of the observations, we also see a different current running through the work. There is the fun of the event and the chance to learn about others' lives. Normally, this is not a part of what we see as the work of a project. While the Londoners involved in *Participants United* were not impressed to be going to a small northern English town known principally for its rainfall, it did cause one man to remember that he had boxed in that town in his youth. This same group had its conditions of participation (that it involved having fun) fulfilled by a group meal followed by drinking and reminiscing at the hotel bar before the next day's work. The stamina, stories and warmth of the three men that came north informed the whole occasion.

So looking at *Participants United* from a care perspective, there is a great deal that normally remains unreported, such as fun, pleasure and enjoyment of each other's company, which became a strong motivating factor for many to continue participating in the research. This is why sharing a meal, drinks, a walk or an informal conversation can often matter in a project, not because of research integrity or obligation, but because these activities can begin to knit a considered way of engaging with one another that is appropriate and specific to that encounter. In taking the time to attune and sensitize to each other, we are able to make connections. These human dimensions may sound peripheral and superfluous to ethical considerations, but care acknowledges the huge role that building trusting relationships plays, shaping our willingness to take part.

If we now look at the mechanics of 'informed consent', which takes nothing on trust, trust can be regarded as a 'faulty' way of knowing because it cannot be publicly verifiable. But the very nature of trust is that it emerges from a personal rather than a professional relationship. It is situated in the moment and in the relations of the encounter as well as the wider social and political frames of our meeting. Arguably, trust is another kind of knowledge into which people develop insight over years of experience with social situations. In the case of *Participants United*, trust pre-existed the project, grown in enduring relationships between research partners.

This kind of knowing is rarely credited. Trusting people is seen as a prerequisite for doing the 'real' project, not a kind of informed judgement. To see it as informed judgement is to invert normal research discourse. Yet, it is sensible and fair that any judgement made in a workshop situation is about the people as much as the activities.

This introduces different responsibilities for the leader of any engagement work, since it delegates some judgements about judgements – we allow our leaders to have expertise on our behalf if we trust them to do right by us. This may be good and proper, and possibly easier and more fun than taking responsibility for understanding – at outset – all the stages to come. We can have trust or we can plough through all the negotiations that such trust replaces.

If our choice is to delegate judgement, there are responsibilities in both directions: when we allow someone to take us on a journey, we can remain alive to the need to revisit what we take on trust and what we can offer as our understanding of the options grows. And for the journey leader, we show care by revisiting our fellows' potential to shape their role in events as their familiarity and knowledge grow. This is the evolving ethics of Meskell and Pels (2005): dynamic and negotiated in context.

However, if we operate with a care ethic as dominant, it is worth remembering that it is not particularly attuned to managing inequalities. It has its own politics, one that flattens hierarchies and emphasizes assemblages, so one weakness levelled at the care ethics position is that it depoliticizes the world by leaving aside structural inequalities and other impacts of persistent social trends. When we consider rights and obligations, we start from a position that emphasizes difference and addresses it; with care we start from commonalities and this may obscure concerns like privilege and access to power.

Navigating obligation and care

If we return to the examples above, we now have a vocabulary for delving further into relations. We can review ethics as obligation and entangle it with a narrative of caring and mutuality.

Back at the Ghanaian village, we can consider the effect of giving disposable cameras to young people, both girls and boys, to record their daily experience. Although previously discussed with the Chief of the village, the actual introduction caused uproar. Cameras of any kind are considered novel and valuable resources by the villagers and thus should be given to the people of greatest status, i.e. older men. It took a few weeks of discussion for relations between the Elders and visitors to settle back down, with younger people allowed to document their lives. It is worth considering whether, without the glamour of visitors from the Global North, this change would have been allowed. And we might also ask whether it should have taken place at all. Is the visitors' notion of gender equality more important than the practices of another culture? The hierarchy is fairly powerful and very fixed in this instance. It almost resembles a workplace, in that there is a management structure to consult. Even so, different opinions emerged, influenced by who was consulted, in what order, and what transpired between requesting permission and carrying out the activities. Discussion on the ground, particularly between mothers, had an impact, as did their sense of what the project team would use the pictures for. This was the more entangled view of what went on. Finally, when the young people of the village went to the town to see their daily lives on the internet, placed alongside school children from the UK, the view in the village changed again and the pictures became a source of pride.

Similarly, in working to support Indigenous nation building in Australia, there are protocols to observe, trust to build, and relations to make and acknowledge. While the Indigenous nations directly involved in the project are located close to urban cities, 'outsiders', such as researchers, must seek permission to visit their country (obligation) and build respectful trusting relationships (acts of care) before any work can commence. Seeking permission in this context is not to follow a regulatory framework, but is undertaken as cultural practice. A 'welcome to country' is given by an Elder or a traditional custodian of the nation to welcome other people to their land. This is usually accompanied by 'acknowledgment of country' by the visitors as a gesture of respect and gratitude. This places the relations at a point where mutuality and obligation meet.

In the same example, the act of documenting stories raises questions of which nation person gets to speak and about what. This is again about rights, though practised through cultural laws and a consciousness of relationships. In discussion with Wiradjuri Elders and nation members, the research team proposed a digital platform where nation members can be invited to upload their stories of nation building. Some of these stories are personal and intimate, speaking of hope, excitement and empowerment through a strengthened nation. Care here features in such stories of connection to one another and to country, and also in the way the digital platform seeks to share and inspire more to join in nation building. However, obligation requires questions on who decides the appropriateness and degree of the cultural knowledge to be revealed. And, once uploaded, who owns the stories? Indigenous people have rights to protect their traditional knowledge, practices and cultures based on the principle of self-determination. Here, we see the tension between obligation and care that is difficult to navigate. The complexity of negotiating different systems is a real and contemporary living experience.

Getting group consent is generally tricky. Making media together is a complex instance of this, because it has the power to represent. What can be shared and made public, who decides and how is of concern. Carelessness can provoke anxiety and give offence, result in exposure where not wanted or ownership neglected (so a thorough approvals process cannot be overestimated[2]). Who gets to speak on behalf of a 'community', group or organization is highly political and may revolve round what people interpret as 'being heard'. Perhaps an individual cannot ethically make this decision on behalf of others but needs to involve a larger cluster of people. Is every voice needed? And if people come and go from a group, are they part of decision-making? Some people may have a hazy picture of what is going on, but that does not stop them from voicing vociferous opinions. Can any informal group absolutely describe its boundaries? Although the language of consent is rights based, again we are back to the fuzzier arena of trust and care.

We have drawn attention to unboundedness already, as a defining quality of working with groups of people, even in seemingly formal settings. Its effects creep into all parts of the design process. For instance, in our work, we have observed very different selection criteria for engagement. Two examples can make this distinction.

In participatory work to research a tool that connects small producers in developing countries with interested consumers across the world (see Light and Anderson 2009), activities took place with a wine collective in Chile and coffee growers in southern India. UK research funding to explore the cultural and technical issues was inevitably limited, but it meant that we had considerable freedom to choose our sites of engagement as studies for a wider implementation. Partners were chosen to give contrast (to investigate the design space), based on existing relations (to benefit from enough trust to make the research possible). But it was always in the researchers' minds that we could have worked with other exemplars and, if we had, the knowledge might have evolved in another direction (Light and Anderson 2009). As important ethically, we might also have grown to understand (care) and intervened in the lives of (obligation) different groups of people. This is not to say that design solutions are generalizable; they necessarily exclude other choices in meeting the challenges that emerge. But in dealing with a large transnational consortium of partners, it is possible to see alternatives that are never realized, revealing both the disruptive nature of design research and the ethics of selection and reach. As no one would directly benefit from the tool within the life of the project, other benefits of collaborating, such as access to new marketing information, were a part of the trade for partners' time. This was felt to be an ethical obligation, but was enacted through time spent informally learning of each other's networks and goals.

By contrast, in Akama's (2015) research on strengthening resilience for disasters there was a clear research rationale for picking a specific group, who are living in geographical areas where risks of fire are high, and sharing this reasoning with participants. As such, decisions are made in order to work with residents to mitigate the specific risks in their locale. This means that in another geographic area, the people and plans for mitigation will be different, but that is not an arbitrary feature – it is a response to the locatedness of the activity. Aspects may be replicable, but no single generalized solution is being sought. The very different purposes of the work produced a very different connection to the people with whom the team worked.

The end point of the activity in which we involve others can therefore be seen as a significant element in the relations we construct – so how we answer to people is partly determined by how we see their role in the project and our longer-term intentions (see Light and Akama 2012 for more detail on how purpose and activities interact).

But we are not in control of how relations evolve, regardless of whether one is talking about one community, many, or whether one eschews the term totally; existing structures and conditions affect who is involved and what can happen. Sometimes it matters which combinations of gender, ethnicity and class are represented. Personal issues such as old rivalries, friendships and networks of support predate anything happening in the moment. These relations are challenged as part of coming together every time any action is proposed or taken. Sometimes the challenge is deliberate. But it can also transpire through happenstance, ignorance and poor planning. Even the mere presence of an outsider can change the trajectory of relations and decisions. And all these considerations are set against an inherited set of norms about our place in the world and society, strengthened or questioned by our behaviour together. All this speaks to a care model.

Conclusion

A view of our work from both obligation and care perspectives produces a fuller and more educative account of designing with people than either one. We do not aim to provide a theoretical synthesis in conclusion, and, instead, summarize our observations that speak to how obligation and care constitute an integral part of our practices. This means that we leave the question open to the reader to consider how these dimensions play out in their own work, without suggesting that one is more important than the other. Instead, responding to the theme of the book, we draw attention to the inversions that exist between the rights-based nature of obligation and the relations-based nature of care. If the figure of the Trickster is to be invoked, it is in turning the politics of engagement through 180 degrees to emphasize a wholly different set of concerns and then require that you keep both in mind.

Articulating this as a marriage, we might argue that the social world is a fluid, emergent and distributed socio-material assembly of actions. We might then regard our unit of engagement as *people taking action together* in social groups, embodied networks, shared locales and communities of interest. Connectedness is forged by the 'doing together', the performance of collective tasks and, through these, the performance of relationships, their tensions and differences.

Within this performance, design can align interests through which 'matters of concern' are negotiated among participants (Bannon and Ehn 2013). Bannon and Ehn ask that participatory design should enable ways in which people can participate in continuous co-creation of socio-material collectives. Doing so would allow for a more profound engagement with designing that goes beyond 'helping out' the designer with his or her project, to sharing ownership of some of the processes and the related negotiations that must accompany collaborative work.

We agree with Greenbaum about the obligation we have to 'provide people with the opportunity to influence their own lives' (see Light and Akama 2014). Yet, we have also demonstrated how this view can inadvertently overemphasize the importance of political obligation, further cementing a particular way of knowing. The discussion of care is also to argue for why building specific kinds of relationships matters in design and to acknowledge their importance when collaborating with groups of people. Care matters because 'we *become* through others' care as well as our own: the participants and partners of our research, our colleagues, peers, students, families and countless other beings and things' (Light and Akama 2014: 159). Recognizing this pre-existing mutuality is fundamental for the participatory designer who cares about taking everyone along in fellow journeying.

Notes

1   In this project, a loose assembly of engineers, artists and others support a group of retired East End men to build water turbines to solve energy problems on the River Thames in an environmental fashion.
2   See http://ccmc.commedia.org.uk/introduction-to-creating-media/guidelines-for-making-media-with-communities/for guidance

Bibliography

Akama, Yoko (2015) 'Continuous Re-configuring of Invisible Social Structures', in A. Bruni, L. L. Parolin and C. Schubert (eds), *Designing Technology Work Organization and Vice Versa*, Wilmington, DE: Vernon Press, pp. 163–183.

Akama, Yoko and Ivanka, T. (2010) 'What community? Facilitating awareness of 'community' through playful triggers'. *Proc. PDC '10*: 11–20.

Anderson, B. (1983) *Imagined Communities: Reflections on the Origin and Spread of Nationalism*, London: Verso.

Bannon, L. J. and Ehn, P. (2013) 'Design: Design Matters in Participatory Design', in J. Simonsen and T. Robertson (eds), *Routledge International Handbook of Participatory Design*, London and New York: Routledge, pp. 37–63.

Bødker, S. (2015) Using IT to 'Do Good' in Communities? *Journal of Community Informatics*, 11, 2. Retrieved from http://ci-journal.org/index.php/ciej/article/view/1151

Clarke, R., Briggs, J., Light, A. and Wright, P. (2016) 'Situated encounters with socially engaged art in community-based design'. *Proc. Designing Interactive Systems (DIS '16)*.

Cohen, A. P. (1985) *The Symbolic Construction of Community*, London: Routledge.

DiSalvo, C., Clement, A. and Pipek, V. (2013) 'Communities: Participatory Design for, with and by Communities', in J. Simonsen and T. Robertson (eds), *Routledge International Handbook of Participatory Design*, London and New York; Routledge, pp. 182–209.

EIA (2014) Everyday Disruptions, Northumbria University, Newcastle upon Tyne, ISBN: 978-1-86135-4570.

Greenbaum, J. (1993) 'PD: A Personal Statement', *Communications of the ACM (CACM)*, 36, 4: 47.

Light, A. (2014) 'Citizen Innovation: ActiveEnergy and the Quest for Sustainable Design, book chapter', in M. Boler and M. Ratto (eds), *DIY Citizenship: Critical Making and Social Media*, Cambridge, MA: MIT Press.

Light, A. and Akama, Y. (2012) 'The human touch: From method to participatory practice in facilitating design with communities'. *Proc. PDC '12*: 61–70.

Light, A. and Akama, Y. (2014) Structuring future social relations: The politics of care in participatory practice. *Proc. PDC '14*: 151–160.

Light, A. and Anderson, T. (2009) 'Research project as boundary object: Negotiating the conceptual design of a tool for international development'. *Proc. ECSCW '09*: 21–42.

Light, A., Egglestone, P., Wakeford, T. and Rogers, J. (2011) 'Participant-Making: Bridging the Gulf between Community Knowledge and Academic Research', *Journal of Community Informatics*, 7: 3.

Light, A., Miskelly, C. and Thompson, S. (2008) 'An analysis of building habitat with networked tools'. *Proc. OzCHI '08*.

Merritt, S. and Stolterman, E. (2012) 'Cultural hybridity in participatory design'. *Proc. PDC '10*.

Meskell, Lynn and Pels, Peter (eds) (2005) 'Introduction: Embedding Ethics', in Lynn Meskell and Peter Pels (eds), *Embedding Ethics*, London: Berg Press.

Pink, S. (2008) 'Re-Thinking Contemporary Activism: From Community to Emplaced Sociality', *Ethnos*, 73, 2: 163–188.

Puig De La Bellacasa, M. (2012) 'Nothing Comes without Its World: Thinking with Care', *The Sociological Review*, 60, 2: 197–216.

Robertson, T. and Wagner, I. (2013) 'Ethics: Engagement, Representation and Politics-in-Action', in J. Simonsen and T. Robertson (eds), *Routledge International Handbook of Participatory Design*, London and New York: Routledge, pp. 64–85.

Robertson, T., Leong, T. W. Durick, J. and Koreshoff, T. (2014) 'Mutual learning as a resource for research design'. *Proc. PDC '14*.

Selasi, T. (2014) Don't ask where I'm from, ask where I'm a local. Ted Global Talk https://www.ted.com/talks/taiye_selasi_don_t_ask_where_i_m_from_ask_where_i_m_a_local).

Sen, A. (2006) *Identity and Violence: The Illusion of Destiny*, London: Allen Lane.

Storni, C. (2012) 'Unpacking Design Practices: The Notion of Thing in the Making of Artifacts', *Science, Technology & Human Values*, 37, 1: 88–123.

Part Three

Tricky Policy

9

Designing Policy Objects: Anti-Heroic Design

Lucy Kimbell

When in 1972 star designers Charles and Ray Eames were asked, 'What are the boundaries of design?' their answer, 'What are the boundaries of problems?' (Eames Office 2016), demonstrated nicely the unboundedness and heroic, hubristic optimism associated with much designerly practice. The problems to which design is now being applied include organizational strategy, social issues such as caring for older people, public health issues such as obesity, humanitarian and development challenges, environmental issues such as food waste and public service redesign. This is design as a field taking on issues facing communities and societies at different scales, moving beyond its entanglement with consumer culture and technological innovation towards actively reconstituting ways of living and being in ways that aim to be participatory, ethical and political (e.g. Armstrong et al. 2014; Binder et al. 2015; Koskinen and Hush 2016).

Against this background, this chapter considers government and public policy making as emerging sites for using design approaches, principles and practices. Using an auto-ethnographic account of my participation in a team of civil servants in the UK government and activism in a political party, I raise some of the ethical implications of this kind of designing. My account draws first on Agamben's (2009) revisiting of the concept of *apparatus*, highlighting the subjectification and desubjectification processes that accompany (co-)designing policy objects. It also invokes the Greek concept of *mētis* (e.g. Singleton 2014) to consider opportunities to resist this subjectification of users, citizens and public servants within an apparatus such as public administration. In so doing, I propose that anti-heroic design, characterized by a *mētic* approach, has the potential to craftily sidestep, decentre or otherwise manoeuvre in relation to an apparatus.

Design in and for public policy

The last few years have seen a rapid expansion of examples of design for policy, alongside other kinds of experimentation in using 'open' and digital data, behavioural science and foresight. As discussed by Bason (2014), design for public policy throws up questions for public servants and politicians about their expertise, organizational capabilities and the logics through which they take action and engage with publics, including voters and beneficiaries of public programmes. The international spread of 'policy labs' in government entities, such as central, regional or local government organizations, mostly in developed countries with stable democracies, has resulted in many more examples of applying design processes, methods, techniques and expertise to policy challenges with, as yet, unclear results (e.g. Bailey and Lloyd 2016; EU Policy Lab 2016).

As a socio-material configuration to be 'designed', policy presents an interesting object of study for scholars of design. Public policy is a diffused social and political phenomenon with complex intersections with other domains including but not limited to politics, economics, social research and legal thought and practice. As the UK Civil Service describes it – in a handbook for civil servants who work directly with elected politicians who are ministers – policy making involves balancing 'politics, evidence and delivery' (Civil Service Learning 2016). Policy making is presented as the active mediation between data and interpretation, in relation to participants and processes inside government departments, parliament, public bodies, civil society stakeholders and also involving where relevant those involved in implementation and evaluation. Within the field of policy studies, concepts such as policy 'cycles' with phases of agenda-setting through to implementation and evaluation (e.g. Howlett 1991), or 'streams' of activity (e.g. Kingdon 1995), have been developed to articulate the object and process of policy design. Reactions to instrumentalist, top-down or rationalist approaches have led to growing interest in designerly approaches within designing policy (e.g. Howlett 2015).

As with the design of other kinds of socio-material thing, policy objects and processes are in flux. Factors shaping policy practice and thinking include ongoing failures to find solutions to complex, dynamic issues; increasing datafication and digitization of public administration; challenges to established means of representing issues and engaging stakeholders; the marketization of public space; and the hold of neo-liberal ideologies arguing for reshaping the role and size of state. These have resulted in new experiments, formats, devices, technologies and kinds of expertise in policy design. New policy development practices have co-emerged with developments in business and management. For example, the push to continuous experimentation in lean start-up and agile software, funded by venture capital ever in search of novelty, has directly informed efforts to make government more agile (e.g. HM Government 2016a).

In short, public policy design is a complex, dynamic context in which designerly practices, and sometimes professional designers, are now evident. The rapid proliferation of formats for bringing designer expertise into policy contexts poses questions about the nature of this emerging practice in public administration. To what extent can designerly optimism in coming up with new solutions to policy challenges engage with the often subtle, and highly politicized, cultural practices of public administration? How do new formats and techniques for policy making intersect with democratic structures and processes? To explore these questions, this chapter makes two moves to consider the opportunities for, and consequences of, public policy being an object for and in designerly practice.

Apparatus and *mētis*

Foucault's concept of *apparatus* has become a widely used analytical device to highlight the production and disciplining of human subjects within institutions. The *apparatus* is defined by Italian philosopher Giorgio Agamben in an essay on this concept (2009: 14) as 'literally anything that has in some way the capacity to capture, orient, determine, intercept, model, control, or secure the gestures, behaviours, opinions, or discourses of living beings'. His discussion highlights a difference between living beings and the apparatuses that capture and thereby seek to govern them. Agamben's examination of the apparatus begins by revisiting the early history of the Christian Church and describing the origins of a foundational split between humans (in the physical world) and god (in the spirit world). An apparatus is what separates us from our immediate environment and constructs subjectivities (how we are to be) in relation to their negation (how we are not to be). For Agamben, the only realistic strategy to resist this split is through *profanation* of the apparatus, saying: 'Profanation is the counter-apparatus that restores to common use what sacrifice had separated and divided' (2009: 19). For Agamben, profanation returns to ordinary life things that were previously considered 'sacred', or apart.

Given the pervasiveness of apparatuses in contemporary life, Agamben notes an urgency 'to bring to light the Ungovernable, which is the beginning and, at the same time, the vanishing point of every politics' (2009: 24). This highlights a key ethical challenge for design for and in public policy: whether design practice will serve to maintain the split between living beings and apparatuses – that result in the subjectification of citizens, users or beneficiaries of government policy, as well as public servants and politicians – or whether design will or can resist this split through profanation.

The second move draws on the ancient Greek concept of *mētis* (Chia and Holt 2009; Mackay et al. 2014; Singleton 2014; Cocker 2016). Often translated into English as 'trickery' or 'guile', *mētis* 'stretches' (Nonaka et al. 2014) the more familiar practical wisdom associated with the Greek term *phronēsis*. It offers an active, but unspectacular, form of engagement with the particulars of a situation or, as Singleton (2014: 14) puts it, not, 'a scheme of domination but … a manipulative gamble, morally complex but also extremely potent in its effects'. Indirect strategic action shaped by *mētis* is 'the ability to absorb contradiction, to display an array of character and a multiplicity of traits, none of which dominate and all of which can be brought into play without any inner fixation that blocks the renewal of one's self' (Chia and Holt 2009: 206).

Unlike *phronēsis, mētis* is morally neutral. Noting histories of distrust of 'crafty' designers and their craft, Singleton points to how: 'If *mētis* incorporates characteristics that are often considered attractive, like foresight, pragmatism and ingenuity, it can also imply insincerity, deceitfulness and manipulation' (2014: 129). From the perspective of organization studies, Mackay et al. (2014) use *mētis* to describe situated resourcefulness in organizational contexts, enabling managers to do their work in contexts of ambiguity, conflict and complexity. In the arts, Cocker (2016: 244) uses the term to describe the work of artists Heath Bunting and Kayle Brandon as a 'critical practice of willful unbelonging, a refusal to passively accept the increasingly limiting or restrictive criteria that denotes a particular kind of social belonging or citizenship, especially as perpetuated by and within contemporary neoliberalism'.

Such explorations of *mētis* point towards organizational practices that are shifty and shifting, both enacting and responding to contradiction and uncertainty. Being attentive to *mētis* in the context of designing policy emphasizes the practical accommodations that enable new kinds of subjectivities to be imagined and brought into play in the work of public administration during dynamic change. *Mētis* has the potential for bringing the 'sacred' back into common use in the way Agamben sketches out, by resisting an apparatus but without doing so dramatically or directly.

In what follows I use these two analytical moves to discuss auto-ethnographic vignettes from a year-long research fellowship in a team of civil servants (Kimbell 2015). Auto-ethnographic research focuses on the writing or performing self of the researcher and how she is constituted in relation to the social worlds she accounts for (e.g. Russell 1999; Spry 2001). For example, Spry (2001) has emphasized performativity and embodiment in research practices, through her affective and poetic intertwining of her 'personal' stories with her 'research' in a scholarly context in which performing is 'academically heretical' (Spry 2001: 708). By presenting such accounts of my participation within government and local politics during my fellowship, I examine the opportunities and consequences of enacting a *mētic* approach within public administration and politics. In writing this I have returned to field notes, photographs, emails and tweets from my participation in many meetings, workshops and events as well as interviews with civil servants in government departments.[1]

Being in transition, being the apparatus

In May 2015 a general election in the UK resulted in a majority of Conservative Members of Parliament (MPs) being voted in. This was unexpected as, even on the day of the vote, polls were predicting a win for the opposition Labour Party. In the week after the election result, I spent several days among civil servants in central London, in the area known as Whitehall where many government departments are located. Over these days the new government took shape as the prime minister selected and announced his team of ministers. The previous government, formed in 2010, was a coalition of two parties, but this election had resulted in a majority for one party. One effect was that although some individual MPs might remain in post as ministers in the same role they had had before the election (such as the prime minister), the overall direction of policy making was now in the hands of a single party. For me, the election result was unwelcome news as I was a member of the Labour Party and had been active in my local area knocking on doors, handing out leaflets and attending meetings.[2]

The second working day after the election, I was present on one floor of the building I had access to as part of my fellowship. I was curious to see what it would be like. My (lightly edited) notes read:

I arrive at the Cabinet Office unfortunately without my pass so I have to wait downstairs until S comes to get me and I can get an unescorted one-day pass. Upstairs the tables are much tidier and it feels tense and excited ... We chat about the election night – sharing different reactions to the surprise result ... I ask who the new minister might be. P says she expects it to be Lord Maude[3] but that 'they' (i.e. the Prime Minister and his team) might have to [appease a different wing of the party] ... 'At least he was really interested in the Civil Service and the Cabinet Office'. A sense of busy-ness. ... I hear one senior civil servant say, 'The angle is the majority is paper thin'.

At this stage it was not clear for the people working in this government department if they will have a new minister – it's up to the prime minister to decide and there was as yet little news. As a researcher, I didn't receive the emails sent to civil servants but was able to pick up what was happening through what people were talking about. Over these days, many of the people around me were often on the phone or checking email, Twitter and news feeds. As ministerial appointments were announced, news spread and I overheard, or joined in with, discussions about the consequences for government departments and policy directions.

The third work day after the election, I was present at an informal meeting when several senior civil servants talked through what was happening, to make sense of the result and the implications for the future. One manager cautioned: 'Don't think it's the same as three weeks ago. They have been through something cathartic and are coming in renewed'. A few days later, I was present in the building when the new minister arrived on the floor I happened to be on. My notes read:

Some clapping round the corner ... I look up. I look at S for an explanation. He says it's the minister. We get up and go round the corner where people are still clapping. [Senior manager N] is standing next to a man in jeans and a shirt – the new minister ... It feels a bit odd to be clapping a Tory minister less than a week after the election but I join in not to be conspicuous. The minister says, 'Thank you for the next five years ... You'll work really hard ... I look forward to working with [you] and taking all the credit'. Laughter. More clapping. We go back to our desks. S comes with me and translates for me: 'We need to do this to make the transition smoother. To build the trust. It didn't happen in 2010 with the incoming ministers and it was a real problem. But you see how we are – jump for the new minister'.

These few days of transition gave me embodied insights into the lived reality of civil servants as part of the apparatus of government. As I stood among a group of people clapping the new minister when he visited the building, I experienced the ambivalence of wanting certainty and a direction, but anxiety about what it might mean. I gained a sense of how civil servants are implicated in the apparatus of government, regardless of and possibly split from their own politics or beliefs. A *mētic* lens suggests such behaviour is part of the craft of public service, requiring resourceful pragmatism in order to maintain the split between public servants and their worlds beyond their professional obligations.

Through temporarily being part of this apparatus and separated from my own commitments, I experienced something of this split. But an unconscious slip-up revealed my own resistance to it. On the first day after the election I went to the office without my access pass – an easy mistake to make, but a rare one. This suggested how unconsciously I was marking out my role and accountabilities as different to those of the public servants. As a researcher my work is publically funded and shaped by academic standards and guidelines. Like civil servants, I am expected not to enact party politics within my work. But within my free time I have been experimenting in bringing designerly approaches into local party politics, which produces insights into the subjectivities constructed through the UK's democratic apparatus.

Opening up participation, manifesting the ungovernable

In July 2015 I co-organized a public meeting to bring people together to find out more about food poverty in my local area, and what can be done about it. All of the organizers were members of a local branch of the Labour Party, but we wanted the event to attract other local residents, not just members. This event was the second in a series of 'open meetings' through which we aimed to open up participation in party politics. Our objectives in organising this meeting were that: more people knew about existing schemes and organizations active in relation to UK food poverty resulting in more donations and new users and volunteers; everyone in the room had the opportunity to generate and share ideas about how to address food poverty; food was gathered for the local voluntary foodbank; and the Labour Party was involved in doing something practical in the area. Ahead of the meeting we designed, produced, handed out and delivered flyers advertising the event, as well using social media. We found and briefed speakers, booked the venue and attended to the other practicalities of such events.

Held on a Saturday afternoon in a community centre, the event was attended by thirty-five people, the majority of whom were party members. Many of the meetings organized by the party in the area adopt a format of a speaker talking in a plenary session to an audience, with opportunities for questions. The format for the open meeting combined hearing from people with direct knowledge of the issue with individuals talking in small groups. As organizers, we believed this opened up more opportunities for people to take part, by sharing their own perspectives, experiences and ideas.

After hearing from speakers from a local food bank, a supermarket that collects food donations and from an elected councillor, participants were invited to talk at tables in small groups to explore the issues in more depth. For some participants, this shift in register, while welcome, led to their checking in several times with us, the organizers: 'What do you want us to do?' But as individuals in the small groups grasped the format and found their voices, the energy in the room from people talking and listening to one another could be heard and felt. Further, the structure we proposed of first discussing the issue, and then coming up with potential solutions, and distinguishing between sites and scales of action (such as campaigning, policy, local government and volunteering) helped distinguish different responses to UK food poverty.

There was, however, one interesting challenge to the format. This came from one of the participants who wanted to share her experience of (food) poverty. For the most part, this participant ignored the invitations to follow the structure for the meeting. Her spoken and embodied interventions were focused on telling her own story, from when she was younger and did not have enough food to eat. She wanted and needed to be heard; this event had seemed to offer the promise of this.

On the one hand, this participant was doing what we had asked – bringing into view the experiences of people in the UK who did not have enough food to eat to understand the conditions, drivers and consequences of food poverty. On the other, she was resisting the rules of engagement of the open meeting, by not talking to the people she was sitting next to, and ignoring the structured activities, including invitations to generate and share ideas. Our format wanted to tidy away – perhaps colonize? – her memories of suffering, anger and sense of injustice, and channel it into the production of 'ideas'.

This woman's responses and the nature of her stories exceeded the format and process of the meeting. Instead of the cordial rationality we, the organizers, required, her response resisted the modes of knowing and being built into our design. The apparatus of our open meeting required particular kinds of disciplined participant for it to work. The affective excess produced by this participant constituted, in Agamben's terms, a profanation of the apparatus. Bringing this participant's feelings, agency and purposes into the workshop revealed something of the 'ungovernable', which was at once thrilling and frightening to me, as one of the organizers. Individual resistance such as this can disrupt the workings of an apparatus in productive ways. But to what extent can organizational practices, such as professional design, enact a collective profanation of an apparatus? Returning to the context of public administration, I explore this by discussing findings from my participation in a team within the UK government (Kimbell 2015, 2016).

Calculating impact, exceeding professional practice

Set up in 2014 as part of efforts to change the work practices of the UK Civil Service (HM Government 2012), Policy Lab is a team consisting of a small number of public servants within central government working with policy officials and others in government departments, sometimes supported by specialist consultancies. As described on its blog:

> Policy Lab is bringing new policy tools and techniques to the UK Government. We are a creative space where policy teams can develop the knowledge and skills to develop policy in a more open, data-driven, digital and user-centred way. … Policy Lab support is best suited to tackling intractable, complex, systemic policy problems that require fresh thinking that can lead to potentially transformative solutions. (Policy Lab 2017a)

The team includes people with backgrounds in policy, design, ethnography, digital and futures. Policy Lab co-exists with other more established players inside the UK government, including the award-winning Government Digital Service (HM

Government 2016a, 2016b), which advocates for designing for user needs and using prototyping in the design of digital public services. Internationally, there is a flourishing ecosystem of people exploring and advocating 'policy innovation' with associated networks, events and research (e.g. EU Policy Lab 2016).

Throughout my research, there was an enduring challenge faced by Policy Lab: how to account for its practices and assess its impact in ways that worked for stakeholders, especially sponsors inside the Civil Service, so it could continue to exist, or possibly grow. The terms of how to make this calculation were not clear. The team was tasked with helping build a culture of open policy making, including getting wider input into defining problems and generating solutions, and by testing policy solutions before they are implemented, to lead to more effective and successful policy making (HM Government 2012). Within a government committed to deficit reduction (HM Treasury 2015), much of the contemporary discussion about 'solutions' was shaped by a political requirement to reduce spending. So on the one hand, the team was part of the apparatus, which requires public servants to be split from their own perspectives, beliefs and commitments, to generate and deliver such solutions. But on the other, innovative practices might go beyond current framings or lead to results that did not fit in existing ways of doing things.

As a new team, with funding initially for one year, headcount equivalent to 2.4 people and a relatively small budget in government terms, Policy Lab had limited resources. Notes from discussions I took part in highlight the ongoing challenge of understanding and describing the frames within which Policy Lab's activities could be assessed. Some of the people cited in these discussions were elected politicians or senior managers with interest in or responsibility for the team's activities. Alongside these conversations, there were many activities through which the team monitored and evaluated its work more formally, for example in regular reports to and meetings with senior colleagues and via an independent assessment by a consultancy.

> You could frame Lab in lots of different ways … efficiency savings, outcomes. T says 'I want to show the monetary benefit' but then says 'I don't believe it'.
>
> T's agenda for [a senior civil servant] is 'Where's the £10 billion solution not the £500,000 solution?' The projects we pick have to be right on the one hand … something captivating, compelling, to demonstrate what others have not been able to do … What can we do in the system that people could point to as an emerging [organisational] technology like 3d printing?

One aspect of this calculation, to which the team returned regularly, was Policy Lab's symbolic value. On occasion, this was seen as having more persuasive power than the team's ability to effect improvements and savings.

> Does a lab serve a symbolic role or does it have to deliver impact?
>
> Lab is distinctive … it's in the global club of labs … its symbolic value is as a lab in addition to its practical ability to deliver change.

Frequent use of the term 'experimental' and the name Policy 'Lab' itself emphasized the provisional, uncertain nature of this new way of working inside government, even if the team drew on established ways of working inside business and social innovation settings. Such experimentality contrasted with that of another, highly visible and much larger team built up from 2010 from within the UK Civil Service, the Behavioural Insights Team (BIT). BIT's work is closely associated with social science research – social psychology and behavioural economics – and with an experimental technique – randomized control trials (RCTs) (e.g. Haynes et al. 2013). Through testing policy interventions that emphasize analytical rigour in the tradition of the experimental sciences, BIT asserts a knowledge base and a methodology. In contrast, Policy Lab's experimentation is more fluid, emphasizes creative engagement with a problem, is pluralist in its intellectual lineages and co-emerges with its context.

> We tried out 12 tools and the approach associated with them. By trying them out we gain licence to try out more things.
>
> We are trying to fine-tune what works in this space.

A brief account of these 'tools' in use in one setting brings into view how such experimentation works in practice.[4] It draws out the ways that Policy Lab carries out this fine-tuning in response to a matter at hand, rather than in relation to a fixed, well-established framing, and opens up discussion about the nature of policy work. In so doing, I suggest this allows participants to manoeuvre in relation to dominant assumptions about policy making practice and the identities associated with public service, resisting the apparatus of which civil servants form a part by connecting them to their purposes, to their emotions and to their wider worlds.

For example, in many workshops run by Policy Lab, an opening move is to engage participants in expressing hopes and fears for their shared project or relating to the policy issue at stake. Typically, a member of the Policy Lab team distributes on the floor or a table a selection of postcards, each with a printed image and an empty space below. Participants are invited to pick one card to express their fear regarding the topic at hand and write a few words on the card. They then share what they have written with one another. This is then repeated for the group to describe their hopes for the topic or project.

During an hour-long workshop I attended, the policy officials who participated spent a few minutes describing their fears for what policy work might look like in central government. A picture of a clock was a chosen to represent the fear of getting behind. A picture of wires was selected to communicate feeling lonely and disconnected. A picture of sky said: 'Too much blue sky, not enough delivery.' When discussing their hopes, participants introduced other concepts in response to the postcards available. A picture of binoculars represented 'short and long range vision'. A pair of shoes were the hope of 'buy in'. A picture of a London department store was chosen to communicate 'world class ideas' and being 'symbolic internationally'. In only a few minutes, this activity connected participants to their own feelings about their work by using a small set of images to elicit responses, privileging subjective experience over evidence and analysis.

This exercise was followed by three more activities. The first was constructing a 'persona' of a civil servant involved in policy making, produced by participants sketching or writing notes in response to characteristics called out by the facilitator.

This was followed by each participant writing down a 'challenge' faced by policy officials inside government, which they then presented to one another. Finally, participants worked in small teams to come up with, sketch, share and discuss solutions to these challenges. One such solution, for example, visualized an iterative policy making cycle with multiple inputs at many points in time. Outcomes of this intense, fast-paced hour included not just insights into current practices, barriers to change, and ideas for how the policy making process might work, but also practical, creative engagement with these topics and a sense of open dialogue between participants.

Through taster workshops such as this, and longer demonstration projects working closely with civil servants on a specific policy issue, Policy Lab invited participants to engage materially and discursively in reconstituting the issue of how policy making could be practised. Emphasizing the visual and performative, rather than the numeric or textual as is more common among policy officials, such activities sidestep the conventional ways of knowing within public administration. The team's practice offers a series of uncertainties in which policy officials were constructed as active participants in exploring issues and imagining collective futures. Much of this was accompanied by self-deprecating, often humorous facilitation and informality, while carefully following Civil Service conventions, such as referring to ministers, senior civil servants and current policy agendas, to legitimize activity. Through its open-ended, generative activities, the team enabled participants to connect with what is often kept apart from their professional practice – their subjective sense of purpose, creating a context in which they can 'experiment' by questioning assumptions about a policy issue, its ecosystem and potential solutions. Policy Lab generates and holds open a space where 'next practice' – a term frequently used by the team – can be co-imagined. This emphasis on subjectivity and not-knowing – or not-yet-knowing – enough about a policy issue or what a solution might be can be seen as a profanation of the apparatus of public administration.

Using the lens of a *mētic* design approach, what comes into view is resistance to presenting an authoritative account of civil service practice. Insights and solutions may be generated by Policy Lab through ethnographic research and co-design. But the team's efforts are also directed towards experimentally co-producing an organizational capacity enabling civil servants to reconnect with their purposes and subjectivities to they can reimagine policy making and collectively explore problems and solutions. Unassuming but provocative, contextual and specific rather than generalizable, Policy Lab's designerly practices inside government hint at an anti-heroic experimentation and partial, ever provisional solutions. By absorbing contradiction and being resourceful, Policy Lab has been able to shift and respond to changes in its environment, sidestepping dominant framings to the extent that the team continues to exist with licence to probe future policy making practices.

Conclusion

Earlier I noted the increasing visibility of designerly expertise within policy contexts, and questioned to what extent it can resist being part of an apparatus and the processes of subjectification and desubjectification that accompany it. Illuminated by the accounts presented above, I now consider the extent to which the optimism associated with design practice in coming up with new solutions to policy challenges can be productive, given the politicized cultural practices of government bodies. Two possible directions for professional design practice emerge in relation to the design of socio-material policy objects.

One option is for design to be enfolded within the work of public administration. Here, designing is a new competence for policy officials to master. This heroic design is on the side of purposefulness and strategic action to address public policy challenges, adding a human-centred perspective and insights into end user experiences. However, it can serve to maintain the split between an apparatus and living beings and is unavoidably implicated in processes of subjectification and desubjectification. Its activities result in producing good or bad citizens, workshop participants, users, beneficiaries or public servants, and indeed policies, which maintain the split that separates living beings from their environment, and give some actors more agency or legitimacy and others less. Such a competence competes with other heroic accounts that produce solutions in accordance with modernist science, and evidence about what works, but fail to reimagine what 'working' might mean.

The second – perhaps more troubling – option is to develop a *mētic* design practice, emphasizing the improvisational and the circuitous. This anti-heroic design for policy has the potential to resist the apparatus and its associated subjectification and desubjectification processes. By profaning the apparatus, anti-heroic design highlights the ungovernable, the unfolding of which may produce new kinds of subjectivities and may result in new ways of living, working, knowing or being. This anti-heroic design eschews the calculability associated with much contemporary design practice that demonstrates 'value' or 'impact' or reflects on its 'role'. Instead, it poses the question of its contribution as something to be explored and re-made.

Given recent political developments that have resulted in unexpected leaders and unanticipated decisions through democratic processes, this anti-heroic design is worth exploring further. Perhaps instead of 'design to the rescue' emphasizing a heroic, active engagement with government, other aspects of designerly practice can be mobilized, as Singleton (2014) argues. Recognizing the potential for profanation enabled by a *mētic* approach positions design as anti-heroic, through cunning, intelligence and unspectacular practical engagement with the particulars of the situation. Acknowledging and enabling this capacity has the potential to produce less alarming ungovernables.

Acknowledgements

This research was funded by a fellowship from the Arts and Humanities Research Council. Thanks to Jamie Brassett for introducing me to Agamben's essay and for suggestions that improved this chapter, and to Jamie, Guy Julier, Noortje Marres and Jocelyn Bailey for ongoing discussions about design, policy and the social.

Notes

1 Details have been changed to retain anonymity, such as names, genders, roles and locations, and in relation to confidential material. Given working in an open plan office and my access to workshops, meetings and interviews, the civil servants who I describe here may work in several government departments.
2 Some civil servants I knew were supporters or members of several different political parties. Their engagement with politics is shaped by clear guidance, in the form of the Civil Service Code, and cultural practices which aim to separate their professional obligations and personal views (HM Government 2013).
3 Francis Maude was a Conservative Member of Parliament and minister who was actively involved in leading the government's Civil Service reform and open government agendas and developing the Government Digital Service.
4 For more on Policy Lab's design tools adapted for policy making see Policy Lab (2017b).

Bibliography

Agamben, G. (2009) *What Is an Apparatus? And Other Essays*, Stanford, CA: Stanford University Press.
Armstrong, L., Bailey, J., Julier, G. and Kimbell, L. (2014) *Social Design Futures: Social Design Research and the AHRC*, Brighton: University of Brighton.
Bailey, J. and Lloyd, P. (2016) 'The introduction of design to policymaking: Policy Lab and the UK Government'. *Proceedings of DRS2016: Design Research Society Conference*, Brighton, UK, 27–30 June 2016.
Bason, C. (ed.) (2014) *Design for Policy*, Abingdon: Routledge.
Binder, T., Brandt, E., Ehn, P. and Halse, J. (2015) 'Democratic Design Experiments: Between Parliament and Laboratory', *CoDesign*, 11, 3–4: 152–165.
Burton, P. (2006) 'Modernising the Policy Process: Making Policy Research More Significant?' *Policy Studies*, 27, 3: 173–195.
Chia, R. and Holt, R. (2009) *Strategy without Design: The Silent Efficacy of Indirect Action*, Cambridge: Cambridge University Press.
Civil Service Learning (2015) *Working with ministers*. Available at: https://civilservicelearning.civilservice.gov.uk/sites/default/files/working_with_ministers_-_a_handbook_-_final.pdf, accessed 6 July 2016.
Cocker, E. (2016) 'Looking for Loopholes: The Cartography of Escape', in K. E. Bishop (ed.), *Cartographies of Exile: A New Spatial Literacy*, Abingdon: Routledge.
Eames Office. Available at: http://www.eamesoffice.com/the-work/design-q-a-text/, accessed 11 December 2016.
EU Policy Lab (2016) Lab connections. Available at: http://blogs.ec.europa.eu/eupolicylab/lab-connections/, accessed 11 December 2016.
Fuerth, L. (2009) 'Foresight and Anticipatory Governance', *Foresight*, 11, 4: 14–32.
Haynes, L., Service, O., Goldacre, B. and Torgerson, D., (2013) *Test, Learn, Adapt: Developing Public Policy with Randomised Controlled Trials*, London: Cabinet Office.
HM Government (2012) The Civil Service reform plan. Available at: https://www.gov.uk/government/publications/civil-service-reform-plan, accessed 11 March 2017.

HM Government (2013) Civil service conduct and guidance. Available at: https://www. gov.uk/government/collections/civil-service-conduct-and-guidance, accessed 11 January 2017.

HM Government (2016a) Gov.uk Service manual. Agile methods: An introduction. Available at: https://www.gov.uk/service-manual/agile-delivery/agile-methodologies, accessed 11 December 2016.

HM Government (2016b) Start by learning user needs. Published 4 April 2016. Available at: https://www.gov.uk/service-manual/user-research/start-by-learning-user-needs

HM Treasury (2015) '2010 to 2015 government policy: Deficit reduction'. Available at: https://www.gov.uk/government/publications/2010-to-2015-government-policy-deficit-reduction, accessed 11 March 2017.

Howlett, M. (1991) 'Policy Instruments, Policy Styles and Policy Implementation', *Policy Studies Journal*, 19, 2: 1–21.

Howlett, M. (2015) 'From Tools to Toolkits in Policy Design Studies: The New Design Orientation towards Policy Formulation Research', *Policy and Politics*, 43, 2: 291–311.

Kimbell, L. (2015) *Applying Design Approaches to Policy Making: Discovering Policy Lab*, Brighton: University of Brighton.

Kimbell, L. (2016) 'Design in the time of policy problems'. *Proceedings of DRS2016: Design Research Society Conference*, Brighton, UK, 27–30 June 2016.

Kingdon, J. W. (1995) *Agendas, Alternatives and Public Policies*, 2nd Edition, New York: Harper Collins.

Koskinen, I., and Hush, G. (2016) 'Utopian, Molecular and Sociological Social Design', *International Journal of Design*, 10, 1: 65–71.

Mackay, D., Zundel, M. and Alkirwi, M. (2014) 'Exploring the Practical Wisdom of Metis for Management Learning', *Management Learning*, 45, 4: 418–436.

Nonaka, T., Chia, R., Holt, R. and Peltokorpi, V. (2014) 'Wisdom, Management and Organization', *Management Learning*, 45, 4: 365–376.

Policy Lab (2017a) 'About Policy Lab'. Available at: https://openpolicy.blog.gov.uk/about/, accessed 11 January 2017.

Policy Lab (2017b) 'Method Bank and Toolkit'. Available at: https://www.slideshare.net/Openpolicymaking/methodbank-and-toolkit-for-design-in-government, accessed 11 January 2017.

Russell, C. (1999) *Experimental Ethnography: The Work of Film in the Age of Video*, Durham, NC: Duke University Press.

Singleton, B. (2014) *On Craft and Being Crafty: Human Behaviour as the Object of Design*. Unpublished PhD thesis, University of Northumbria.

Spry, T. (2001) 'Performing Autoethnography: An Embodied Methodological Praxis', *Qualitative Inquiry*, 7, 6: 706–732.

10

'Tricky Like a Leprechaun' – Navigating the Paradoxes of Public Service Innovation in the Context of Austerity

Adam Thorpe

We use the term 'wicked' in a meaning akin to that of 'malignant' (in contrast to 'benign') or 'vicious' (like a circle) or 'tricky' (like a leprechaun) or 'aggressive' (like a lion, in contrast to the docility of a lamb). We do not mean to personify these properties of social systems by implying malicious intent.

Rittel and Webber (1973, p. 160)

Introduction

This chapter explores the challenges facing those designing to ensure equitable access to public goods in times of austerity. It briefly describes the wider context of the financial austerity seen to be driving the reform of local government services in the UK between 2010 and 2020 and warns against an efficiency-led approach to public service reform that forgoes experimentation that might improve effectiveness.

This chapter illustrates the impact of these reforms on public service innovation by reflecting on examples of the 'collaborative design experiments' of the Public Collaboration Lab, an action research partnership between a London council and researchers, staff and students from the University of the Arts, London that explored a new way of building and developing local design capacity for service, policy and social innovation.

This chapter proposes that public service innovation in a climate of austerity is 'tricky', rather than solely complex or 'wicked', in that challenges appear to be deceitfully and craftily constructed. It concludes by reflecting on the relationship between 'designerly' approaches and practices and the 'trickiness' of this design context.

Background

Facing intensifying financial austerity within UK local government, those responsible for the quality and continuity of public services recognize that innovation in service design and delivery is critical if effective public services are to be secured. The UK

Local Government Association (LGA 2013) suggests that massive financial savings could be achieved by a collaborative approach to service delivery that aligns different agencies' objectives, activities and resources. Current research and practice in design (Manzini and Staszowski 2013) suggest that greater involvement of, and collaboration with, citizens and other agencies may also foster improvements in service quality by involving end users in research, prototyping and testing of services, and engaging citizens and other agencies in the co-production (design and delivery) of services, enabled and supported by public agencies.

The approaches offer particular potential when considering 'relational services', those services which are 'deeply and profoundly based on the quality of interpersonal relations *between* participants' (Cipolla et al. 2009: 46). However, despite growing interest in and appreciation of the potential of these approaches, the design and delivery of 'public and collaborative' relational services are not straightforward, should not be uncontested, and require the consideration and navigation of complex and sometimes wicked (Rittel and Webber 1973) scenarios in the process. Worse still, these scenarios are further compounded by conditions of austerity, giving rise to some new 'tricky' characteristics; desirable outcomes that are not contested by different publics involved in their deliberation and delivery, but denied by available resources, as illustrated by the examples shared later.

Something wicked this way comes

Public service innovation is complex, integrating as it does the constituent complexities of service innovation (Gallouj et al. 1997), human interactions (Cipolla et al. 2009) and public goods. This complexity and unpredictability is further compounded by the diversity of people's perspectives and the subjectivity of people's expectations and experiences. As societal scenarios become more complex, interventions and their effects become more contested since addressing one element of the system is likely to impact another. The more we understand of the complexity in societal systems, the more we understand the limitations of ambitions to plan or manage them. Rittel and Webber (1973, p. 160) explain that 'plurality of objectives held by a plurality of politics make it impossible to pursue unitary aims', suggesting that social problems are not for solving, or not in ways that can satisfy all the diversity of publics within society. According to Rittel and Webber, the best we can hope for is resolution – not solution, 'societal problems are never solved only re-solved – over and over again'. This frames the addressing of 'wicked' problems in society as an open-ended and 'agonistic' (Mouffe 2007) process of argument and contestation.

It is agonistic dissent that enables pluralism to survive and diversity to thrive. And it is this diversity – with its myriad potential for success and failure – that ensures some 'right' answers for some of the people some of the time, if never all of the people all of the time. Wicked problems are resolved through an 'argumentative process in the course of which an image of the problem and the solution emerges gradually among the participants, as a product of incessant judgement, subjected to critical argument' (Rittel and Webber 1973, p. 162). Resolutions to wicked problems are always incomplete, they are examples of 'satisficing' – 'good enough' answers to the problems addressed (Simon 1996: 27). This understanding rejects the hubris of solutionism and control, accepting the uncertainties of society as a complex adaptive system. So, public service innovation can be seen as a wicked challenge given the complexity and contestation that accompany its proximity to the social. As navigators in this ocean of uncertainty we do not hope to tame the sea but to learn to sail.

However, in the current context of austerity there may be something more to be said about the wickedness or otherwise of this design scenario. As the epigraph to this chapter makes clear, Rittel and Webber's use of the term 'wicked' to describe these problem properties does not imply the problems are themselves 'ethically deplorable', nor do they seek to imply 'malicious intent' in the problems they describe. However, they do suggest to us that 'we may agree that it becomes morally objectionable' for the planner (politician/designer) to treat a wicked problem – a problem with no clear definition and no clear resolution 'as though it were a "tame" one, or to tame a wicked problem prematurely, or to refuse to recognise the inherent wickedness of social problems' (Rittel and Webber 1973, p. 161). When we look to public service innovation imposed by austerity it appears that we are dealing with just such a 'morally objectionable', 'ethically deplorable' design scenario, one created with 'malicious intent'.

Tricky challenges – constructed contradictions in desirable outcomes

Advocates of marketization argue that public services are more efficient and effective when stimulated by competition. However, this position ignores the fundamental contradiction between the desired outcomes of accumulating private wealth and realizing public goods. The neo-liberal[1] proposal denies the paradox of this wicked scenario, characterized by contradictory desirable outcomes and suggests that the marketization and financialization of public services will deliver both private and public value. However, an examination of the context in which public services are seen to be failing reveals a 'malicious intent' on the part of the advocates of marketization that frames the challenge of public service innovation in the current climate not as a wicked challenge but as a *tricky* one, characterized by the 'deceitful and crafty' (Oxford English Dictionary) nature of its conception. So, the assertion here is that the challenges faced by local government reforming public services are not solely wicked challenges but rather 'tricky' challenges. They are not insolvable by dint of their complexity and subjectivity but as a consequence of malicious intent.

Local government has four main sources of funding: the revenue support grant from central government, monies from local business via the business rates retention scheme, council tax paid by residents, and fees and charges for council services. Public servicing of private debt linked to bank bailouts and fiscal initiatives such as the Private Finance Initiative (PFI) have seen central government increase the burden of debt servicing on local government, at the same time reducing funding to them by an estimated 37 per cent between 2011 and 2016 (National Audit Office 2014) with a predicted further £7.8bn or 78 per cent reduction up to 2020.

This is anticipated to drive an unprecedented number of councils into financial crisis (Nolan and Pitt 2016: 4).

The poisonous fruit of this austerity is a drive for efficiency. The Local Government and Accountability Act 2014 has driven many councils headlong into cost saving measures, and round after round of restructuring and cost cutting, attempting to make financial savings while improving outcomes for residents. This sounds like a sensible response, as waste is not a virtue, but this pursuit of efficiency appears to ignore the 'wicked' nature of the scenario, making the challenge a 'tricky' one, constructed in such a way that to engage with it from the dominant-hegemonic position[2] – that is, to strive for efficiency to save services – will thwart its resolution. Efficiency is not the same as effectiveness. Furthermore, when pursuit of efficiency means people's needs are left unmet in one public service area it often increases demand, and costs to the public, in another.

This is especially true in the case of 'relational services' defined earlier, such as adult social care and mental health services for which demand is increasing as life expectancy[3] and incidence of mental health treatment[4] increase. Adult social care services account for roughly 30 to 35 per cent of total local government expenditure, expenditure which it is feared could be significantly reduced in coming years. The LGA (2016) estimates that adult social care in England and Wales will face a funding gap of £1.3 billion by the end of the decade. This funding gap is already seen to have led to unmet need among some of the UK's most vulnerable citizens, and increased costs to National Health Services, a grim illustration of the folly of prioritizing efficiency over effectiveness. Evidence to the House of Commons health select committee states this plainly:

> Cuts to social care funding over a number of years have now exhausted the capacity for significant further efficiencies in this area. We have heard that the savings made by local councils in the last parliament have gone beyond efficiency savings and have already impacted on the provision of services. Based on the evidence we have heard we are concerned that people with genuine social care needs may no longer be receiving the care they need because of a lack of resource. This not only causes considerable distress to the individuals concerned but results in significant additional costs to the NHS. (Health Select Committee 15th July 2016, para 86)

Perhaps 'trickier' still is the way in which efficiency limits innovation by driving out redundancy – the 'space' to experiment, reflect and learn. In the language of local government, 'redundancy' typically points to reductions in staffing rather than 'superabundance',[5] a useful surplus that offers multiple ways to achieve objectives and goals in a resilient system. On this positive view, redundancy delivers what Talib (2012) calls 'anti-fragility', 'layers of redundancy [that] are the central risk management property of natural systems'. As an attack on redundancy, efficiency is an enemy to innovation in that it denies the public sector the opportunity to experiment to find new ways to deal with the complexities of demographic change.

In this scenario the drive for 'efficiency' prevents public servants innovating alternatives to financialization and privatization of public services. Without redundancy, space for reflective learning and innovation will be denied to public services and no new ways of delivering public goods to citizens will be forthcoming. In this scenario the neo-liberal prophecy that the public sector does not have the capability or capacity to deliver public services becomes self-fulfilling, as the pursuit of efficiency prohibits innovation that might deliver effectiveness. Unable to balance the books, councils will have no choice but to abandon public services and public infrastructure to private ownership, at the cost of equitable access to public goods. New models are required. But, the development of these new models demands space to experiment, reflect and learn – redundancy is required for service innovation to occur.

Design education is a bastion of superabundance in thinking and doing that are essential to experimentation, reflective learning and innovation. It is a social resource with the capacity to share redundancy with those to whom it is denied. By collaborating with local government and the citizens they serve, design education can extend learning and practice in collaborative, socially responsive design, for students and researchers, and those they collaborate with within society, as an action-learning environment. This practice can offer the redundancy necessary to address the *tricky* challenge of public service innovation in the context of austerity. This is the practice which the Public Collaboration Lab explores.

Introducing the Public Collaboration Lab

The Public Collaboration Lab (PCL) is a prototype public social innovation lab focused on collaborative design for service, social and policy innovation. It shares characteristics with other public social innovation labs in that:

- Project teams are typically multi-stakeholder and multidisciplinary.
- Projects seek to understand the wider system while prioritizing human experience.
- Collaboration and co-creation with end users of services and stakeholders are central to the work of the lab.
- Approaches are iterative and agile following a robust design process framed as action research in 'real life' scenarios.

However, PCL is differentiated by its primary emphasis on collaboration between local government and design education, specifically, local government officers (LGOs) and design students supported by tutors and academic research staff. Residents and other stakeholders become involved via participatory design activities, including creative and collaborative exploration, visualization and visioning of new ways of meeting societal needs and goals. PCL considers design students and university staff to be societal assets and the community context to be an action-learning environment for all those involved. Participants share knowledge, skills, experience and expertise, working collaboratively to address local goals and challenges linked to finding new ways to deliver improved public services and outcomes in the face of austerity.

PCL projects offer participants an opportunity for the experimentation and reflection that contribute to innovation, providing greater capacity for local government to work with residents and other stakeholders. Together participants apply methods and approaches derived from human-centred design, service design, and participatory and collaborative design to discover the diversity and complexity of experiences, concerns, needs and desires in relation to a particular service or issue; co-define and prioritize the challenges and opportunities for intervention; and combine expertise and assets in addressing them. The outputs of these activities include rich qualitative insights that support decision-making and priority setting by LGOs and politicians. Alternative possibilities for delivery of services and achievement of outcomes are also explored and proposed, feeding into public service innovation and transformation. Depending on the nature of the projects, the activities may raise awareness and change behaviours or redefine and redesign ways of developing and delivering services. An LGO described the benefits of the PCL approach like this:

> PCL offers us the chance to explore new ways of collaborating with our partners and our communities, to design services that are based around the needs of residents [and] tap into the creativity and energy of Central Saint Martin's staff and students.

Projects address diverse operational scenarios and service areas, including how to consult more meaningfully with citizens on public issues, such as the future of libraries and the planning process, through to ways of increasing recycling rates, dealing with the effects of overcrowded housing, exploring synergies and alternatives for home care support and reshaping youth centres to facilitate new ways of delivering youth services. Our work in this area has brought us face-to-face with several *tricky* challenges – characterized by mutually desirable outcomes made antithetical by politically imposed austerity. Two examples are shared below.

Observations from the lab – '*tricky* challenges' in the day-to-day

Since 2015 PCL has worked with council officers, residents and other stakeholders in a London borough to co-deliver a series of 'collaborative design experiments' exploring potential social and service innovations that can improve outcomes for residents and reduce costs to meet medium-term financial targets.[6]

Example 1. 'This is not a courier service' – relational losses in home library services

Many public authorities provide a home library service (HLS) to ensure equitable access to library services for housebound residents. The partnering London borough provides this service to 400 to 500 residents at a cost of around £140,000 per year, which it is required to reduce by 60 per cent. Many HLS users find it difficult to access public services outside their homes because of age or medical conditions and receive visits from home care providers, being 'individuals with multiple complex needs' (UK

Public Service Transformation Network Service's Transformation Challenge Panel 2014). The HLS refers to these residents as 'readers' and their interests and literary preferences are known to the home librarians who visit them on a fortnightly basis. The council was seeking new service models for the HLS to deliver cost savings.

The brief for this collaborative design experiment was to explore alternative, public and collaborative service models. During the research phase, designers shadowed the librarians and observed their interactions with readers, supported by council officers and research and teaching staff from the PCL. This revealed that the services provided by the HLS librarians go far beyond the selection and delivery of reading books. The same librarian had visited some readers for several years, being welcomed into their homes and building trusting relationships with benefits beyond the remit of the HLS. A reader's request for larger print triggered a referral for an eye test and revealed that the instructions on medication were illegible to the reader. The temperature of a reader's home led to a conversation about heating allowances. A request for 'talking books' led to an impromptu training session on how to use a CD player. A reader's request for information around care homes led to a discussion around care options and a referral to relevant council support. The librarian's role as a trusted information provider influenced the interactions between them and readers, with books and their delivery providing a platform for trusted encounter and exchange. The service is predicated on recognizing the reader as an intellect as well as a body, foregrounding their individual interests rather than their needs.

The project made visible the deeply relational service support that the HLS team provided to readers. The design team's proposals amplified the unique value observed within the service, to improve outcomes and create cost savings in the long term through early intervention. They assigned 'back office' functions such as sorting, packing and loading books to volunteers, so HLS staff could concentrate on relating to their readers, supported by a digital platform to help them make timely and appropriate referrals to other support services. The platform also coordinated informal care support from family members and those who shared interests with the readers – to make volunteering more mutually rewarding through exploring shared interests – inside and outside the home. The new name for the redesigned service, the home and community library service (H&CLS), referred to the way the transformed HLS model extended interest-oriented home care into the community. The service was recognized to be uniquely positioned to deliver 'interest-oriented early intervention' whereby home librarians could be trained and supported in making referrals to community activities and support, as well as council services – explicitly amplifying the tacit roles and values that had been identified as being present in their current role.

This service innovation responded to recent research findings in this area:

> Civil society organisations have pressed for a person-centred approach to care ....
> Social relationships, allowing for frequent face-to-face interaction, are recognized
> as vital to older people's health and well-being. Experts say more development on
> these lines is needed .... Opportunities exist for businesses to expand in the area
> of long term care. For example, ... to invest in internet-based systems designed to
> promote social interception and combat loneliness. (Tinker et al. 2013: 5)

No one inside or outside the service and stakeholder network denied the value of the service innovation, the relationships that were at its core, or the potential for these relationships to support early intervention in social care. Some effort was made to explore alternative business models, including the 'Buurtzorg' 'public service mutual' approach that has delivered exceptional value and performance in home care in the Netherlands.[7] However, sufficient funding was not available to implement this service innovation due to the necessity of cost savings. Related service areas, under similar pressures to make savings, were unwilling to bear what was perceived as a 'cost shunt' from one service area to another and budgetary pressures denied sufficient time to find alternative business models. Consequently, the solution selected was that of a courier delivery model, losing the relational value and its potential to fulfil public service reform objectives around early intervention in adult social care and public health. This was not the result of a 'wicked' social challenge born of human subjectivity and conflicting desirable outcomes of actors but of the *tricky* withdrawal of public funding from the pursuit of public goods.

Example 2. Finding ways to combine 'hoping' with 'coping' – addressing the challenges of overcrowded living

Many of the UK's cities are densely populated. With a high demand for housing driving up the price of accommodation, increased costs combined with lack of investment for new social housing means that for many families, to remain in their communities means living in overcrowded conditions. Overcrowding directly and indirectly affects residents' well-being, contributing to a number of negative outcomes (Table 10.1).

Sixty-seven per cent of families in social housing in the borough live in overcrowded accommodation, with little prospect of rehousing. Recognizing the challenges this presents to families, the council has taken action to support families in addressing them and aims to reduce the impacts of overcrowding for all households in the borough, especially:

- households with children (particularly children aged under 5)
- households with people with mental health problems or learning disabilities
- households with people with other health problems
- households that are part of the Complex Families programme

A council officer responsible for supporting overcrowded families led a design team, comprised of design students and researchers, to work with overcrowded families to identify ways to lessen the impacts of overcrowding on their lives. Designers shadowed the council officer visiting families in their homes to see and hear about how they were living, the actions they were taking to alleviate the challenges they faced, and the support that they felt could further help to address their unmet needs. In each visit the designers applied different tools: visualizations, including maps and models of neighbourhood services and support networks, 'design probes' 'evocative tasks meant to elicit inspirational responses from people' (Gaver et al. 2004), and personas that helped residents to identify the challenges and responses most relevant to them.

Table 10.1 Impact of overcrowding on residents living in overcrowded conditions.*

Indirect or direct effect	Symptom of overcrowding
Direct	Sleep disturbance
Direct	Lack of privacy generally
Direct	Lack of storage space
Direct	Lack of privacy and space to study or job hunt/work
Indirect	Lack of space to socialize or play
Indirect	Stress levels and wider mental health impact
Indirect	Physical health (illness and infection)
Indirect	Family exclusion
Indirect	Relationship breakdowns
Indirect	Anti-social behaviour
Indirect	Educational attainment

* (Source: London borough briefing for the PCL Overcrowded Living Project 2016)

These tools supported the officer and residents through a process of reflection and planning in response to their overcrowded situation. Through successive visits, the team iteratively developed and tested these tools and used them to first identify and then prioritize the challenges residents faced. The work also explored the assets and resources available to the residents through their own networks and those provided by the council and other agencies, and finally set out a plan of action to make improvements. To understand how council services were supporting the overcrowded families, the team spoke to officers and front line staff across the council who came into contact with them. These consultations explored how the tools could help the officers support residents and point them towards further help outside the officers' specific service area.

The team delivered collaborative workshops with residents and officers in libraries and community centres to gather feedback on the prototype tools to ensure their utility and usability for officers and overcrowded residents. The project's main challenge was to support constructive conversations with concerned and frustrated residents, the majority of whom wanted engagement with council officers to result in rehousing. Unfortunately, rehousing was impossible in the majority of cases so the team had to come up with different ways to engage with residents, rethinking home visits and how to support and advise overcrowded households. The design of these interactions needed to be engaging and useful for residents, but also insightful to the council. The resulting tools structured conversations that were meaningful to residents, allowing their challenges to be heard and helping them to understand the limitations of what the council could do for them. The tools helped the council to find areas for intervention as well as referrals to further support. They helped to support the relationship between the council officer and the residents so that they could work together to address a situation that neither felt was 'right' but that they had to deal with nonetheless. This frustration was evident in feedback from the council officer leading the project:

The probes worked really well on yesterday's visit. We left quite late because it helped the mother to think of the positives for her, about home and community – she said that it made her realise that the best option for her family would be to stay and make the most of the space. Of course, her ideal option would be to move to a 3 bed.

The project revealed the complexity of the residents' situation. Residents sometimes set aside attempts to improve their living conditions to avoid reducing their chances of rehousing by being seen to be 'coping'. A deficit-focused 'points system' that attributes points to residents according to indicators of need gave the impression that residents would be rehoused if things got bad enough. However, some severe cases of overcrowding, producing negative outcomes relating to the health and well-being of family members, resulted in less than half the number of points required for rehousing. While no one wants to crush 'hope' for the long term, residents need support to act to 'cope' in the short term, alleviating some of the negative outcomes of overcrowding. The tools developed helped to structure a conversation around coping that was otherwise difficult to have.

Tricky problems and *tricky* practices

Disentangling the contradiction between coping and hoping, finding ways to deliver early intervention with long-term benefits when deprived of even short-term investment, these are examples of the *tricky* day-to day challenges facing public service innovation in the context of austerity.

These challenges are 'tricky' rather than 'wicked' because they are the result of devious intent and because they force contradiction between *uncontested* desirable outcomes in the day-to-day operations of local government. As might be expected, designing service and social innovations in this context is itself 'tricky' in that it is difficult and awkward (*Oxford English Dictionary*). Worse still, designers risk their practices being perceived as 'tricky', complicit in the deceitful and crafty action of austerity, if they are not negotiated transparently and inclusively with all the actors involved. Open, participatory and responsive design approaches can help to navigate this tricky scenario:

> At the heart of design is the need to mobilize cooperation and imagination. The design process needs to be kept open to requirements that by necessity are evolving, as well as to be able to arrive at novel, and sometimes unexpected, solutions. Openness implies that decisions about possible design trajectories are not made too quickly, and requires that the various stakeholders involved present their work in a form that is open to the possibility of change. It puts emphasis on the dynamics of opening and expanding, fixing and constraining, and again reopening. (Binder et al. 2012: 22)

When dealing with 'tricky' challenges, shared visions may be perceived as deceptions if left unrealized. And every shared vision in the context of public services is beyond the gift of the designer alone. While designers have a role in the conception, configuration, communication and ultimately construction of one or other of diverse and sometimes contradictory future imaginaries, theirs is at best a *constitutive* power rather than a *constituted* one (Follett 1924 cited in Durose and Richardson 2016: 15) – a *power with* rather than a *power over* others (and therefore outcomes). The designers' actions can therefore be viewed by those they collaborate with either as a 'duplicitous' advocacy of contradictory outcomes or as a 'holistic' countenance of possible futures that might be achieved. Deception is subjectively entwined with expectation and realization.

The designer is comfortable countenancing seemingly paradoxical possibilities, suspending decision and disbelief, empathizing with diverse accounts of the present and imagining myriad possible futures, 'mediating between research and action and between potentialities and actualities' (Julier and Kimbell 2016: 39). Whether navigating the contradiction between the dominant-hegemonic neo-liberal position of the present while designing for a socially just public and collaborative future, or working together with diverse actors, with potentially contradictory perspectives, to address the challenges of the present at the same time as shaping possibilities for the future, it is the designer's comfort with contradiction, their ability to hold contradictory present realities and possible futures in the same gaze, that equips them to be able to work with, and within, tricky scenarios without cognitive dissonance (Festinger 1957) limiting their ability to act. But, to avoid the appearance of 'trickiness' in this scenario, to ensure that comfort with contradiction and openness to possibility are not mistaken for double dealing, it is suggested by some that designers 'manage expectations' of participating actors. But, to do so would belie the designer's actual agency in the design process at the same time as closing down rather than opening up the extent and array of future possibilities. Thus, to avoid the appearance of trickiness at the same time as preserving openness, designers should seek to mediate and negotiate rather than manage the expectations of participating actors, in as open and accessible a way as possible, so that the 'trickiness' of the challenge is understood and not projected onto the practices of the designer.

> Diverse values are held by different groups of individuals – that what satisfies one may be abhorrent to another, that what comprises problem solution for one is problem generation for another. Under such circumstances, and in the absence of an overriding social theory or an overriding social ethic, there is no gainsaying which group is right and which should have its ends served. (Rittel and Webber 1973: 168)

So how is the designer meant to operate ethically within this contradictory climate? Postpone judgement and harbour contradictory possibilities certainly, but also recognize themselves as *responsive* not responsible, at the risk of appearing 'tricky' in their inability and unwillingness to take responsibility for a situation over which they only have a contributory agency.

Recognizing the designer's role in this scenario as that of the *socially responsive* designer, we are able to mobilize understandings discussed elsewhere (Gamman and Thorpe 2006, 2011) that locate the designer as 'a co-actor within a co-design process – sometimes leading as an expert and sometimes not' – displaying 'pluralism and adaptability'. Recognizing that 'it is not clear which ethical design drivers, or stakeholder agendas, the design[er] should be responsible to' and given 'that there may be no "right answer", or none that can address all drivers and actors equally' the socially responsive designer applies 'a co-design approach' that seeks to be 'plural and equitable regarding the agency of actors within the design process'. Co-design processes 'integrate the individual and collective agencies of the actors within them, and necessitate negotiation of collective goals. Thus, the individual agency of the designer, and other actors, over both the processes and products of (co)design are inevitably subject to compromise'. Consequently, designers are only able to be responsive rather than ultimately responsible in the way they engage with, and deliver social objectives through design – and this limitation needs to be understood by other actors in design processes and acknowledged as 'good enough'.

i) Innovating democracy as a response to trickiness in democratizing innovation

As soon as the words 'Big Society'[8] left former prime minister Cameron's lips (2010), one of the 'trickiest' ethical dilemmas facing the social designer active in public service and social innovation arose. Using design to meet publics' needs was feared by many to inadvertently support the neo-liberal destruction of public services. By helping to find ways and means of meeting the needs that the destruction of public services leave unmet, designers risked making something that is very wrong appear alright. However, to seek to remedy is not to condone. The co-design of public and collaborative services is intended not to support the destruction of the public sector but to find alternatives to privatization, to ensure equitable access to public goods despite politically induced austerity.

Now more than ever, we need to work together to find new ways to deliver public services that safeguard equitable access to public goods, to outmanoeuvre the 'tricky' challenges posed by the austerity and efficiency end game that sees impossible odds stacked against the public sector as stewards of public goods.

The limitations of designerly responses are clear. The partial agency of the socially responsive designer renders them impotent to deliver the required service and social innovation alone. Even together with other societal actors, the 'tricky' nature of these challenges means that what is achievable in the short term is 'the best of a bad job' – a good enough resolution given the context at hand – overcrowded families forced to choose between hoping and coping; housebound readers forced into a transactional rather than a relational home library service, losing the potential for interest-oriented early intervention that the latter affords; a society forced into a choice between prevention and cure rather than afforded both. The dominant-hegemonic position of neo-liberalism appears to have captured even the social designer, limiting her or his ability to reach beyond the trickily constructed present-day 'reality' of austerity towards a more socially constructive future where wealth distribution ensures equitable access to public goods.

Despite this bleak reckoning, the designer's open embrace of ambiguity and uncertainty, and of the plurality of present realities and future possibilities, has a key role to play in going beyond present constraints. To work collaboratively in the assembly and service of publics to find new ways to meet the needs of the present offers a prototype for the future. Design's contribution to a social account of 'democratizing innovation' via participatory and collaborative design approaches, finding equitable and inclusive ways to bring a diversity of skills, competencies and resources to bear on collective visioning in response to challenges, is simultaneously a prototype for 'innovating democracy', opening the possibility of finding equitable and inclusive ways to bring a diversity of skills, competencies and resources to bear on the 'tricky' causes of austerity, not just its effects. Erling Björgvinsson articulates a role for design researchers in 'infrastructuring agonistic public spaces mainly by facilitating the careful building of arenas consisting of heterogeneous participants, legitimising those marginalised, maintaining network constellations, and leaving behind repertoires of how to organise socio-materially when conducting innovative transformations' (Björgvinsson et al. 2012: 143).

While much of the activity described above has been focused on facilitating and finding resolutions to tricky day-to-day challenges via public and collaborative service innovation, in fulfilling this role, designers may help to address what DiSalvo articulates as 'the problem with politics'. Citing Honig (1993) and Mouffe (2000) he states:

> ...the structures and mechanisms of governance often hide or mitigate the essential contests of life. In benign forms, this occurs in an effort to lessen public strife and smooth the processes of governance. In less benign situations, politics become the very methods of extending hegemony by feigning to provide opportunities for expression and action, thereby re-directing or sublimating contestation and reinforcing the status quo. (2010: 3)

Assembling publics for collaborative experimentation in public and collaborative service innovation supports the sharing of different experiences and perspectives. The day-to-day shortcomings of the dominant-hegemonic viewpoint, that neo-liberalism is legitimate and austerity appropriate, are made more visible. Visualization of these shortcomings from human-centred perspectives makes them more accessible while collective visioning changes expectations of what is possible. Framed this way, collaborative design for public service innovation becomes a kind of 'political design' that 'identifies new terms and themes for contestation and new trajectories for action' (DiSalvo 2010: 4). Building on this understanding, design universities can contribute to the infrastructuring of a 'space' of redundancy, a space in which publics can assemble and act, stepping outside the dominant-hegemonic position of neo-liberalism to counter the hegemonic discourse of austerity and its drive for efficiency that leads to privatization of public services.

Collaborative design approaches can support the constitutive power of publics to both *democratise innovation* and *innovate democracy*. Co-producing public services by prioritizing effectiveness over efficiency addresses the *tricky* challenge of demographic shifts combined with austerity, *at the same time as* collectively making visible, visualizing and envisioning alternatives to the neo-liberalism that fundamentally contributes to inequality of access to public goods.

Notes

1 In an article on personalization in health provision, Savard (2013) defines neo-liberalism as 'the (re)privileging of liberal principles, including the notion that individuals are atomistic, rational agents whose existence and interests are prior to society', citing Petersen and Lupton (1996).
2 The term 'dominant-hegemonic position' is used here to describe the scenario in which efficiency is taken for granted as desirable in relation to public services, such that to respond in a different way, especially one that is oppositional, is deemed illegitimate.
3 Between 2015 and 2020, over a period when the general population is expected to rise 3 per cent, the number aged over 65 are expected to increase by 12 per cent to 1.1 million, the number aged over 85 by 18 per cent to 300,000 and the number of centenarians by 40 per cent to 7,000 (Parliament.uk 2015).
4 One in three adults aged 16–74 (37 per cent) with conditions such as anxiety or depression, surveyed in England, was accessing mental health treatment in 2014. This figure increased from one in four (24 per cent) since the last survey was carried out in 2007 (McManus et al. 2016).
5 Oxford English Dictionary defines 'redundancy' as 'the state or quality of being redundant, superabundance, superfluity'.
6 The identity of the borough is not shared as the opinions expressed are those of the author and cannot be attributed to collaborating stakeholders.
7 For a summary of Buurtzorg ('care in the neighbourhood') see Huijbers (n.d.).
8 *'David Cameron launches Tories' "big society" plan',* http://www.bbc.co.uk/news/uk-10680062 archived, accessed in December 2016.

Bibliography

Binder, Thomas, De Michaelis, Giorgio, Ehn, Pelle, Jacucci, Giulio, Linde, Per and Wagner, Ina (2012) 'What Is the Object of Design?', *Chi 2012*, 5–12 May 2010, Austin, Texas. Available at: http://perflensburg.se/p21-binder.pdf
Björgvinsson, Erling, Ehn, Pelle and Hillgren, Per-Anders (2012) 'Agonistic Participatory Design: Working with Marginalised Social Movements', *Co Design*, 8, 2–3: 127–144.
Cipolla, Carla and Manzini, Ezio (2009) 'Relational Services', *Knowledge Technology and Policy*, 22, 1: 46.
DiSalvo, Carl (2010) 'Design, Democracy and Agonistic Pluralism', in D. Durling (ed.). *Design and Complexity. Proceedings of the Design Research Society Conference*, 7–9 July 2010, Montreal (Quebec), Canada: Université de Montréal.
Durose, Catherine and Richardson, Liz (2016) *Designing Public Policy for Co-Production; Theory, Practice and Change*, Bristol: Policy Press.
Festinger, Leon (1957) *A Theory of Cognitive Dissonance*, Evanston, IL: Row & Peterson.
Gallouj, Faïz and Weinstein, Olivier (1997) 'Innovation in Services', *Research Policy*, 26, 4-5: 537–556.
Gamman, Lorraine and Thorpe, Adam (2006) 'What Is Socially Responsive Design – A Theory and Practice Review', *Wonderground, Proceedings of the 2006 Design Research Society International Conference*, Forum Tecnologico do Polo Tecnologico de Lisboa, Lisbon, 1–4 November 2006.

Gamman, Lorraine and Thorpe, Adam (2011) 'Design with Society: Why Socially Responsive Design Is Good Enough', *CoDesign International Journal of CoCreation in Design and the Arts*, 7, 3–4: 217–231.

Gaver, William, Boucher, Andrew, Pennington, Sarah and Walker, Brendan (2004) 'Cultural Probes and the Value of Uncertainty', *Interactions*, 11, 5: 53–56.

Honig, Bonnie (1993) *Political Theory and the Displacement of Politics*, Ithaca, NY: Cornell University Press.

House of Commons Health Select Committee (2016) *Impact of the Spending Review on Health and Social Care*, Published 19 July 2016, HC 139.

Huijbers, Peter (n.d.) '*Care in the neighbourhood: Better home care at reduced cost*', *Interlinks Health systems and long-term care for older people in Europe. Modelling the interfaces and links between prevention, rehabilitation, quality of services and informal care.* Available at: http://interlinks.euro.centre.org/model/example/ NeighbourhoodCareBetterHomeCareAtReducedCost

Julier, Guy and Kimbell, Lucy (2016) *Co-producing Social Futures through Design Research*, Brighton: University of Brighton.

Local Government Association (2013) *Whole Place Community Budgets: A Review of the Potential for Aggregation*, London: Local Government Association.

Local Government Report: The Impact of Funding Reductions on Local Authorities (National Audit Office, November 2014). Available at: https://www.nao.org.uk/wp-content/ uploads/2014/11/Impact-of-funding-reductions-on-local-authorities.pdf, accessed on 1 November 2016.

McManus, S., Bebbington, P., Jenkins, R. and Brugha, T. (eds) (2016) *Mental Health and Wellbeing in England: Adult Psychiatric Morbidity Survey 2014*, Leeds: NHS Digital.

Manzini, Ezio and Staszowski, Eduardo (2013) *Public and Collaborative*, New York: DESIS Network.

Mouffe, Chantal (2000) 'Deliberative Democracy or Agonistic Pluralism', in C. Neuhold (ed.), *Working Papers*, Vienna: Department of Political Science, Institute for Advanced Studies (IHS).

Mouffe, Chantal (2007) 'Artistic Activism and Agnostic Spaces. Art and Research: A Journal of Ideas', Contexts and Methods, 1, 2. (n.p.) available at: http://www. artandresearch.org.uk/v1n2/mouffe.html.

Nolan, Sean and Pitt, Joanne (2016) *Balancing Local Authority Budgets*, London: CIPFA. Available at: http://www.cipfa.org/policy-and-guidance/publications/b/balancing-local-authority-budgets-online

Parker-Follet, M. (1924) *Creative Experience*, New York; Longmans, Green & Co, p. xiii.

Parliament.uk. (2015) *Political Challenges Relating to an Aging Population: Key Issues for the 2015 Parliament*. Available at https://www.parliament.uk/business/publications/ research/key-issues-parliament-2015/social-change/ageing-population/

Petersen, Alan and Lupton, Deborah (1996) *The New Public Health: Health and Self in the Age of Risk*, St. Leonards: Allen and Unwin.

Rittel, Horst W. J. and Webber, Melvin M. (1973) 'Dilemmas in a General Theory of Planning', *Policy Sciences*, 4: 155–169.

Savard, Jacqueline (2013) 'Personalised Medicine: A Critique on the Future of Healthcare', *Bioethical Enquiry*, 10: 197–203.

Service Transformation Challenge Panel (September 2014) *Bolder, Braver and Better: Why We Need Local Deals to Help Save Public Services*. Available at: http:// publicservicetransformation.org/images/2902929_ChallengePanelReport_acc3.pdf, accessed in December 2016.

Simon, Herbert (1996) 'The Sciences of the Artificial', 3rd Edition, Cambridge, MA: MIT Press.

Taleb, N. (2012) *Antifragile: How We Live in a World We Don't Understand*, London: Allen Lane, p. 44.

Thorpe, Adam and Gamman, Lorraine (2016) 'What Is "Socially Responsive Design and Innovation"?' in Penny Sparke and Fiona Fisher (eds), *The Routledge Companion to Design Studies*, London: Routledge, pp. 317–329.

Tinker, Anthea, Ginn, Jay and Ribe, Eloi (2013) *Assisted Living Platform – The Long Term Care Revolution: A Study of Innovatory Models to Support Older People with Disabilities in the Netherlands*, Technology Strategy Board, Knowledge Transfer Network, Housing LIN.

11

Understanding Suicide and Assisted Dying – Why Is 'Design for Death' Tricky?

Lorraine Gamman and Pras Gunasekera

A girl calls and asks, 'does it hurt very much to die?'
'Well, sweetheart', I tell her, 'yes, but it hurts a lot more to keep living'.
Chuck Palahniuk, Survivor (1999)

We cannot escape the reality of dying; it will happen to all of us. At least 0.8 per cent of the planet's population (55 million people) are estimated to die each year (De Sousa 2015). But how to design for death is very tricky considering that 'assisted dying' (a system that allows a person the choice to get help to control their death if they decide their suffering is unbearable) is a taboo subject and 'suicide' (taking one's own life) even more so. In daily life, most people don't often talk about *suffering* (men find this particularly difficult, see Galdas et al. 2005) nor about death, suicide or assisted dying because of cultural customs and other repressive mechanisms that prevent open discussion. In the global context, death is usually connected with the sacred rather than profane material issues and suicide transgresses assumptions about the sanctity of life. So, policy concerning how to dispose of our bodies in new ways when we don't need them and how to design the end of ourselves doesn't happen that often. The subject of death is sacrosanct, particularly if the person concerned chooses to commit suicide. Also the differences between lonely 'do-it-yourself' suicide and assisted/accompanied dying (as in the Swiss 'assisted dying' model) are rarely the subject of easy discussion.

Designing is acknowledged as inherent to human beings (Dilnot 2014; Fry et al. 2015). It shapes power relations, and it can (re)write pasts, reconfigure presents and prefigure futures (Prado de O. Martins and Vieira de Oliveira 2016). It has the potential to be a catalyst for intentional material and philosophical change, but outside of specialist design education circles the world talks about design as much as it talks about death, that is, not that often (with a few notable exceptions!). So, this chapter will try to address the gap in knowledge of how 'design', which is about pragmatic arrangements that can be envisioned and created, can be a space that can facilitate autonomy for end-of-life and assisted dying decisions in the context of 'sanctity of life' discourses. Of course, legally binding advance healthcare directives (to refuse treatment) are not per se 'assisted dying', even if it is an end-of-life decision that is legal in the UK. It is also one that can leave some individuals with no other choice, when medical treatment is stopped, than to starve to death.

The context of our discussion therefore is that developments in medicine and our lifestyles have made human lives longer, yet some with poor health conditions would prefer not to experience long life. In fact some research indicates that increasing longevity for many people over the age of sixty-five could mean nothing but adding poor-quality years to their lives (Crimmins et al. 2016). An earlier European Court of Human Rights ruling (2002) in the case of *Pretty v. the United Kingdom* (paragraph 65) went further and pointed out: 'In an era of growing medical sophistication combined with longer life expectancies, many people are concerned that they should not be forced to linger on in old age or in states of advanced physical or mental decrepitude which conflicts with strongly held ideas of self and personal identity.'

Of course the human desire to control death, even in difficult scenarios, raises all sorts of ethical and political questions about the 'right to die' and also about 'abnormal' mental health conditions. For example, Cavanagh and colleagues (2003) have argued that the majority of people who die by suicide suffer from mental disorders. Many other authors, following Durkheim (1897), describe diverse causal factors, including weak social ties and social isolation issues that result in suicide or requests to assist suicide, and inevitably these accounts have informed protective social policies. With assisted dying, however, the evidence is such that the individuals being helped have nothing in common with people suffering from mental disorders. The data from the state of Oregon, USA, for example, shows that it is not the weak and vulnerable who opt for assisted dying, but rather the health-insured, and the above averagely educated (Public Health Division 2017).

In a 2014 debate for MA Communication Design students at Central Saint Martins, UK, Baroness Mary Warnock recognized the diverse reasons and factors for suicide, when she spoke *for* changing policy to support assisted dying. Baroness IIora Finlay spoke *against* this position, explaining why so many disability groups oppose 'assisted dying'. Speakers at the same debate from the Samaritans, the British Humanist Association, and Survivors of Bereavement by Suicide and other social innovation networks (documented at www.macdextendingempathy.wordpress.com) demonstrated that the issues raised by suicide and policies about it are equivalent to a 'wicked' design problem (defined and outlined by Rittel and Webber 1973; Buchanan 1992). No agreement or easy discussion regarding the issues raised by suicide appears to be available that suits all actors in the political and social landscape. Consequently, this chapter considers discourses that have informed this existential debate by first reviewing 'design against suicide' initiatives and secondly, reviewing issues raised by designing for assisted dying and voluntary euthanasia. The final section of our chapter will consider why it is important to open up agonistic discussion on this topic in the way Chantal Mouffe (2013) describes when thinking about the world politically. Ultimately this chapter will look beyond the design of existing humanist anti-suicide policies, to consider broad questions about how more design engagement regarding end-of-life rituals could aid in the development of pragmatic ways to make new suicide policies work by design to better serve democratic purpose.

Design against suicide

To understand why we often speak about suicide in hushed tones, the cultural taboos that surround death along with its euphemistic language like 'passed away' need to be examined and understood. Elsewhere we have discussed how future visions of death care design, generated by a 2013 *Designboom* competition, offer important new ways of thinking about how to design for death (Gamman and Gunasekera 2015). In a similar way, the social design research team in Hong Kong led by Yanki Lee, the *Fine Dying* project, used participatory/critical design methods to engage communities to codesign dying matters (Lee 2015). This included new ways to dispose of their own bodies or to commemorate or remember those who have died by introducing the concept of a Death Jewellery Collection, designed to hold synthetic diamonds made from human ashes (Figure 11.1).

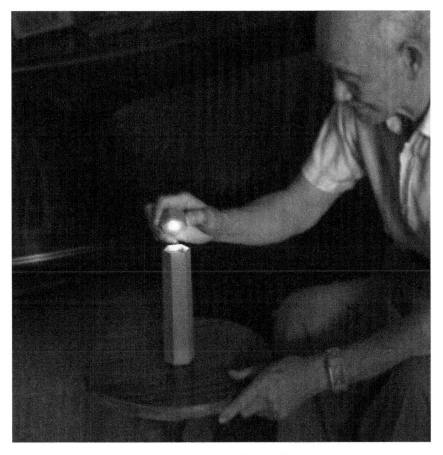

Figure 11.1 The Light of the Death Jewellery Collection (design research by Yanki Lee of HKDI DESIS Lab) designed by Pascal Anson.

In seeking to identify new forms of human body disposal, the *Fine Dying* project has worked with community groups, including groups of senior citizens, to create sustainable strategies and possible new futures for cities. Hong Kong like other cities struggles to find space for people to live as well as to die. Yet neither the *Fine Dying* project nor the *Designboom* competition addressed design for suicide or assisted dying, perhaps because these concerns (despite the dominance of neo-liberal profit logic) are difficult to discuss. With a few global exceptions, such as Hollywood portrayals of Japanese Samurai (or their wives) committing 'seppuku' (also called 'hara-kiri' in English) for honourable purposes in films like *The 47 Ronin* (1941), *The Last Samurai* (2003) and James Clavell's TV mini-series, *Shōgun* (1980), suicide is rarely represented as a form of death that design could engage with. Nor is it taken to be a way of dying that deserves positive commemoration, not least because of concerns about suicide 'contagion' and 'copycat' suicides.

While there are websites that promote suicide and discuss details of best suicide methods, including the most painless ways to die, most search engines are designed to display prevention discourses associated with the Samaritans when the word 'suicide' is used as a search term. This may be because in 2012 suicide accounted for 1.4 per cent of all deaths worldwide, making it the 15th leading cause of death (World Health Organisation 2014: 22). In 1998, suicide constituted 1.8 per cent of the total disease burden; this is estimated to rise to 2.4 per cent by 2020 (Bertolote and Fleischmann 2009). It is now one of the three leading causes of death among young people (both male and female) aged 15–44 (Public Health Action for the Prevention of Suicide 2012: 4). Suicide is traumatic for those left behind, affecting parents and families dealing with the loss of children to suicide as well as communities when suicide occurs in social spaces. Bridgend in Wales unfortunately became known for its attempts to make sense of teen suicides when between January 2007 and December 2008 twenty-six people committed suicide in their homes, many of whom were aged between 13 and 17. 'Suicide clusters' and ideas about 'suicide contagion' have been investigated in a number of other geographical regions, including Palo Alto High School in Silicon Valley, with inconclusive results.

Suicide attempts are up to twenty times more frequent than successful suicides (Preventing Suicide: A Global Imperative 2014: 26). The World Health Organization (WHO) identifies that almost 800,000 deaths by suicide occurred in 2015, making it the second leading cause of death by injury after road traffic injuries (World Health Statistics 2017: 32). Prevention discourses are paramount in discussion, with the WHO Mental Health Action Plan 2013–2020 aiming for a 10 per cent reduction in the suicide rate in countries (World Health Organisation 2014: 09). However, the cultural sensitivities that surround suicide mean that attempts to design against it in the built environment often have to be covertly implemented. Even at suicide hotspots, we don't want to be reminded of suicide or death by any means. Consequently, discourses that promote safety and protective designs to prevent suicide attempts usually contain hidden target hardening metaphors, rather than operating as part of an open discussion about suicide, mental health or social isolation issues.

In most countries suicide is no longer a crime, but an ethical issue. In the UK, the Suicide Act of 1961 decriminalized the act of suicide in England and Wales so that those who failed in an attempt to kill themselves would no longer be prosecuted. Given the criminological context associated with the history of suicide, it is not surprising that some of the measures from the Design Out Crime (DOC) movement were taken on board by those who promoted suicide prevention because agenda setting promotions by the UK Home Office were influential and connected both approaches. In 1988, criminologists Ronald Clarke and Pat Mayhew, employed by the Home Office, showed that gas suicides in Britain in the 1960s and 1970s (literally putting your head in the oven to die) were reduced when the carbon monoxide content of domestic gas changed. When coal gas was replaced by natural gas from the North Sea, suicides by cookers virtually stopped altogether. By the 1990s, such accidental 'designs' against suicide inspired the DOC movement (see Clarke 1983, 1992). Clarke made a strong case that physical design can provide opportunities to commit suicide, or make them more difficult. See also Gamman and Thorpe (2017) on issues raised by design for behaviour change.

The idea underlying this work – that suicide and death need to be prevented and that public places need to be safe – can be extended to humanistic and empathic design understandings (Gamman and Thorpe 2016). In addition to protecting those who may feel suicidal from harming themselves, preventive design protects the relatives and operatives who have to live with the impact of successful suicide events. Public Health England (2015) puts this bluntly, noting that when 'a suicidal act takes place outside the deceased's or another's private home or in a public location, it offers potential for the act to be witnessed by members of the public, or for the body to be found by someone unknown to the deceased'. The secondary impacts of suicide not only involve financial clean-up costs, as highlighted in the DIGNITAS (a Swiss member society – To live with dignity To die with dignity) inquiry (2017: 11), but can cause immense emotional suffering, not just to the loved ones of the suicide victim, but also to workers and bystanders, such as the drivers of trains that hit suicide victims.

Harm to others clearly can't be ignored by those designing *against* suicide even if this focus might result in the sort of target hardening design that often adversely affects the aesthetic of the built environment, as Minton (2009) describes. Design for suicide prevention has not yet delivered the sort of empathic designs associated with healing places like the Maggie's Centers (drawing on nature to reduce alienation) because often suicide prevention design is an 'add on' or retrofitted to pre-existing built environments. The designers of spaces/places that become suicide hotspots will not have anticipated such spaces/places would aid or facilitate people killing themselves. One positive side effect of retrofitting such spaces to make them less convenient for suicides is that anti-suicide design strategies raise issues about the need for human agency as well as physical design. In locating telephone helplines at such hot spots, or designing in human inspections, there is a recognition of the need for human contact to aid prevention – a recognition that reliance on physical barriers or remote and distant crime prevention strategies such as CCTV (or surveillance of spaces via drone activities) is not enough.

The Samaritans, a UK charity that supports troubled and suicidal individuals, has delivered some excellent anti-suicide campaigns, including the 'We Listen' campaign, designed by Mullen Lowe in 2016. They point out that despite best practice prevention design strategies, more lives are lost in public space to suicide than to road traffic accidents. They recently brought together over fifty stakeholder organizations to try and address this problem. Among the actions they reviewed was the need to regulate internet sites used by high-risk networks and individuals. These sites contain statements such as '*You may be reading this looking for information on methods to commit suicide. They are here*' (lostallhope.com) and '*planning ahead greatly improves your chances of a good death*' (finalexodus.org) which could be seen as promoting suicide. This example of the ethical consequences of digital public space offers a particular instance of tricky dilemmas about how best to design or regulate it, given a broadly liberal desire for freedom of information that seeks to tolerate diverse and controversial views.

Is it possible to ethically assist dying by design?

Debates around 'assisted dying' and 'voluntary euthanasia' remain more controversial than designing against suicide. 'Euthanasia', which is prohibited all over the world, and voluntary euthanasia, which is possible in the Netherlands, Belgium, Luxembourg and to some extent in Canada (where it is defined as Medical Assistance in Dying or MAID), are of course very different approaches. Assisted dying and voluntary euthanasia *always* require the explicit wish/consent of the patient (and acceptance in law of this process), without which the doctor administering the drug would be committing euthanasia which is a criminal offence of murder/manslaughter.

Those who are in pain and want to put their affairs in order by managing their own 'end of life' and/or designing their own merciful death are rarely allowed to do so legally. These are very different situations to people who attempt or commit suicide, while the balance of their mind is/was 'disturbed', as Barraclough and Shepherd (1976) point out. Even when mental illness is not the main reason for suicide, dealing with the aftermath of suicide is very distressing to the families left behind, for moral, emotional and religious reasons. Yet this distress also constrains open discussion about assisted dying for fear of offending those who have already lost loved ones to suicide or are worried about this happening. There is also concern about whether or not the design of systems for assisted dying can avoid criminal misuse and abuse, and manage the potential for an individual to be manipulated by others to commit 'voluntary' suicide. However, this focus on the potential 'misuse' of law is not always helpful because concerns about murder of the vulnerable, rather than design of systems that could prevent this, tend to block open discussion. For example, living wills (also called 'advance directives' or 'advance decisions') with clear, actionable parameters (e.g. 'I only want to be given a lethal injection if I can no longer consistently recognize any members of my family when consulted over a specified period') could be implemented by carefully designed strategies that include checks by medical and other professionals. At a future date, if the law changes, advance directives made by individuals when 'compos mentis' might mean those of us who do not wish to experience advanced stage dementia, for example (where we cannot recognize loved ones), can have our wishes to end life at this point heard and implemented.

Of course, design could be used in many ways to assist dying or prevent suicide. Yet discussion of design and suicide is limited perhaps because the capacity of design is poorly understood outside of design circles. Designers are rarely invited to discuss how to prevent suicide in terms of service provision where radical social innovation is needed. Here, empathy with the potential distress of those whose lives have already been harmed by suicide may repress truly agonistic debate or social innovation benchmarks by design being developed. Paul Bloom's *Against Empathy* (2016) suggests democratic debate can be hijacked or blocked by stigmatized interest groups – for example, those with disabilities who are worried changes to the law on suicide (and the design opportunities this could bring) will eventually impact on them in negative ways, possibly in worst case scenarios, linked to eugenic narratives.

Open discussion is also compromised by the fact that suicide attempts are viewed as a 'cry for help' and actual suicides are often understood by the therapeutic community as 'missed opportunities' to provide that help or social contact. Consequently, the debates about suicide and, by extension assisted dying and voluntary euthanasia, run into a number of powerful and tricky ideological conflations about preserving life at all costs that even a legal order to allow someone to die cannot override. Cathy Rentzenbrink's brother existed in a vegetative state for over eight years, and when his family decided the last act of love would be to let him die, they obtained a court order that agreed to the withdrawal of life support, as a form of passive euthanasia. There then ensued an ordeal for the family as withdrawal of life support did not provide assistance with death. As Rentzenbrink observes: 'There are kinder ways to end life than starving someone to death' (Rentzenbrink 2015). This merciless situation occurs (and reoccurs) in the UK because our medical practice primarily aims to 'save lives, not tend to their demise' (Gawande 2014) and Cathy Rentzenbrink and her family had to prove her brother's prior mental disposition to refuse life support rather than accept palliative care.

At the time of writing, voluntary euthanasia is legal in the Netherlands, Belgium, Colombia and Luxembourg. Assisted dying is legal in Switzerland, Germany,[1] Canada and in the US states of Washington, Oregon, Colorado, Vermont, Montana and California. In other geographical regions such as the UK, requests to seek assistance with dying are not supported by policy and are deemed 'criminal' (linked to manslaughter or murder charges).

Designing for autonomous dying and against youth suicide

Many of the themes and issues we have introduced so far in relation to suicide and assisted dying were explored in 2014 by a group of Communication Design postgraduates at CSM. Their brief gave them a choice: to design a campaign *against suicide* aimed at preventing harm to the young, or to work on a policy campaign *for assisted dying* aimed at individuals with only six months' life expectancy. Although the cohort that engaged with the project was nearer in age to the target group for the brief against suicide, the majority chose to design campaigns that were 'pro' or in support of assisted dying.

Figure 11.2 'Living Wills' project, © MA Communication Design, Central Saint Martins, 2014.

Overall, students hotly debated ways of creating 'safeguards' in systems to support assisted dying that would preclude abuse. At the moment all living wills/advance directives can do is outline an individual's wish to refuse treatment (or not to be revived) by medical practitioners. But even this request is not always assured: in 2017 a UK stroke patient (Brenda Grant) who made a living will was found to have been kept alive and fed through a stomach peg for two years, despite her wishes, because her living will/advance directive had been 'mis-filed'. Designs for future living wills by our students anticipated building in more sophisticated options than just the choice of not being revived or refusing treatment but also with firm constraints to prevent abuse – for example, not going ahead with broader options for assisted dying or voluntary euthanasia until certain conditions are met. The students also produced communication campaigns to support assisted dying organizations that help individuals live and die with dignity and to help the public understand why some people demand the 'right to die'.

The low-key visual responses from our students, such as that shown in Figure 11.2, took place in a context where there is not only a need for designs of new campaigns but also a demand for the design of new *policy*. But shortly after this student project was completed (in September 2015) UK MPs rejected Lord Falconer's assisted dying bill in England and Wales, which was based on the Oregon model that has been in place, and judged to have been effective since 1997 (see Sullivan et al. 2000, for a full review). This was the UK's first vote on the issue in almost twenty years (Gallagher and Roxby 2015) and it failed, despite polling evidence conducted by Populas for Dignity in Dying recording that 82 per cent of publics they canvassed supported the bill! The parliamentary debate heard impassioned views and personal experiences from both sides and the bill was rejected with 330 votes against and 118 votes in favour.

A clear distinction can be made between 'euthanasia' and 'assisted dying'. Legal ethics expert Penney Lewis reviewed the law in a number of countries in 2015 for the BBC. She showed that euthanasia is defined as an intervention undertaken with the intention of ending a life to relieve suffering – e.g. a lethal injection administered by a doctor. 'Assisted dying' is the more commonly used term in the United States and United Kingdom. The UK organization Dignity in Dying are pushing for the Oregon model to become legal in the UK and almost copy its wording, referring to a terminally ill, mentally competent adult, who makes the choice to die early of their own free will to avoid what they would consider an undignified death, after meeting strict legal safeguards. This could occur through the individual, taking prescribed medication which will end their life (www.dignityindying.org.uk/assisted-dying) or arranging for an appointed medical practitioner or other representative to administer it. (Organizations in the UK, such as MDMD [https://www.mydeath-mydecision.org.uk] tend to prefer this latter approach.)

The key difference between the two is that in assisted dying the individual, rather than medical professionals, makes the decision to end their life. We should clarify that **we are for choice and for assisted dying/voluntary euthanasia** but *against* euthanasia. We support those who who want and need varying types of end-of-life care and we value their democratic decisions, but we also want choice.

The UK is surrounded by countries that take different, arguably more rational, views on end-of-life choices. In Europe, the Netherlands was the first country to legalize voluntary euthanasia and assisted dying, in 2002, after nearly thirty years of parliamentary debate. Belgium and Luxembourg have followed and also implemented end-of-life choices. In October 2016, the Dutch government went further and announced plans to draft new laws to extend assisted dying to those who feel their **'life is complete'** (Sterling 2016). The health and justice minister advised that the extension should only be made available to the elderly who have met 'strict and careful criteria' (Sterling 2016) and that their choices should dominate. This provision includes developing systems that design out potential abuse or misuse to ensure that vulnerable patients who claim the right to die are adequately protected from those who might wish to inherit property or assets.

The Swiss society, DIGNITAS - To live with dignity - To die with dignity (in short: DIGNITAS), provides a space and designed means to end one's life through legal doctor-supported accompanied suicide. It is the only legal option available for UK citizens wishing to end their life via assisted dying, and involves travel to Switzerland. The process itself requires membership of DIGNITAS, and a formal request including medical evidence to be reviewed by DIGNITAS and by Swiss doctors (independent of DIGNITAS). It also involves follow-on payments to cover running costs (although there is a sliding scale and possible exemption for those who do not have the financial means). In addition two consultations take place before a lethal dose of powdered Pentobarbital is administered by a doctor, dissolved in water for the patient to drink. In Switzerland, assisted dying is legal and generally takes place in the home of the individual. When this is not possible (e.g. patients who live in care homes that do not allow such assistance to take place), and for people from abroad, DIGNITAS provides a room in a house for this purpose (Figure 11.3). Because of complaints by residents (about

Figure 11.3 Garden with pond in front of the DIGNITAS house, 2013 (Image © Dignitas).

undertakers and hearses), the space provided by DIGNITAS has been moved from an inner-city location to the city's edge. This move may be a failure of design from the point of view of the experience of the clients involved and the stakeholder associations who support it, but it became a necessity. It has also raised broad questions about who would rather die where – in the familiar comfort of one's own home, or far away.

Design interventions to assist dying in the UK could develop future visions of spaces that could offer a service like DIGNITAS, creating scenarios about how things could work pragmatically. Linking such designs to the use of *ritual* could make a difference by helping the public to explore their pre-death wishes through increased cultural understanding of, and participation in, such processes.

Rituals have a long cultural history. Durkheim (1957: 225–226) showed that religious rituals unite individuals into collective groups, serving to 'strengthen the bonds attaching the individual to the society of which s/he is a member'. We seek to make the case not just for the design of new policies but also for ritualistic end-of-life systems using design (Figure 11.4). This is because ritual enables enduring patterns of social organization and cultural symbolic systems to be brought to bear on real events that are assessed and negotiated in ways that can transform these traditional patterns or structures (Bell 1997: 77).

Every religion has a structured approach to dealing with death. The Jewish community has communal activities as well as clearly defined periods of mourning (Parkes et al. 1997: 112). In Buddhist Japan, there are prescribed measures as to how a

Figure 11.4 Futuristic service tools to create pre-death rituals. Pras Gunasekera (MA Industrial Design, Central Saint Martins), 2012 (Author's photograph).

body should be laid out and with what objects in preparation for the soul to transcend to the next life (Grimes 2000). As Catherine Bell outlines, rites of passage known as 'samskaras' within Hinduism are intended not only to purify but also to 'make over or transform' (Bell 1997: 99). These ceremonies denote a series of actions that progressively refine and prepare the inner and outer person for the ultimate goal in Hinduism of 'better rebirth and final release from the cycle of life and death in this world' (Bell 1997: 99). Such rituals provide important ways to make sense of death, making tangible the stages that we encounter throughout life and offering the potential to explore the stages pre-death for those that wish to die, perhaps to aid better decision-making.

The events leading up to death and the recognition that someone has died can be traumatic and often produce ambiguous moments. Mary Douglas (1999: 111) has pointed out that many societies regard death as a stage of meaning that is polluted by ambiguity. Fear about ambiguity, and a lack of control, produces all sorts of effects for those left behind. Consequently, rituals used within rites of passage to mark death could help people make sense of the trauma death often causes, particularly in the context of assisted dying. Innovative design might usefully draw upon ritual in the implementation of assisted suicide policy, achieving better social understandings about managing the threshold of the end of life.

Designing for death and the future: What is the role of design?

In our view design that is plural, responsive, political, delivering ideas that may not find affinity with market-led strategies has a place in 'design for death' that supports humanist accounts. There can be no single solution to end-of-life management that suits everyone and this fact is accentuated in the wicked and distressing problem of suicide, particularly of young, vulnerable people. As we have already identified, suicide as a subject is linked to stigmatization and any new policy or pragmatic design for assisted dying and voluntary euthanasia must address fears that policy could lead to decisions being made that 'creep' towards practices that were not intended. Design's ability to envision possible new futures, including those that concern assisted dying, can therefore have a positive role. By offering pragmatic options and visualizing them, design can make a difference by engaging publics in democratic debate about those options and solutions. Perhaps design activism and even user-centred design for new future users have a role to play, not least because given the rising trends of agnosticism, atheism and those who are not affiliated with religion (Bullard 2016), because there are new social needs to be served.

Such 'user needs' are not being addressed and prevailing taboos, about death, suicide and assisted dying, indicate that religion continues to influence many of our 'choices'. Debates, for example, over capital punishment draw upon some of the same ethical principles. The humanist golden rule of 'treat others how you wish to be treated' is hard to make real in design terms when not everyone in the world agrees on what an 'appropriate' treatment actually is! Amnesty International's view that the death penalty is 'the absolute irreversible denial of human rights' (2013) is not shared by fifty-eight countries in the world that retain capital punishment.[2] Yet it is possible in those countries, with marked differences resulting from their democratic systems, to make arguments against the death penalty to demand change – to be part of what Chantal Mouffe (2013) proposes as the space for positive contestation and 'agonistic democracy' to occur. So why are accounts of assisted suicide in the UK still compromised by cultural taboos?

By making marginal voices heard and visible, presenting choice scenarios, designs for death and assisted dying can be delivered as ethical design. Such community engagement and discussion that uses design skills to offer better visions of the future and solutions about how to deal with end-of-life choices is currently absent. There is no engagement with how to make assisted dying easier, or to protect vulnerable individuals at risk from suicide. Designers could be involved in making that debate heard and visible; they are skilled future visionaries, strong at making future scenarios understandable through design prototyping and visualization. Such envisioning of how assisted suicide could work could have an important role to play in democratizing innovation regarding end-of-life choices and also in answering the challenge of achieving communities' engagement with the complexities of legal debates on this subject.

When faced with life or death decisions, all designers recognize how small they really are, and how different contexts raise different issues. After the death of his father, IDEO's Chief Creative Officer, Paul Bennett, wrote an article in September 2014 titled 'Can Death Be Designed?'. Bennett's experience made him realize that his father was trying to take control of his last moments and, ultimately, to design his death, to make it acceptable. But Bennett found this difficult to bear, as have those of us who have powerlessly witnessed parents dying (from dementia, for example) who could not take control of their last years. Dementia leaves many families and friends with little to do except watch loved ones living and dying in ways we know they would not have wanted when they were their full selves. Such lived experiences have inspired many of us to look our own death in the face and to try to figure out how best to design for it in the future. Some of us want to use living wills/advance directives and other methods to allow us as individuals more democratic choice and agency, if, and when, we as citizens are not capable of making those final decisions.

'Reinventing death for the twenty-first century' is such an agenda, promoted by Marie Curie's *Design to Care* programme. It asks tough questions that highlight a tension between humanist and laissez faire neo-liberal discourses that often make people uneasy. James Pallister has reviewed the Marie Curie programme and highlights a range of further start-ups, corporations, venture capitalists and health providers who see designing for death as a positive thing. Together many involved in design are trying to devise new and more meaningful ways of dying, including for assisted dying, by suggesting *design* should have a role in the arrangements for death – a role that is socially responsive to human suffering, participatory and collaboratively linked to democratizing innovation and choice (Lee et al. 2015) rather than simply a logical extension of economic concerns. The articles by both Bennett and Pallister emphasize our current medicalized view towards death and suggest that we need to move beyond this. Given that design is employed readily to create the nuances of our *living*, it is argued that the same opportunities for design should be sought and applied to our inevitable *dying* (Pallister 2015).

Conclusion

It may seem cynical to see death or assisted dying as a design opportunity, but many social design innovation groups are making strong arguments about the need to help society see different future visions and design *for* death. Groups like Modern Loss (www.modernloss.com) and the Death Café (www.deathcafe.com) have been growing across the globe. The audience at a Southbank Death Café (March 2017) were told that over 4,000 café events have already happened and that Death Café events have occurred in twenty-six countries across the globe. Understanding these conversations about death may be a key factor in improving how society deals with end-of-life decisions, including issues raised by assisted dying (and also voluntary euthanasia) – discussions that are central to Death Café group activities.

Speculative and critical designers have also joined the design for death debate and are trying to present new possibilities too. Unfortunately, most of the examples from critical design such as 'Afterlife' by Auger Loizeau (October 2009), the 'After Life Euthanasia Device' by Dunne and Raby (March 2011) and the 'Euthanasia Coaster' by Julijonas Urbonas (2010) (see Figure 11.5) sit in publicly inaccessible spaces, such as art galleries. Also they do not present 'preferable futures' or the sort of strategic future thinking that accounts of socially responsive design (Gamman and Thorpe 2011) or design activism (Julier 2013) offer. Instead, they engage with death as a spectacle, presenting uncomfortable mysterious technologies designed to disgust and shock

Figure 11.5 Euthanasia Coaster by Julijonas Urbonas (Royal College of Art), 2010 (Author's photograph).

audiences through their uncanniness (DiSalvo 2012; Tonkinwise 2014; Prado de O. Martins and Vieira de Oliveira 2016). If such critical design approaches are able to start public debate it appears to be delivered with little pragmatism, in terms of broad community engagement, or any account of further actions that might be needed.

We think design can do better. We must use design visioning, including speculative and critical design faculties, in proleptic or positive ways to address death. Instead of generating self-indulgent as well as self-contained narratives exhibited in a gallery space (accessible only to a few who may already support liberal, pro end-of-life choices), we need to open up conversations about death, beyond cynical economic arguments, so that broad audiences and publics as well as multiple stories can be involved, revealed and followed (Prado de O. Martins and Vieira de Oliveira 2016). We argue that the diverse possibilities for death and assisted dying in the future can be reimagined, by design, discussed and conceived, as new choice. If the contemporary moment of 'difficult and dangerous times' (Manzini and Margolin 2017) has taught us anything, it is that designers need to be able to visualize in material ways objects, systems and services that address *conflicts* regarding our understanding of human rights and values that characterize our times (not just the values we support). We need to use design to design different things; not just to 'solve' problems, but to speak disparate truths that will support real democratic debate, and help us to understand wicked problem scenarios. Well-designed technology is not only for living moments; technical and design skills can also be drawn upon and stepped up, to greet our inevitable death. Of course, thinking about how to prevent or aid suicide may be painful and never less than tricky, but designers should have the courage to invent and visualize new possibilities and help to design new policies and ways of pragmatically implementing them in the real world. All this, to paraphrase the lyrics of Johnny Mandel and Mike Altman's *Suicide Is Painless* (1970), is aimed at allowing us to 'take or leave them, as we please'.

Notes

1   Since November 2015 with some restrictions, namely that only a one-off assisted suicide would be legal. Professional help is therefore restricted from repeated acts by Section 217 of the German Criminal Code.
2   In 2016, 102 countries have completely abolished the death penalty for all crimes, 6 have abolished it for ordinary crimes (while maintaining it for special circumstances such as war crimes) and 32 are abolitionist in practice. Consequently, almost 60 per cent of human beings live in democracies such as the United States, India, China and Indonesia and experience the death penalty as a reality.

Bibliography

Barraclough, B. and Shepherd, D. (1976) 'While the Balance of His Mind Was Disturbed', *British Medical Journal*, 39: 128.

Bell, C. (1997) *Ritual: Perspectives and Dimensions*, New York and Oxford: Oxford University Press.

Bennett, P. (2014) IDEO Stories. *Can Death Be Designed?* Available at: https://medium.com/ideo-stories/can-death-be-designed-c002f4bcb383#.f22x60xp4 (accessed 14 December 2016).

Bertolote, J. M. and Fleischmann, A. (2009) '*A Global Perspective on the Magnitude of Suicide Mortality*', in D. Wasserman and C. Wasserman (eds), *Oxford Textbook of Suicidology and Suicide Prevention: A Global Perspective*. Oxford: Oxford University Press, 91–98.

Bloom, P. (2016) *Against Empathy: The Case for Rational Compassion*, London: The Bodley Head.

Buchanan, R. (1992) 'Wicked Problems in Design Thinking', *Design Issues*, 8, 2: 5–21.

Bullard, G. (2016) *The World's Newest Major Religion: No Religion*. Available at: http://news.nationalgeographic.com/2016/04/160422-atheism-agnostic-secular-nones-rising-religion/ (accessed 29 December 2016).

Cavanagh, J. T., Carson, A. J., Sharpe, M. and Lawrie, S. M. (2003) 'Psychological Autopsy Studies of Suicide: A Systematic Review', *Psychol Med*, 33: 395–405.

Clarke, R. (ed.) (1992) *Situational Crime Prevention: Successful Case Studies*, Albany, NY: Harrow and Heston.

Clarke, R. V. (1983) 'Situational Crime Prevention: Its Theoretical Basis and Practical Scope', *Crime and Justice: An Annual Review of Research*, 4: 225–256.

Clarke, R. V. and Mayhew, P. (1988) 'The British Gas Suicide Story and Its Criminological Implications', in M. Tony and N. Morris (eds), *Crime and Justice: An Annual Review of Research*, Chicago, IL: University of Chicago Press.

Crimmins, E. M., Zhang, Y. and Saito, Y. (2016) 'Trends over 4 Decades in Disability – Free Life Expectancy', *American Public Health*, 106, 7: 1287–1293. doi:10.2105/AJPH.2016.303120. Epub 2016 Apr 14.

De Sousa, A. N. (2015) '*Death in the City – What Happens When Our Cemeteries Are Full*'. Available at: https://www.theguardian.com/cities/2015/jan/21/death-in-the-city-what-happens-cemeteries-full-cost-dying (accessed 12 October 2016).

DIGNITAS (2017) *Joint Select Committee on End of Life Choices Inquiry into the need for laws in Western Australia to allow citizens to make informed decisions regarding their own end of life choices*. Available at: http://www.dignitas.ch/images/stories/pdf/diginpublic/stellungnahme-submission-end-of-life-choices-western-australia-23102017.pdf (accessed 27 October 2017).

Dignity in Dying (2015) 'Largest ever poll on Assisted Dying shows 82% of public support Lord Falconer's proposed change in the law'. Available at: https://www.dignityindying.org.uk/news/poll-assisted-dying/ (accessed 20 October 2017).

Dilnot, C. (2014) 'Is there an ethical role for the history of design? Redeeming through history the possibility of a humane world', *in Tradition*, Transition, *Trajectories: Major or Minor Influences?*. *9th Conference of the International Committee for Design History and Design Studies*. Aveiro, Portugal, 8–11 July. doi:10.5151/despro-icdhs2014-0003.

DiSalvo, C. (2012) *Adversarial Design (Design Thinking, Design Theory)*, 1st Edition, Cambridge, MA: MIT Press.

Dorst, K. (2015) *Frame Innovation: Create New Thinking by Design*, Cambridge, MA: MIT Press.

Douglas, M. (1999) *Implicit Meanings: Essays in Anthropology*, 1st Edition, London: Routledge, p. 111.

Dunne, A. and Raby, F. (2009) *After Life Euthanasia Device*. Available at: http://www.dunneandraby.co.uk/content/projects/486/0 (accessed 20 October 2017).

Durkheim, E. (1897 [1951]) *Suicide: A Study in Sociology*, New York: The Free Press.

Durkheim, E. (1957) *The Elementary Forms of Religious Life*, 2nd Edition, London: Allen & Unwin, pp. 225–226.

Fry, T., Dilnot, C., and Stewart, S. (2015) *Design and the Question of History*, 1st Edition, London: Bloomsbury Academic.

Galdas, P. M., Cheater, F., and Marshall, P. (2005) 'Men and Health Help-Seeking Behaviour: Literature Review', *Journal of Advanced Nursing*, 49, 6: 616–623.

Gallagher, J. and Roxby, P. (2015) *Assisted Dying Bill: MPs reject 'right to die' law*. Available at: http://www.bbc.co.uk/news/health-34208624 (accessed 6 February 2017).

Gamman, L. and Gunasekera, P. (2015) 'Some Context: Designing for Death'. Available at: https://macdextendingempathy.wordpress.com/brief-elements/some-context-designing-for-death/ (accessed 15 February 2017).

Gamman, L. and Gunasekera, P. (2016) *Design against Suicide: Background Strategies*. Available at: https://designagainstcrime.com (accessed 3 March 2017).

Gamman, L. and Thorpe, A. (2011) Design with Society: Why Socially Responsive Design Is Good Enough', *CoDesign International Journal of CoCreation in Design and the Arts*, 7, 3–4: 217–231.

Gamman, L. and Thorpe, A. (2016) 'Design for Empathy – Why Participatory Design Has a Contribution to Make Regarding Facilitating Restorative Values and Processes', in T. Gavrielides (ed.), *Offenders No More: New Offender Rehabilitation Theory and Practice*, New York: Nova Science Pub.

Gamman, L. and Thorpe, A. (2017) 'Is Nudge as Good as We Think in Designing against Crime? Contrasting Paternalistic and Fraternalistic Approaches to Design for Behaviour Change', in Kristina Niedderer, Stephen Clune and Geke Ludden (eds), *Design for Behaviour Change: Theories and Practices of Designing for Change (Design for Social Responsibility)*, London and New York: Routledge.

Gawande, A. (2014) *What doctors don't learn about death and dying*. Available at: http://ideas.ted.com/death-and-the-missing-piece-of-medical-school/ (accessed 22 December 2016).

Gould, M., Jamieson, P. and Romer, D. (2003) 'Media Contagion and Suicide among the Young', *American Behavioral Scientist*, 46: 1269–1284.

Grimes, R. L. (2000) *Deeply into the Bone*, 1st Edition, Berkeley, CA: University of California Press.

Jacobs, J. (1961) *The Death and Life of Great American Cities*, New York: Random House.

Julier, G. (2013) 'From Design Culture to Design Activism', *Design and Culture*, 5, 2: 215–236.

Lee, Y. et al. (2015) *Fine Dying: Let's Co-design Our Dying Issues HKDI DESIS LaB, ISBN: 978-988-13961-43*.

Lewis, P. (2015) *Assisted dying: What does the law in different countries say?*. Available at: http://www.bbc.co.uk/news/world-34445715 (accessed 1 October 2016).

Loizeau, A. (2009) *Afterlife*. Available at: http://www.auger-loizeau.com/projects/afterlife (accessed 20 October 2017).

Manzini, E. and Margolin, V. (2017) Open Letter to the Design Community: *Stand up for Democracy*. Available at: www.democracy-design.org (accessed 20 October 2017).

Mason, R. (2015) *Assisted dying bill overwhelmingly rejected by MPs*. Available at: https://www.theguardian.com/society/2015/sep/11/mps-begin-debate-assisted-dying-bill (accessed 21 November 2016).

Minton, A. (2009) *Ground Control: Fear and Happiness in the Twenty-First Century City*, London: Penguin.

Mouffe, C. (2013) *Agonistics: Thinking the World Politically*, London: Verso Books.

Palahniuk, C. (1999) *Survivor: A Novel*, Chapter 40, 1st Edition, New York: Anchor Books.

Pallister, J. (2015) *Reinventing death for the twenty-first century*. Available at: http://www.designcouncil.org.uk/news-opinion/reinventing-death-twenty-first-century-0 (accessed 1 October 2016).

Parkes, C. M., Laungani, P., and Young, B. (1997) *Death and Bereavement across Cultures*, 1st Edition, London: Routledge, p. 112.

Prado De O. Martins, L. and Vieira De Oliveira, P. J. S. (2016) 'Breaking the Cycle of Macondo: Design and Decolonial Futures', *ACM Crossroads*, 22, 28–32.

Pretty v. The United Kingdom (2002) European Court of Human Rights, case 2346/02 [online]. Available at: https://hudoc.echr.coe.int/eng#{"itemid":["001-60448"]} (accessed 26 October 2017).

Public Health Division, Center for Health Statistics (2017) *Oregon Death with Dignity Act. Data Summary 2016*. Available at: http://www.oregon.gov/oha/PH/PROVIDERPARTNERRESOURCES/EVALUATIONRESEARCH/DEATHWITHDIGNITYACT/Documents/year19.pdf (accessed 26 October 2017).

Public Health England (2015) *Preventing Suicide in Public Space: A Practice Resource*. Available at https://assets.publishing.service.gov.uk/government/uploads/system/uploads/attachment_data/file/481224/Preventing_suicides_in_public_places.pdf

Rentzenbrink, C. (2015) *The Last Act of Love: The Story of My Brother and His Sister*, 1st Edition, London: Picador.

Rittel, H. and Webber, M. (1973) 'Dilemmas in a General Theory of Planning', *Policy Sciences*, 4, 155–169.

Sterling, T. (2016) *Dutch may allow assisted suicide for those who feel life is over*. Available at: http://www.reuters.com/article/us-netherlands-euthanasia-idUSKCN12C2JL (accessed 19 December 2016).

Sullivan, A. D., Hedberg, K. and Fleming, D. W. (2000) 'Legalized Physician-Assisted Suicide in Oregon – The Second Year', *The New England Journal of Medicine*, 342: 598–604.

Tonkinwise, C. (2014) 'How We Intend to Future: Review of Anthony Dunne and Fiona Raby, Speculative Everything: Design, Fiction, and Social Dreaming', *Design Philosophy Papers*, 12, 2: 169–187.

Urbonas, J. (2010) *Euthanasia Coaster*. Available at: http://julijonasurbonas.lt/euthanasia-coaster/ (accessed 20 October 2017).

World Health Organization (2012) *Public Health Action for the Prevention of Suicide: A Framework*, Geneva.

World Health Organization (2014) *Preventing Suicide: A Global Imperative*, Geneva.

World Health Organization (2017) *Suicide Data*. Available at: http://www.who.int/mental_health/prevention/suicide/suicideprevent/en/ (accessed 26 October 2017).

Referred Websites

Amnesty International on Corporal Punishment: www.amnesty.org/en/what-we-do/death-penalty/

Death Café: www.deathcafe.com

Designboom Design for Death competition: www.designboom.com/competition/design-for-death/

DIGNITAS: www.dignitas.ch/index.php?lang=en

Fine Dying: www.enable.org.hk/details/2017/8/15/fine-dying
Humanists UK: www.humanism.org.uk
Maggie's Centres: www.maggiescentres.org/about-maggies
Modern Loss – Candid Conversations about Grief: www.modernloss.com
The Samaritans: www.samaritans.org
Survivors of Bereavement by Suicide: www.uksobs.org

12

The Quest for Purity, 'Clean' Design and a New Ethics of 'Dirty Design'

Jeremy Kidwell

The contemporary designer is forced to grapple with an ever-increasing range of forces and agencies, which may be revealed or concealed in the design process. In this chapter, I analyse a cluster of design paradigms that hover around the idea of 'clean design'. Though my ultimate pursuit of tricky design is an ethical one, I begin with a historical excavation of the ways that the modern ideals of hygiene and purity conceal malevolent and anti-ecological design agendas. As I see it, 'clean' design arose in relationship with the rise of hygiene science and though the latter has been significantly revised, the former has not yet seen the same level of critique. In this chapter, I will follow some of the historical tributaries of clean design, noting some of the ways in which seemingly benevolent intentions, towards accessibility and clarity can mask a much broader (and more problematic) range of cultural mobilizations like purity and hygienic mass-death. I will commend an alternative 'tricky' approach – *dirty design* – in order to promote a mode of design that may promote social innovation in design while upholding a more broadly ecological result.

There is an unavoidably complex web of agencies at work in design and I will contend that the designer will either react to encounters with foreign presences and the tricky agendas of non-human other by grasping for control, and by extension some measure of exclusion and sanitary killing, or choose to accept the task of accommodating the lively relationships that tricky substances promote. Through three design case studies that engage with a range of tricky substances, I suggest that this *dirty design* offers a re-orientation which ultimately comes as an acceptance of 'growth' and the extension of welcome to the unpredictable other.

The birth of clean design

In the early twentieth century 'streamlining' also went by another name, 'cleanlining'. Alongside the new awareness of aerodynamics and the desire for speed, streamlining was driven by anxiety about dirt and cleanliness, generated in part by new scientific knowledge about disease and immunology. Miasma theory of disease had given way to the germ theory of disease just before the turn of the twentieth century – Louis Pasteur's experiments ran between 1860 and 1864 and Robert Koch confirmed the causative relationship between microbes and disease in 1890. In Britain, the Public Health Acts of 1874 and 1875 emphasized public sanitation as an avenue towards health. These discoveries and public policy innovations implanted an awareness of bacteria and its relation to disease in the popular imagination. Concurrently, the early decades of the twentieth century (Hoy 1995: 104ff) saw the rise of aerodynamics, with scientific work on aerodynamics and gliders by Otto Lilienthal between 1891 and 1896 and the first flight by the Wright Brothers in 1903. The increased influence of streamlining in design is evidence for an emerging partnership between science, social welfare and design stimulated by knowledge of dangerous bacteria.

Several examples demonstrate designers working to promote purity and hygiene. As Adrian Forty points to the paradoxical streamlining (or cleanlining) of stationery objects like Raymond Loewy's redesigned refrigerator:

> Loewy's design, the Coldspot, with its pressed steel casing and seamless finish ... conveyed an image of absolute cleanliness and hygiene. The seamless exterior and rounded corners, the brilliant white finish, and the absence of dust-catching crevices and mouldings ... all meant that when it was clean, it looked the physical embodiment of health and purity. (Forty 1992: 156)

The thinking behind cleanlined design held that pure surfaces were those where 'flow' that allowed for efficient movement (i.e. speed) might repel dirt, and eventually by extension, microscopic life, providing 'pure' surfaces which generated healthful living conditions. Le Corbusier's design principles in his 'Manual of the Dwelling' demonstrate the comprehensiveness of this vision for design as a vehicle for hygiene:

> Demand a bathroom looking south one of the largest rooms in the house or flat ... One wall to be entirely glazed ... An adjoining room to be a dressing-room in which you can dress and undress. Never undress in your bedroom. It is not a clean thing to do and makes the room horribly untidy ... Demand a vacuum cleaner ... Demand ventilating panes to the windows in every room ... Bear in mind economy in your actions, your household management and in your thoughts. (Le Corbusier 1986: 122–123)[1]

There isn't space in this brief chapter to unpick all the associations and collusions that arose with the rise of modernism, but it is important to note that these seemingly benign associations between clean space, hygiene and dwelling seen in the late nineteenth century also saw a more sinister deployment in the form of 'racial hygiene'. It is here that the association of an aesthetic of cleanliness is explicitly connected to 'whiteness', but as Judith Williamson and others have noted, the integration of an ideology which brings together 'clean', 'white' and 'hygienic' works across science, advertising and design in more subtle ways as well (Proctor 1988; Williamson 2001).

Alongside this designed hygienic exclusion of the non-white there is a second less well-documented exclusivity, and this lies in the forms of design which deliberately sought to exclude other-than-human agencies. Just one generation before Le Corbusier, before it became widely understood that pathogenic microscopic life might dwell on surfaces, Alois Riegl argued for a positive appreciation of the accumulation of things on surfaces, that is, patina as part of the so-called 'age value' of a building (Riegl 1982). A number of Romantic theorists emphasized the importance of the accumulation of patina as part of the beauty of a designed object.[2] Perhaps in an even more fundamental way, this early association of bacteria exclusively with disease and not also with healthfulness (as I will suggest below may now be more appropriate) underwrote a new perception of the other not only as malevolent but also as *implicitly distinct from oneself.*

Charles Taylor suggests that the premodern conception of self was a 'porous' entity, that is, it was generally accepted that other creatures and consciousnesses could traverse the boundaries of an individual person. In Taylor's view, the modern Western view of the self replaces this porosity with a more bounded conception – what he calls a 'buffered self': 'As a bounded self I can see the boundary as a buffer, such that the things beyond don't need to "get to me" … This self can see itself as invulnerable, as master of the meanings of things for it' (Taylor 2007: 38ff). One of the results of this, in Taylor's analysis, is a resulting sense of 'the utter flatness, emptiness of the ordinary' (Taylor 2007: 309). The crucial point here is not that our domestic reality is actually flat or empty, but that hygiene and purity-driven rationalist design paradigms seek to create this condition by establishing a new boundary around the self, policed through design interventions. Yet, as I will go on to suggest below, the world is full of 'tricky substances' which defy this desire to keep all the forms of life in airtight containers.

This newly 'pure' self has a range of consequences. Bruno Latour argues that the drive towards purification resulted in an array of dichotomies which eventually accumulated into a 'great divide'. As he puts it, 'moderns are serious bifurcators' and this tendency facilitated a wilful cultural separation of art and science, facts from values, theory from practice and nature from culture (Latour 2013: 174). This quest for purity was worked out in the domestic space, on the national political stage and in the space of self-consciousness. What theorists such as Latour and Taylor along with others such as Michel Foucault, Donna Haraway, Deleuze and Guattari have shown us in the latter decades of the twentieth century is the degree to which this sense of the bounded self represents a self-destructive and self-denying quest. The modern imagination describes the human body as a site which does not bear co-inhabitation, and hygienic narratives defend, often violently, the purity of the body against infiltration. By denying the tricky hybridity that defines human agency and liveliness more broadly, hygienic, 'clean' design undermines life itself.

In recent decades, the sciences of immunology and bacteriology have provided the basis for a decisive reconsideration of hygiene and health. As regards the former, recent discoveries regarding the human microbiome suggest that the human body is not only inhabited by a majority of foreign DNA, but that the other creatures which it includes are not merely benign presences but are essential to basic human health and likely co-evolutionary partners (Dethlefsen et al. 2007). There is a growing body of examples which show that the homogenizing and cleansing work of hygiene described above undermines human well-being (Cho and Blaser 2012). In a resonant scientific discourse, late-twentieth-century immunologists struggled to take into account the seemingly strange tolerance of the human body for 'foreign' inhabitants. This resulted in a revision of the general theory of immune system function. Our immune system does not function on the basis of a distinction – as F. M. Burnett influentially framed it in 1949 – between 'self' and 'non-self'. Rather, the body's immune system works on the basis of perceived danger (Crist and Tauber 1999; Matzinger 2002; Medzhitov and Janeway 2002). In essence, over the course of the twentieth century, immunology has come full-circle, concluding that our bodies are a lively meta-community and that only those community members who misbehave are candidates for killing (Leibold 2011; Mihaljevic 2012).

These discoveries about microscopic life challenge modern dichotomies of bodily integrity and design's campaign to exclude the 'non-self', and are in contrast to the hygienist's desire to protect the human body from invasion. Consequently, I will argue for a form of design that can convey an ecological appreciation of tricky hybridity and otherness alongside a re-appreciation of the porous self and the enchanted world. In seeking to mobilize this way of thinking based on this critique of the ideological roots of clean design I have outlined above, I will argue for a form of 'dirty design' and tricky hybridity that I connect back, in the conclusion of this chapter, to the *tricky* focus of this book in terms of the understanding of complex designed systems. As I will go on to suggest, this is not merely meant to serve as a mirror image of clean design, rather, dirty design seeks to reshape design practice in several overlapping ways. Dirty design is characterized fundamentally by the acceptance of two things: hybrid space and death. In seeking to demonstrate this I turn to three examples from design practice that illustrate dirty design, each in a different way.

Inhabiting hybrid space: Shared mineral narratives

As I have argued above, at the heart of the clean paradigm is a sense of policed boundaries, rendered purity and bodily integrity. Looking back a century we can now see many ways in which this modern impulse, which rested on theory which was formalized in the late nineteenth and early twentieth centuries, represents a profound mismatch with the ecological rhythms and structures which the human animal inhabits alongside other forms of life. Ironically, a design paradigm which was built on cutting-edge scientific insight is now significantly at odds with the suggestions of immunology, ecological science, bacteriology and earth systems science. What a host of voices across all these domains of inquiry are suggesting is that life and all its patterns cannot be enclosed by pure categories nor its mechanisms described by well-bounded relationships. 'Clean' has become an anachronism. One way of promoting a more ecological (and by implication also a more relational) approach is to highlight the ways in which the world is saturated with hybridities (Whatmore 2002). The first step towards a dirty design lies in embracing this fact of tricky hybridity.

In recent decades, a range of scholars including Donna Haraway, Bruno Latour, Michel Foucault, Gilles Deleuze and Felix Guattari have argued for a reconsideration of the nature of agency. Their approaches have generally been described as non-essentialist or post-dualist (Haraway 2008). The significance of the post-dualist turn for this chapter lies in an awareness of the presence and activity of non-human others in the *agency* of designs and the importance behind acknowledging these others in the *activities* of design. Another way of putting this is that we make things in ways which are inextricably entangled with other creatures. As Bruce Braun puts it, 'attending to the "double circulation of objects that create social relations and social relations that create objects" … has meant placing non-humans in our stories from the start, as part of the collectivities within which human life is constituted' (Braun 2008: 670).

Scottish Artist, Ilana Halperin, designs objects which explore this entangling of agencies on a geological scale. This is a particularly helpful example here, given the ways in which supposedly inanimate matter, as expressed in soil, rocks, mountains and other geological forms can so often be mistakenly distinguished from animate *life*. In describing her collection, Between Formation, which includes a sustained reflection on body stones, Halperin teases apart this distinction:

> I am a biological organism. I am alive. I am not rock, or earth, though now my father is. Last week my sister was in the hospital for risk of possible gallstones. They found traces of a stone in her body; a process of erosion had taken place and the stone was gone. We expect that we are not made of geology, but our bodies produce mineral evidence that says otherwise. Elephants, snails, horses, dogs all form stones. We are animal and mineral at the same time. We form geology. (Halperin 2015: 21)

In an era where we are confronted so frequently with problems of 'deep time' and resource extraction, exploring tricky hybridity with mineral creatures is quite helpful. As Halperin presents the collection, Between Formation, it represents a kind of narrative or an excerpt from a 'library of rocks and minerals – composed of books of mica, limestone volumes laid down in sheets, etched stone surfaces 800 million years old' (Halperin 2015: 22). Halperin's attending to the work of rocks and the hybrid ways in which humans and minerals co-exist provides a helpful critique of the myth of human power. It points to a mode of design which seeks to surmount the purification of human agency by integrating 'found' narratives, that is, those which are constituted outside the realm of human action and are told within a particular place and time. This principle of tricky hybridity can be exposed in a variety of other design contexts and is threaded through my next two examples.

Designing with death and life: Cor-Ten steel and plastic-eating bacteria

Another example of co-creation can be seen in the earliest use of Cor-Ten steel by neo-futurist architect Eero Saarinen in his design for the John Deere World Headquarters in Moline, Illinois. What is often seen as a key design problem for steel is that it will eventually rust. Showing signs of decay is a particularly sharp problem for the 'clean' ethos and thus steel has proved to be a problematic material. As Cairns and Jacobs observe, modern architecture has oriented much of its work around the idea of a 'persistent natalism' (Cairns and Jacobs 2014: 24). The notion of a human product which might never decay, developed and refined in the Renaissance, represented the ultimate creative achievement for some early modern thinkers. One can see many ways in which the desire for immortal creation culminated in the twentieth century.

In the early 1930s US Steel Corp. developed Cor-Ten as a low-cost departure from the tendency to manufacture steels (as with 'stainless steel' or other alloys) to avoid rust through treatments and painting, by designing a steel intended to rust in a particular way. What George Smith called 'weathering steel' oxidizes for a particular duration and eventually produces an outside layer which protects the remainder of the material from rusting any further. On paper, the benefits of Cor-Ten are numerous: it resists corrosion without being costly, requires little maintenance and the process of oxidization actually improves the mechanical strength (Smith 1971: 211). In spite of the benefits Cor-Ten, which was patented in 1932, it wasn't used for several decades outside specialized industrial applications. It seems likely that a material which was designed to weather ran directly counter to Le Corbusier's vision of 'white cathedrals' and struggled to find appeal in the midst of design hygienists. Saarinen took design rationalism to a logical conclusion, and in his own tricky way initiated 'dirty design'. In approaching the headquarters of John Deere, an agricultural equipment manufacturer, Saarinen sought to design a building which would suit the rural locale and clientele of John Deere. This was not an easy sell, either to his client or to the material supplier. Yet Saarinen persisted on both fronts and was successful in making his case on the basis of an aesthetic argument. Rust need not be considered unlovely, especially when designing in symmetry with nature. As Smith explains in a *New Scientist* article extolling the aesthetic virtues of Cor-Ten:

> These steels weather on exposure to the atmosphere to form an adherent protective oxide coating of a dark attractive colour. The exact tone depends on the time of exposure and the kind and amount of atmospheric contamination present, and ranges form a deep reddish brown to a warm purple grey–somewhere between pine bark and rosewood. These steels are likely to prove of particular value for construction work in rural environments, for they blend unobtrusively into a natural background of trees and shrubs. (Smith 1971: 211)

Seen in this way, Cor-Ten offered a decisive break from the tendency within clean design to make use of materials and structures that eschew environmental inhabitation. This design intervention went on to generate what Lowenthal calls 'a taste for rust' (1985: 163).

In their marvellously provocative book *Buildings Must Die* (2014), Cairns and Jacobs present Cor-Ten as an example of decay which they contrast with the 'persistent natalism' embedded in modern architecture that their book seeks to critique. This is certainly true to a certain extent, but I am not entirely satisfied with the juxtaposition of organic and mineral agencies as they present it (as my mention of Halperin's work above already indicates). I agree with their critique of natalism but want to resist the temptation to conflate natalism with liveliness – a category which might well include both birth and death as part of a wider cosmological understanding of entangled creaturely agencies. On this basis, I would argue that as a material which deliberately embraced weathering as part of its aesthetic and function, Cor-Ten fits the criteria of what sculptor Oliver Andrews calls 'living materials'. As Andrews suggests:

> The concept of 'living materials' acknowledges that every material has an active presence, a character, a capacity for change, that entitles it to be considered 'alive'. Any piece of wood, though no longer part of a growing tree, has a grain pattern and a resiliency that causes it to respond characteristically when struck, bent, or cut. Every stone has its structure, granular or crystalline, flawed or sound, which will make it chip or split in certain ways, but not in others. Steel has its rusty willingness, silver its penetrating molten fluidity. To understand and work with these living qualities, and occasionally to counter and transcend them, is the task of every artist and craftsman. (1988: 1)

While Andrews remains focused on the designer who *acts upon* materials (with a nevertheless more astute understanding of their liveliness), Jennifer Gabrys resituates material attentiveness in the broader context of more-than-human politics. Focusing on the often-maligned material, plastic, Gabrys seeks to transcend the critique of synthetic materials as toxic, invented and ultimately *other* in order to appreciate 'materiality as process'. Seen in this way, causality is not merely linear, instead, as Gabrys argues, 'our material processes and politics are always undertaken in collectives. These collectives are sites of ethical relation and obligation' (Gabrys 2013: 218). In this way of thinking, the designer's response to environmental change should accommodate the work already underway by more-than-human carbon workers such as microbacteria which are breaking down plastics, and move beyond life-cycle thinking which seeks to disappear the unruly other and find a way of reclaiming materials which 'works with those historical remains of our lived plastic materialities to begin to generate new approaches to how plastics orient material practices and politics in the present' (Gabrys 2013: 220).

Ultimately, it is important to appreciate how any embrace of 'living' materials implies an acceptance of death and decay as latent within materials and ultimately part of the telos of any designed object. This stands in some contrast to the desire to design 'new immortals' as Michelle Bastian describes them (2017), or in Timothy Morton's words, 'hyperobjects' (Morton 2013). The twentieth century encompasses a radically changing perspective towards persistent designed objects, whether those early plastics which seemed to innocuously repel dirt and bacteria, or in the more sinister forms we now see in the form of radioactive waste, islands of plastic floating across the ocean, persistent organic pollutants such as DDT or indissoluble microbeads from scented liquid soaps. Morton goes so far as to suggest that these 'hyperobjects … are directly responsible for … the end of the world' (2013: 2). What he means is not that they have literally destroyed terrestrial life (though it remains to be seen whether this might be the case), but rather that these objects generate logical and scalar paradoxes as they congeal into larger and more incomprehensible wholes which render our comprehension of a concept such as 'the world' epistemologically impossible. With its focus on lively entanglements, the mode of dirty design shown in rusting steel provides a more robustly coherent material paradigm for design which might offer a way around some of these plastic paradoxes.

Reconciliation ecology through living walls and roofs

My first two examples of tricky hybridity focus on the need for designers to accept that we design in cooperation with (or in opposition to) other-than-human agencies. In this sense, dirty design is about playing in the midst of a mess of divergent intentions and possibilities. However, the flip side of this hybrid coin is an ethical one, namely that acceptance of the other-than-human should be paired with an intention to make space for them. In this way, I would argue that we *should* make things which provide space for and account for the agency of these others. In this sense, dirty design is also about opening the door to invite a messy encounter. A group of urban ecologists and geographers have recently begun using the term 'reconciliation ecology' in an attempt to capture the dimension of hospitality that this self-extension represents.[3] For my final example of dirty design, I would like to present the living roof as a form of design which reconciles.

Given all the discussion I have already presented surrounding what is some form of 'ecological' design, it is important to appreciate the plasticity of the term 'sustainability'. Sustainability has tended to work out in variety of sometimes opposed ways, though two primary modes could be distilled down to (1) sustainability through (often hubristic) management or restoration schemes which appropriate other-than-human creatures as a 'resource' and (2) sustainability through preservation programmes designed to avoid anthropogenic impacts on 'wild spaces' which often conversely establish urban spaces as anthropogenic reserves. The latter of these two can often be found expressed in a form of sustainable design which is really just eco-consumerism, producing products which are less harmful than their alternatives, but do nothing in themselves to promote 'sustainability' in a broader sense. This kind of sustainability-"lite" shows the influence of 'clean' thinking inasmuch as it reveals a tendency to discount urban space as an ecological context. Inhospitality towards other-than-human creatures is indicated through urban design in a variety of ways, from the act of architectural outfitting of buildings with spikes to prevent birds from roosting to the design of landscapes filled with pesticide-washed urban plant monocultures primarily for decoration (with the lawn as the most pervasive example). Against this tendency to bifurcate space into human/other-than-human realms, a growing range of writers in both sciences and humanities have begun to argue that we must begin to treat every corner of the earth as recently put by Pope Francis as 'our common home' (Pope Francis 2015).

One of the basic tenets of reconciliation ecology is the recognition that any space represents a possible habitat. This stands in direct contrast to the clean sensibility that any space, particularly if it is proximate to human living or working space should be made into a biological vacuum. Following a more thoroughly hybrid notion of human living space, reconciliation ecologists are particularly interested in urban spaces as a site for the regeneration of ecologies. Thus, Francis and Lorimer define reconciliation ecology as 'the modification and diversification of anthropogenic habitats' (Francis and Lorimer 2011: 1429). As these authors suggest, a paradigmatic example of dirty design at work in architectural design practice is the living roof. There are a range of options for building design which can integrate a living roof; this can accommodate an existing structure, though increasingly green facades and roofs are integrated into the design of a building's envelope. The advantages of this kind of design are numerous. As one study reports:

> Covering buildings with vegetation, when applied in a significant urban scale, can improve the urban environment by contributing to urban biodiversity, stormwater management, air quality, temperature reduction and mitigation of the heat island effect. At the same time, the application of greening systems can have, besides the environmental aspects, social and economic benefits. These systems encourage the fruition of urban areas, have a therapeutic effect by inducing a psychological wellbeing through the presence of vegetation, improve cities image [sic], increase property value and function as a complementary thermal and acoustic protection. (Manso and Castro-Gomes 2015: 864)

There are additional benefits which are political in nature. A wide range of conservation principles require top-down delivery and thus are politically very costly. The deployment of living roofs and facades can be coordinated on a small local scale and then stitched together into a network forming ecological corridors. It is important to keep in mind the tricky principle which lies behind dirty design here, as my deliberate use of the term 'living roof' over 'green roof' already implies. As Henry and Frascaria-Lacoste note, green roofs have been deployed for purely aesthetic purposes without necessarily having a positive ecological impact (2012: 91). As these authors imply then, it may be possible to design a green roof to be quite literally green – and by extension decorative – but not *habitable*. In this way a green roof may represent a literal form of green-washing, and akin to the whitewashed and 'cleanlined' surfaces I described above. In terms of conservation priorities, many of the creatures that are threatened are not those which thrive in the liveliest habitats, but actually in brownfield sites, that is, more marginal habitats. In this way, reconciliation ecology can be as its progenitor Michael L. Rosenzweig suggests a 'win-win' option, but only if designers avoid the temptation to create a new form of hygienic green space which is decorative but not habitable. The appeal of bright green may need to give way to a 'dirtier' brown.

A new dirty design ethic

As I have already hinted above with my discussion of Cor-Ten steel and the use of lively materials, dirty design implies that designers must come to terms with death. One of the advantages of a design paradigm which places tricky hybridity at the centre is that it compels an appreciation of the necessary cohabitation of humans with other creatures. This will necessarily include some measure of 'terminal literacy' within one's design practice (Cairns and Jacobs 2014: 47). But it is important to emphasize that dirty design is not exclusively about death, grime or bacteria, but rather about expanding our design to express a wider and more holistic range of liveliness. It is my hope that this broadening out for design in a deliberate departure from emphasis on 'clean' will deliver two important step changes. First, it may promote a transition away from the design paradigms that underwrote so much of the hygienic mass-death which was a result of modern manufacture in the twentieth century, and instead give way to more complex understanding of lively entanglements. Second, in embracing hybridity as part of design discourse, it will help give way to more complex understandings of lively and tricky engagements that recognize complex systems and wicked problems (Rittel and Webber 1973). Here, no single design definition exists as to the causal mechanisms of the problem I have identified in this chapter. Further, any attempt to find a solution will invariably fail if such proposals do not accept the complex interplay of diverse actors as well as the complex interplay of discourses such as hospitality, violence and cohabitation that lie at the heart of dirty design.

Notes

1   It is interesting to note that for Le Corbusier cleanliness ultimately resulted in an architecture which showed no signs of ageing, as outlined in Le Corbusier (1964).
2   Cf. David Lowenthal, *The Past Is a Foreign Country* (Cambridge: Cambridge University Press, 1985), 149–182.
3   For more on the philosophical underpinnings to reconciliation ecology, see my article 'Hybrid Encounters in Reconciliation Ecology' in *Worldviews: Global Religions, Culture, and Ecology*, Vol 20, Issue 3, (October 2016).

Bibliography

Andrews, Oliver (1988) *Living Materials: A Sculptor's Handbook*, Berkeley, CA: University of California Press.
Bastian, Michelle and Van Dooren, Thom (2017) 'The New Immortals: Immortality and Infinitude in the Anthropocene', *Environmental Philosophy*, 14, 1: 1–9.
Braun, Bruce (2008) 'Environmental Issues: Inventive life', *Progress in Human Geography*, 32, 5: 667–679.
Cairns, Stephen and Jacobs, Jane M. (2014) *Buildings Must Die: A Perverse View of Architecture*, Cambridge, MA: MIT Press.
Cho, Iseung and Martin, J. Blaser (2012) 'The Human Microbiome: At the Interface of Health and Disease', *Nature Reviews Genetics*, 13, 4: 260–270.
Corbusier, Le (1964) *When the Cathedrals Were White*, New York: McGraw-Hill.
Corbusier, Le (1986) *Towards a New Architecture*, New York: Dover Publications.
Crist, Eileen and Alfred, I. Tauber (1999) 'Selfhood, Immunity, and the Biological Imagination: The Thought of Frank Macfarlane Burnet', *Biology and Philosophy*, 15, 4: 509–533.
Dethlefsen, Les, Margaret McFall-Ngai, M. and David A. Relman (2007) 'An Ecological and Evolutionary Perspective on Human–Microbe Mutualism and Disease', *Nature*, 449: 811–818.

Forty, Adrian (1992) *Objects of Desire: Design and Society since 1750*, New York: Thames & Hudson.

Francis, Robert, A. and Lorimer, Jamie (2011) 'Urban Reconciliation Ecology: The Potential of Living Roofs and Walls', *J Environmental Management*, 92, 6: 1429–1437.

Gabrys, Jennifer (2013) 'Plastic and the Work of the Biodegradable', in Jennifer Gabrys, Gay Hawkins and Mike Michael (eds), *Accumulation: The Material Politics of Plastic*, London: Routledge.

Halperin, Ilana (2015) 'Between Formation', in P. Sawdon and R. Marshall (eds), *Drawing Ambiguity: Beside the Lines of Contemporary Art*, London: I.B. Tauris.

Haraway, Donna J. (2008) *When Species Meet*, Minneapolis, MN: University of Minnesota Press.

Henry, Alexandre and Frascaria-Lacoste, Nathalie (2012) 'The Green Roof Dilemma – Discussion of Francis and Lorimer (2011)', *Journal of Environmental Management*, 104: 91–92.

Hoy, S. M. (1995) *Chasing Dirt: The American Pursuit of Cleanliness*, New York: Oxford University Press.

Latour, Bruno (2013) *An Inquiry into Modes of Existence: An Anthropology of the Moderns*, Cambridge, MA: Harvard University Press.

Leibold, Mathew, A. (2011) 'The Metacommunity Concept and Its Theoretical Underpinnings', in Samuel M. Scheiner and Michael R. Willig (eds), *The Theory of Ecology*, Chicago, IL: The University of Chicago Press, pp. 163–184.

Lowenthal, David (1985) *The Past Is a Foreign Country*, Cambridge: Cambridge University Press.

Manso, Maria and João Castro-Gomes (2015) 'Green Wall Systems: A Review of Their Characteristics', *Renewable and Sustainable Energy Reviews*, 41: 863–871.

Matzinger, Polly (2002) 'The Danger Model: A Renewed Sense of Self', *Science*, 296: 301–305.

Medzhitov, Ruslan and Charles, A. Janeway (2002) 'Decoding the Patterns of Self and Nonself by the Innate Immune System', *Science*, 296: 298–300.

Mihaljevic, Joseph R. (2012) 'Linking Metacommunity Theory and Symbiont Evolutionary Ecology', *Trends in Ecology & Evolution*, 27, 6: 323–329.

Morton, Timothy (2013) *Hyperobjects: Philosophy and Ecology after the End of the World*, Minneapolis, MN: University of Minnesota Press.

Pope Francis (2015) *Laudato Si: On Care for Our Common Home*, Vatican City: Encyclical Letter.

Proctor, Robert N. (1988) Racial Hygiene: Medicine under the Nazis, Cambridge, Mass: Harvard University Press.

Riegl, Alois (1982) The Modern Cult of Monuments: Its Character and Its Origin, *Oppositions*, 25: 20–51.

Rittel, Horst W. J. and Melvin M. Webber (1973) 'Dilemmas in a General Theory of Planning', *Policy Sciences*, 4: 155–169.

Smith, George (1971) 'Steels Fit for the Countryside', *New Scientist*, 23: 211–213.

Taylor, Charles (2007) *A Secular Age*, Cambridge, MA: Harvard University Press.

Whatmore, Sarah (2002) *Hybrid Geographies: Natures, Cultures, Spaces*, London: Sage.

Williamson, Judith (2001) 'The Rise of the White King', *New Statesman*, 14: 28–29.

Conclusion: Design's Tricky Future

Lorraine Gamman and Tom Fisher

The more I think, read, do and see, the more I view design as it is as part of the prob-
lem of an unsustainable mode of world-making. For this situation to change, what
design is understood to be has to be remade.

Tony Fry (2016: 363)

Or put simply, we need to challenge what design designs.

Pedro J. S. Vieira de Oliveira and Luiza Prado
de O. Martins (2018, this volume)

The idea that design needs to *change* following the global financial crisis of 2008 and
that market-led design may have had involvement in delivering 'an unsustainable mode
of world-making' is accepted by all the authors in this book. They have pursued this
idea by engaging with the concept of 'trickiness', discussing design in the sense of being
able to address 'awkwardly tricky' or 'misleading tricky' things and problems with the
ambition of offering an account of one aspect or another of this change. Following Guy
Julier's acknowledgement that design's 'variegated practices' mean we must acknowledge
that 'no one definition is enough' (2017: 2), several of the chapters including Srinivas
and Staszowski's (on p. 59) discuss the fact that definitions of 'design' are themselves far
too tricky to be expressed in the singular. Moving from definition, to 'reach' – in terms
of agency – Jeremy Kidwell (p. 195) observes that design discussions should 'focus on
the need for designers to accept that we design in cooperation with (or in opposition
to) other than human agencies'. This is an argument supported by Tonkinwise (p. 81)
and challenged by Dant (p. 69). Both authors in different ways engaging with Latour's
account that 'design things'– the socio-material entities explored in the introduction –
mediate our relation to the world. Put simply, this perspective proposes that design
mediates by giving description to the world through applied form that feels like it is
reality but which is artificial (Herbert Simon (1996 [1969]) and constitutes merely a
version of the possible.

The chapters in this collection therefore unashamedly embrace the complexity of
design's mediation and offer no simple focus on the past role of design in making and
delivering (inadvertently or otherwise) unethical and unsustainable patterns of life.
Nor do they focus on the designer as a negative Trickster or 'cunning plotter laying his

traps' (Flusser 1999: 17) to make huge profits for the few. Instead, in different ways, the authors explore 'trickiness' not as deceit and/or deception, but as a critical aspect of the indeterminacy of *things*, as well as a much needed and ethically charged twenty-first-century design focus, able to review what Keshavarz discusses as 'tricky shape shifting artefacts' (on p. 45) and problem contexts.

In trying to find new ways to address 'wicked problems' (Rittel and Webber 1973; Buchanan 1992), and to make the case for ethical and decolonized design approaches to social challenges, all the chapters attempt to identify why today's design and research landscape is awkwardly tricky. The chapters also explore why design practices that deliver the socially situated actions that are necessary to 'design things' (Suchman 1987: 3; Haraway 1988: 591) require unavoidable ethical or unethical choices that have political ramifications.

The state we're in

Writing ten years before the financial collapse of 2008, Will Hutton (1996) was one of a number of authors who raised concerns about the spatial distribution of the banking system in global economy. His book described the negative effects that post-war experiments in neo-liberal economics were having on social cohesion. Clearly, capitalism has also had positive effects, its 'creative destruction' (Schumpeter [1975] 1942: 82) triggering the biggest and fastest surge in development the world has ever seen since 1750, improving living conditions for the majority in the West. However, neo-liberal economics has brought many problems, into which design is tightly bound. As Guy Julier has eloquently explained, beginning in the 1980s, neo-liberalism has the following features:

> The deregulation of markets and the privileging of market forces; the privatisation of state-owned enterprises; the foregrounding of financial interest over others (commutarian, civic, social, environmental etc.); an emphasis on competitiveness and on individual, entrepreneurial practices. (2013: 217)

Design has had a leading role in neo-liberalism. It is entwined with its values and where neo-liberalism thrives, so does a design culture that is implicated in the identities neo-liberalism makes possible. The design economies of the last forty years of capitalism have helped make the intensification of the free market possible giving credibility to the cultural and scientific narratives on which such economics have been built. Design has mainly operated to embody, and to reify, a world view based on competition and individualism, its hegemonic discourses have privileged profit logic ('I', before 'we') obscuring the value of collective action and the advantage of altruism (Wilson and Wilson 2007), and its critical ambitions often amounting only to flirtation with utopian narratives.

Yet since the 1970s this economic mode of organization and industrial paradigm has started to falter, due to instabilities deriving from movements of global capital relating to industrial production that made it hard for some communities to survive without meaningful work. It is difficult to hold on to the dream that the free market can resolve all our complex problems, particularly after the collapse of financial markets in 2008. The exponential development of information technologies in the last twenty years has also impacted on global certainties. These innovations have delivered constant digitally connected communication and shifted numerous boundaries and expectations causing some traditional definitions about how best to do things to blur and blend. As Paul Mason points out, these changes have brought 'inequality to a state of that close to 100 years ago and ... triggered a survival-level event' (2015: xii). Neo-liberalism has produced a privileged 1 per cent elite, who despite the collapse of financial markets in 2008 have more wealth, and consequently power, than 50 per cent of the rest of the world combined (Hardoon et al. 2016). In 2010 Davies and colleagues published similar conclusions having measured the distribution of global household wealth in the year 2000, showing that 10 per cent of adults in the world owned 71 per cent of all household wealth, with massive inter-country differences.

To the extent that design 'is a process of change more than an endpoint' (Julier 2013: 8), it should be no surprise that design is a handmaiden of neo-liberalism. As a practice, design has the inherent ability to envision and therefore help to bring about a positive future, conjuring up positive possibilities, different futures. However, this is a very different 'brief' from reifying the present, which is what design for the market does. Consumerism has produced a design culture that has helped to transform production into consumption, simultaneously embedding a set of values that have colonized the world. While this has provided physical well-being to many in the West, its material dimension is environmentally unsustainable, and its relationship to wealth disparity is socially unacceptable. Consequently, design needs to reinvent itself and offer new visions that are feasible, rather than utopian. As Tonkinwise points out, understanding design's magical 'constructivist powers ... can make seemingly impossible things [equitable social change] not just possible, but materialized as what people take for granted'.

Yet historically design seems to have imagined itself as a process with no inherent moral character. Tom Fisher takes up this point in detail in Chapter 1, when he reviews design's negative but normalized manifestations as part of the arms industry. Tim Dant's chapter also explores different normalizing manifestations of guns and firearms, reinforcing the point that every artificial thing upon which civilization is built is mediated and produced by human values. The effects of design are everywhere and some of these are decidedly unheroic and tricky, awkward. While design might often pretend to be neutral, there are tricky responsibilities linked to designing things that kill, that demand ethical review.

The trickster v tricky design reasoning (as part of ethical design)

The Trickster might seem an unlikely place to start such an ethical review, given that in the history of different cultures, tricksters play amoral tricks and personify instability as much as positive change. Yet the trickster figure offers powerful metaphors about how change happens. Lewis Hyde (2008) points to the trickster's boundary-crossing and occupation of hybrid cultural spaces, the ones where innovation can occur. The trickster is linked to mischief, transgression, disruption, deception, moral ambiguity, magic and play, drawing on a type of cunning intelligence, both inside and outside of the establishment, to deliver transformation. As Fisher (2012) emphasizes, tricksters carry 'critical potential' that should not be underestimated. Lucy Kimbell's chapter draws on a similarly ancient concept in her discussion of the Greek concept of *metis*, wisdom, cunning, practical action in the moment, as a quality that can push against 'apparatus' in the Foucauldian sense. She suggests a metic approach to an 'anti-heroic design' that 'has the potential to craftily sidestep, decentre or otherwise manoeuvre'.

While casting the designer as a cunning trickster may not be an obvious way to rethink what the world needs from designers and design, the tricky potential of design reasoning to ethically make, remake and unmake change, is certainly worth consideration, as it has the ability to impact on all that design touches. Janet McDonnell defines design reasoning through the words of Ian Hacking as 'reasoning that is done in public as well as in private by thinking, also by talking, by arguing and by showing' (Hacking (1992) in McDonnell 2015: 108). She also quotes Horst Rittel's (1987) account of the 'Reasoning of Designers' a critical aspect of which is the way that by reasoning through making designers are easy with working with states of ambiguity or uncertainty. She points out that because their 'form-giving' operates in this way, designers are also 'highly skilled in reasoning critically and are well placed to challenge societal assumptions' (McDonnell 2015: 117). But designers as makers are not always clear about how to best manage the expectations of participating actors, and while the ambiguities that arise around this do not constitute duplicity, as Ann Light and Yoko Akama in Chapter 8 remind us, 'if we are looking for trickiness, we have found it here'.

Being easy with holding competing and paradoxical perspectives as a way to bring about change is neither duplicity nor a lack of leadership, rather as Adam Thorpe argues in Chapter 9, it indicates 'comfort with contradiction and uncertainty, and familiarity with present realities and possible futures held in the same gaze', which 'equips the designer to be able to work together with diverse actors'. These elements of designers' creative skills that inform design expertise feature prominently in accounts of 'design thinking' (Schon 1984: 76–103; Brown 2009), a focus of Kimbell's chapter. She cites Mackay et al.'s (2014) accounts of organization studies to describe the 'metis' – the wisdom in practical action – that is behind 'situated resourcefulness in organisational contexts'. Certainly, this requires feeling at ease with working in a state of what Keats called 'negative capability'. In a letter to his brothers of 1817 he talked about how the greatest writers had the ability to accept 'uncertainties, mysteries, doubts, without any irritable reaching after fact and reason'. This tricky ability to absorb contradictory ideas while not allowing any discourse to dominate or block creative response is not duplicity but comfort with ambiguity. Edward de Bono's *Lateral Thinking* (1999), Brian Eno and Peter Schmidt's *Oblique Strategies* (1975) and IDEO's Methods Cards (2003) are other creative approaches available to design that embody tricky sideways thinking to both defamiliarize, or 'make strange' reality and potentially to deliver a critical view.

Tricky design approaches oscillate between different modes of operation and can be applied to many matters of concern, in various fields. For Janet McDonnell (2015: 112), the 'drawing, thinking and examining .... generating ideas, gathering information modelling and evaluating', involved in designing lead to 'better quality outcomes' that include new design forms and 'things' as social material assemblies (Björgvinsson et al. 2012). The latter in particular can envision futures by materializing how the *probable* can become *possible* and thus help transform systems and people by making change seem *reasonable*. The current need for positive visions of change makes these design skills very relevant now. Herbert Simon (1996 [1969]) reminds us that such skills have always been transferrable and present as many different professions including medicine, law, business apply their thoughts to designed outcomes.

While a focus on such interventions in Simon's 'artificial' is important, it also requires recognition that the designer's actual agency in whatever field is very limited, and that expectations of competing actors and discourses need to be managed carefully, and ethically, in the design making process to avoid losing trust and to share power. Answering this tricky challenge, designers help to materialize the probable next world, while living in this one, which raises a series of paradoxes (Rodgers et al. 2017), and they need to be transparent in order to avoid being labelled deceitful. An ethical approach is therefore essential to be able deal with the contradictions that are part of the contemporary design landscape. However, such contradiction is the beginning not the end of tricky design because it requires change, implying that the designing subject is de-centred and the objectivity of the 'hero designer' is called into question. Practice is opened up in this way through dialogue, and questioning what design should engage with or address through practice, and who should be included in that process.

Social design: Collaboration as a response to complexity

Concern with design's ethics and activity currently directed at making 'change happen towards collective and social ends, rather than predominantly commercial objectives' (Armstrong et al. 2014: 15) has antecedents that can be traced back to the 1970s. Part of the same strand of critical thinking about the purpose of design that produced the 'First Things First' manifesto covered in the introduction, Victor Papanek introduced *Design for the Real World* (1971) with the now-famous warning there are 'few professions more harmful than industrial design', and suggested designers should address social issues. He was not alone in these thoughts and his recommendation coincided with various design initiatives during the 1970s. While a complete overview is not appropriate here, the Italian radical design efforts from Archizoom, Superstudio and UFO that imagined the changes that information systems could bring to consumer culture and to work and leisure are a prominent example. The contributions of community architecture and permaculture movements, summarized by Nick Wates and Charles Knevitt (1987), and Scandinavian design engagements with the trade union movements from the 1970s (see Ehn 1992) are also relevant background to design's current preoccupations. Papanek and other designers who shared his views about their time and for the future attempted to transform the market-led paradigm by designing against poverty and for need rather than profit. Their perspective was radically 'user centred', designing for people, even if it has needed more recently emerged participatory and social design initiatives for designers to work *with* people, as reported in a number of the chapters in this volume.

Social design refuses easy definition, as Armstrong and colleagues (2014) discuss at length, and perhaps because it overlaps with some aspects of 'design activism' (Markussen 2013) there is little meaningful data about it. In a 2014 paper for Nesta,[1] Geoff Mulgan points out that 'there is very little hard evidence on what works'. Over twenty years ago, Nigel Whitely (1993) showed that a social design philosophy existed in some aspects of commercial and public sector operations, when he reviewed accounts of social responsibility. However, he could not gauge to what extent this was significant, nor the real impact of design that seeks to avoid market determination and to change the world. Such approaches remain hard to quantify precisely in terms of actual effects on the world, even today. Yet despite the difficulty of gauging such evidence about actual impact, this has not stopped numerous design challenge movements emerging over the last 15–20 years to address a multitude of issues, energy crisis, housing crisis, environmental impacts of product lifecycles, accessibility and inclusivity, challenges in healthcare and education, crime prevention, ageing, marginalized people and communities in the developing world, sustainability, poverty and democracy, among them. These approaches have delivered innovative design strategies and numerous toolkits to address social issues, in ways that are highly creative, and potentially useful, but their methodological diversity offers a fragmented overall picture. The definition of their objectives in 'social innovation', 'social entrepreneurship' and 'social design' are also often entangled. Markussen's (2017) paper analyses the aims, methods and effects of these approaches to addressing the wicked problems that are part of today's tricky design landscape.

While there are clearly some shared collaborative and participatory design understandings embedded in competing social design approaches, between them, they have yet to instigate the 'massive change' that Bruce Mau advocates (2004). Within design education the design approaches identified above have changed some of the ways design is taught not least because 'challenge based education programmes' are popular (Mulgan et al. 2016). Many design projects that address social issues draw on participatory techniques, as the global DESIS labs demonstrate, in order to promote openness and find new ways to democratize innovation, that are not reliant on market forces (Björgvinsson et al. 2012), inspiring young designers to take such ideas into mainstream practice. As can be seen from the entries to the 2017 Beazley Design Awards[2] at the UK's Design Council, successful design agencies are addressing social issues, some using alternative finance such as crowd funding to get their projects off the ground.

Scaling up such initiatives is problematic, but Manzini (2015: 11–12) nevertheless suggests design for social innovation is becoming more widespread because people in many parts of the world find themselves in situations where they need to reinvent their lives. This could be due to financial crisis where they need to find a way to live well, if possible, with less income and less consumption, or it could be due to people being displaced. Chen and colleagues (2016) offer a different perspective on why design is embracing social issues. They suggest that the financial crisis of 2008 pushed designers to look for new opportunities from the public and non-governmental sectors because of the shrinkage of design's traditional home in manufacturing. The growth of design education too may have impacted on the push towards designers engaging with complex social challenges, with education initiatives promoting engagement with social challenges and providing designers with tools to address services and communities. One consequence of this shift is that many designers recognize the ethical challenges ahead and are inspired to design for good, seeking new sectors to engage with, and proactively forging new opportunities to use their training on alternatives to the market-led design that they no longer see as ethically valid.

Design for democracy: Reframing political issues as design problems

Design understandings, methods and perspectives (Martin and Harington 2012) are *multiple*; they draw on many possible points of view held by a variety of potential stakeholders/actors. This means that design engagement with social issues inevitably embraces tricky encounters with issues raised by complexity, indeterminacy and democracy. What is most tricky about design's predicament is not just that there are multiple ways to address and barriers to resolving social issues, but because the degree to which capitalism is embedded in every type of human meaning linked to self and society, design culture most often does not function to bring about change but tends to reify prevailing customs. This reification is rearticulated via the 'intimate level' at which design's 'visual, spatial and temporal qualities' engage with economic action (Julier 2017: 21). Neither the process of this engagement nor its ethical consequences are necessarily evident, a fact that aligns with Clive Dilnot's characterization of ethics as 'a concept does that not contain within itself the operative criteria by which it can become manifest' (2017), so the job of design can be to visualize and make transparent the ethical contradictions at work in the settings that normally determine it.

Designers have easy access to strategies that can be appropriated for social good, involving designers in visualizing contradiction, or creating spaces for revealing and challenging power relations. This offers a form of design for what Chantal Mouffe (2000) calls agonistic democracy – a condition of political contestation and dissensus, between different actors and competing discourses, that involves disagreement and confrontation. As Mouffe puts it:

> What is specific and valuable about modern liberal democracy is that, when properly understood, it creates a space in which this confrontation is kept open, power relations are always being put into question and no victory can be final. However, such an 'agonistic' democracy requires accepting that conflict and division are inherent to politics and that there is no place where reconciliation could be definitively achieved as the full actualization of the unity of 'the people'. (Mouffe 2000: 15)

This process is not necessarily *ant*agonistic, but intends to engage with political debate through diverse struggles over meaning. According to Carl DiSalvo, 'those who espouse an agonistic approach to democracy encourage contestation and dissensus' (2012: 4). When design visualizes such contradictions, generating alternative ways of living and being, often as part of critical participatory design approaches, it is rarely given significant mainstream attention, unless as part of some profit-led production, for example a film, a housing development project, product range or brand promotion.

Consequently, as the chapter by Thorpe explains today's designers increasingly draw on participatory or collaborative methods to address wicked challenges, as useful ways to address their complexity and also to encourage participatory democracy. For many designers involving diverse actors in design processes is a way of giving them agency to respond to complex problem contexts and offers a way of empowering them as citizens – the design objective may simply be to make contradictions apparent. This puts 'social' designers and design activists in a tricky position, for engaging with a design processes may 'reframe' (Dorst 2015) dominant accounts by making diverse voices manifest and so identifying more equitable relationships underlying 'what we want less of and what we want more of'. As Agid points out Chapter 7, 'shifting the understanding of the problem shifts ideas of who might be best positioned to address or rethink it, and shapes possibilities for imagined futures'. This shifting and re-shaping means that small-scale social design and innovation projects are able to rehearse 'large changes' (Manzini and Rizzo 2011). They can offer agonistic approaches through participatory design that accommodates diverse voices and can produce new ways of working via contestation to achieve a participatory democracy.

Reframing political issues as design problems that need to be understood, addressed or challenged through design activism and participatory engagement is a radical approach. However, the need for it may never have been more urgent, given that our democratic systems are under threat as Ezio Manzini and Victor Margolin have recently pointed out (see the introduction) (2017). But nor has it ever been trickier to deliver effective design in this way, in highly networked consumer-orientated societies. While activists may be able to organize quickly they may not be able easily to prevent the decimation of the public realm, the welfare state (cf Julier 2013; Mulgan 2014; Chen et al. 2016) or, ultimately, 'spaceship earth' (Buckminster Fuller 1968). Nonetheless, social issues, the multiple causes of which are unfolding in time *are* being raised and addressed by designers. Consequently, signals of concern and ideas about what to do to bring about change emerge from within design education, design activism as well as design theory and practice.

Design as dialogue

The chapters in this collection, in different ways, confront diverse dilemmas and ethical design challenges that require dialogue. By enacting new ways of doing design, design research and designing new futures, such design projects offer hope regarding ways of organizing ourselves and the public realm, including cooperative, self-managed, non-hierarchal and sustainable approaches. As Tom Fisher observes in Chapter 1, designs construct expectations about the future, 'expectations which themselves have agency'. This is, of course, part of the *power* of applied thinking through design and the use of design dialogue in the sort of community engagements, with its consequent political influence, that design can deliver. This applied capacity to dialogue the tricky issues of the day through design visualization and participatory design workshops can help us better understand what design can offer and what its future role might be.

As Light and Akama suggest in their chapter, in opening up such discussions design is accompanied by an obligation to help to find new ethical ways. That is to 'to devise courses of action aimed at changing existing situations into preferred ones' (by the majority), to paraphrase Herbert Simon (1996 [1969]). But design must seek to facilitate emergent solutions not simply provide them, and relinquishing control in this way de-centres the power of the designer as a consequence of building collaboration. This is *design as dialogue*, as the process of collaboration rather than the monologue of the perfect/object, system or building.

While the chapters in this collection do not address all the political challenges of our times or even the issues different communities are grappling with, the accounts of (i) *tricky thinging* (by Dant, Fisher, Kersharvarz, Srinivas, Staszowski and Tonkinwise), the descriptions of (ii) *tricky processes and tricky principles* (by Agid, Akama, Light, Martins and Oliverier) as well as discussion of the (iii) potential of design to help address *tricky policy* issues (by Gamman, Gunasekera and Kidwell, Kimbell and Thorpe) signal new design approaches and agendas. All the chapters therefore engage with the shared understanding that design must address social issues in new ways, with new forms of collaboration, and use its political influence beyond current consumer market profit-led limits to innovate for social change and social good. We locate change as being fashioned within already existing environments rather than being imposed by experts from on high or from outside.

There is no finished object here, instead we want to open up the space between the designer and the designed *for*. Ultimately, we question the function of this space. For that reason, we hope this collection, on many levels, begins to offer accounts of how to reinvent what sort of 'world making' design can deliver, as Tony Fry (2016) quoted at the beginning of this chapter demands. While the chapters herein certainly do not conform to the prescriptive requirements of design that Fry promotes in *Design as Politics* (2011) we hope our chapters offer a glimpse of what sort of tricky design thinging and reasoning sustainable modes of world making might need to consider. If design has any 'gifts to the future' (to paraphrase McDonnell (2015) who paraphrased Tony Fry (2011)), it is to embrace, discuss and understand the ethical complexity all actors need to understand to adequately address the tricky challenges involved in creating the new times to come.

Notes

1 Nesta is the UK's National Endowment for Science, Technology and the Arts.
2 https://designmuseum.org/exhibitions/beazley-designs-of-the-year

Bibliography

Armstrong, Leah, Bailey, Jocelyn, Julier, Guy and Kimbell, Lucy (2014) *Social Design Futures: HEI Research and the AHRC*, Brighton: University of Brighton.
Björgvinsson, Erling, Ehn, Pelle and Hillgren, Per-Anders (2012) 'Design Things and Design Thinking: Contemporary Participatory Design Challenges', *Design Issues*, 28, 3: 102.

Brown, Tim (2009) *Change by Design: How Design Thinking Transforms Organizations and Inspires Innovation*, New York: Harper Collins.

Buchanan, Richard (1992) 'Wicked Problems in Design Thinking', *Design Issues*, 8, 2: 5–21.

Chen, Dung-Sheng, Cheng, Lu-Lin, Hummels, Caroline and Koskinen, Ilpo (2016) 'Social Design: An Introduction', *International Journal of Design*, 10, 1: 1–5.

Davies, James, Sandstrom, Susanna, Shorrocks, Anthony and Wolff, Edward (2009) 'The Global Pattern of Household Wealth', *Journal of International Development*, 21: 223–254.

De Bono, Edward (1990) *Lateral Thinking: Creativity Step by Step*, New York: Harper Perennial.

Dilnot, Clive (2017) '"Care" as a problem: How to begin to create, for design, an adequate theory of model of care'. *Proceedings of Does Design Care … ?*, Imagination, Lancaster University, 12 and 13 September.

DiSalvo, Carl (2012) *Adversarial Design*, Cambridge, MA: MIT Press.

Dorst, Kees (2015) *Frame Innovation: Create New Thinking by Design*, Cambridge, MA: MIT Press.

Ehn, Pelle (1992) 'Scandinavian Design: On Participation and Skill', in Paul S. Adler and Terry A. Winograd (eds), *Technology and the Future of Work*, New York: Oxford University Press, pp. 96–132.

Ehn, Pelle, Nilsson, Elizabeth and Topgaard, Richard (2014) *Making Futures – Marginal Notes on Innovation, Design and Democracy*, Cambridge, MA: MIT Press.

Eno, Brian and Schmidt, Peter (1975) Oblique strategies, hand produced deck of cards. Available at: http://www.rtqe.net/ObliqueStrategies/retrieved (accessed 31 October 2017).

Fisher, Tom (2012) 'Design as Trickster'. *DRS Conference DRS2012*, Chulalongkorn University, Bangkok, Thailand, 1–4 July.

Flusser, Vilem (1999) 'About the Word Design', in *The Shape of Things A Philosophy of Things*, London: Reaktion Books.

Fry, Tony (2011) *Design as Politics*, Oxford: Berg.

Fry, Tony (2016) 'Configuring Design as Politics Now', in Penny Sparke and Fiona Fisher (eds), *The Routledge Companion to Design Studies*, Oxon: Routledge.

Fuller, Buckminister (1968) *Operating Manual for Spaceship Earth*, Baden: Lars Muller Publishers.

Haraway, Donna (1988) 'Situated Knowledges: The Science Question in Feminism and the Privilege of Partial Perspectives', *Feminist Studies*, 14, 3: 575–599.

Hardoon, Deborah, Fuentes-Nieva, Ricardo and Ayele, Sophia (2016) *An Economy For the 1%: How Privilege and Power in the Economy Drive Extreme Inequality and How This Can Be Stopped*, Oxford: Oxfam International.

Horst, W. J. Rittel (August 1987) The Reasoning of Designers (Working Paper, International Congress on Planning and Design Theory in Boston). Available at http://www.cc.gatech.edu/fac/ellendo/rittel/rittel-reasoning.pdf.

Hutton, William (1996) *The State We're in: Why Britain Is in Crisis and How to Overcome It*, London: Vintage Books.

Hyde, Lewis (2008) *Trickster Makes This World: How Disruptive Imagination Creates Culture*, Edinburgh: Canongate Book.

IDEO (2003) *Method Cards*, Richmond, CA: William Stout Publishers.

Julier, Guy (2013) 'From Design Culture to Design Activism', *Design and Culture*, 5, 2: 215–236.

Julier, Guy (2017) *Economies of Design*, London: Sage.

Keats, John (1817) 'Letter to George and Tom Keats, December 1817', in Robert Gittings (ed.), *John Keats Selected Letters*, Oxford: Oxford University Press, pp. 41–42.

Klein, Naomi (2015) *This Changes Everything*, London: Penguin Books.

Mackay, D., Zundel, M. and Alkirwi, M. (2014) 'Exploring the Practical Wisdom of Metis for Management Learning', *Management Learning*, 45, 4: 418–436.

Manzini, Ezio (2014) 'Making Things Happen; Social Innovation and Design', *Design Issues*, 30, 1: 57–66.

Manzini, Ezio (2015) *Design When Everyone Designs: An Introduction to Design for Social Innovation*, Cambridge, MA: MIT Press.

Manzini, Ezio and Rizzo, F. (2011) 'Small Projects/Large Changes: Participatory Design as an Open Participated Process', *CoDesign*, 7, 3–4: 199–215.

Markussen, Thomas (2013) 'The Disruptive Aesthetics of Design Activism: Enacting Design between Art and Politics', *Design Issues*, 29, 1: 38–50.

Markussen, Thomas (2017) 'Disentangling 'the Social' in Social Design's Engagement with the Public Realm', CoDesign, 13, 3: 160–174.

Martin, Bella and Hanington, Bruce (2012) *Universal Methods of Design*, Beverley, MA: Rockport Publishers.

Mason, Paul (2015) *Postcapitalism: A Guide to Our Future*, London: Penguin.

Mau, Bruce (2004) *Massive Change: A Manifesto for the Future Global Design Culture*, London: Phaidon.

McDonnell, Janet (2015) 'Gift to the Future: Design Reasoning, Design Research and Critical Design Practitioners', *She Ji, The Journal of Design, Economics and Innovation*, 1, 2: 107–117.

Mouffe, Chantal (2000) *The Democratic Paradox*, London: Verso.

Mulgan, Geoff (2014) 'Design in Public and Social Innovation: What Works and What Could Work Better', London: Nesta. Available at: https://www.nesta.org.uk/sites/default/files/design_in_public_and_social_innovation.pdf.

Mulgan, Geoff (March 2016) 'Oscar Townsley and Adam Price The Challenge-driven University; How Real-life Problems can fuel Learning'. *Nesta*, https://www.nesta.org.uk/blog/the-challenge-driven-university-how-real-life-problems-can-fuel-learning/

Papanek, Victor (1971) *Design for the Real World*, New York: Pantheon Books.

Ramirez, Mariano (2011) 'Designing with a social conscience: An emerging area in industrial design education and practice'. *International Conference of Engineering Design ICED11*, Technical University of Denmark, 15–18 August 2011.

Rittel, Horst and Melvin Webber (1973) 'Dilemmas in a General Theory of Planning', *Policy Sciences*, 4, 2: 155–169.

Rodgers, Paul, Innella, Giovanni and Bremner, Craig (2017) 'Paradoxes in Design Thinking', *The Design Journal*, 20. Available at: http://dx.doi.org/10.1080/14606925.2017.1352941.

Schon, Donald (1984) *The Reflective Practitioner – How Professionals Think in Action*, New York: Basic Books.

Schumpeter, Joseph (1975 [1942]) *Capitalism, Socialism and Democracy*, New York: Harper.

Simon, Herbert (1996 [1969]) *The Sciences of the Artificial*, Cambridge, MA: MIT Press.

Suchman, Lucy (1987) *Plans and Situated Actions: The Problem of Human Machine Communication*, Cambridge: Cambridge University Press.

Thorpe, Adam and Gamman, Lorraine (2013) 'Walking with Park: Exploring the "Reframing" and Integration of CPTED Principles in Neighbourhood Regeneration in Seoul, South Korea', *Crime Prevention and Community Safety Journal*, 15, 3: 207–223, Palgrave Macmillan.

Wates, Nick and Knevitt, Charles (1987) *Community Architecture: How People Are Creating Their Own Environment*, London: Penguin.

Wilson, David S. and Wilson, Edward O. (2007) 'Evolution: Survival of the Selfless', *New Scientist*, 31: 10.

Index